BIKER BILLY'S HOG WILD ON A HARLEY COOKBOOK

BIKER BILLY'S HOG WILD ON A HARLEY COOKBOOK

200 Fiercely Flavorful Recipes to Kick-Start Your Home Cooking from Harley Riders Across the USA

Bill Hufnagle

The Harvard Common Press | Boston, Massachusetts

The Harvard Common Press
535 Albany Street • Boston, Massachusetts 02118
www.harvardcommonpress.com

A Few Words About Words
Many of the folks who contributed recipes and I have used words and names that are the trademarks of the Harley-Davidson Motor Company and/or the Buell Company. All possible efforts have been made to use these words in a descriptive manner. The Harvard Common Press and I respect the trademarks of the Harley-Davidson Motor Company and the Buell Company and are grateful for the permission to use them within this book. Those trademarks are:

Aluminator, Bad Boy, Badlander, Bazooka, Biker Blues, Buddy Seat, Diamond Back, Disc Glide, Dyna Glide, Eagle Iron, Electra Glide Road King, Enthusiast, Evolution, Fantail, Fat Boy, FXR, FXRG, HD, H-D, H.O.G., Hog, Harley, Harley Chrome, Harley Owners Group, Harley Women, Harley-Davidson, Heritage Softail, Heritage Springer, Howitzer, Hugger, Ladies of Harley, Low Rider, Motorclothes, Revolution, Road Glide, Road King, Roadster, Screamin' Eagle, Softail, Sport Glide, Sportster, Springer, Sturgis, Super Glide, The Legend Rolls On, Thunderstar, Tour Glide, Tour-Pak, Ultra Classic, V-Rod, Wide Glide, Willie G., and the Harley-Davidson bar and shield logo are trademarks of H-D Michigan, Inc. Blast, Buell, Cyclone, Dynamic Digital, Firebolt, Fuel Injection, Lightning, and Thunderbolt are trademarks of Buell.

Printed in the United States of America
Printed on acid-free paper

Library of Congress Cataloging-in-Publication Data

Hufnagle, Bill.
  Biker Billy's hog wild on a Harley cookbook : 200 fiercely flavorful recipes to kick-start your home cooking from Harley riders across the USA / Bill Hufnagle.
      p. cm.
  ISBN 1-55832-250-7 ((hc) : alk. paper)
  1. Cookery. I. Title.
  TX714.H82 2003
  641.5—dc21   2002154184

ISBN- 13: 978-1-55832-250-9
ISBN- 10: 1-55832-250-7

Special bulk-order discounts are available on this and other Harvard Common Press books. Companies and organizations may purchase books for premiums or resale, or may arrange a custom edition, by contacting the Marketing Director at the address above.

10   9   8

For interior photo credits see page 312.
Cover design by Night & Day Design
Book design by Richard Oriolo

This book is dedicated to an American Icon, the proud Company that builds them, the thousands of people who compose that Company, the founding four men who started it all, their families who carried the dream through good times and bad, and to you the American people who have made Harley-Davidson a symbol of America and freedom.

CONTENTS

ACKNOWLEDGMENTS

This book has been a labor of love for me, an idea I carried around for many years. For a long time I kept it a secret, discussing it rarely with only a select few people. Once the contracts were signed and appropriate permissions had been requested and received, it was time to share the idea, roll up my sleeves, and begin the work.

Along the road to completion, many people helped me and played a part as this work progressed to the book you have in your hands. I owe a deep debt of gratitude to all the wonderful people who helped to move it along from concept to completion. This is one part of writing a book that is, for an author, both extremely satisfying and very scary. It is sweet to bring a large project to completion and to reflect on and thank all the great people who have helped. The scary part is that I know from experience I will miss somebody, so first off, let me thank you, the helpful soul who was there at my time of need and whose name this tired soul has misplaced.

Before starting to acknowledge everyone I can remember, there is one simple reality I wish to acknowledge. While I tried to reach everyone I know in the motorcycle industry, all the friends I have ridden with over the years, and all the Harley enthusiasts out there, I am sure that, as with any project of this type and magnitude, some folks did not get the message or missed the deadline, yet would have

wanted to be part of this book. To all of you, all I can say is, I am sorry you were not included—it was not by intention.

This book is all about sharing. So many people shared their recipes, stories, and pictures with me for your enjoyment and to honor Harley-Davison and its motorcycles. There are too many to list here, but you know who you are and your names are proudly attached to your wonderful contributions—thank you.

I would like to send my heartfelt thanks to Dan Klemencic of the Harley-Davidson Motor Company. Dan has been my primary Company contact through this process; it was his hand that delivered my request for permission to use the trademarked Harley and HOG names in my title. It was his hand that delivered the permission when granted. I think this is why we continue the handshake as a greeting, for it is with the helping hands of our friends that we accomplish things greater than ourselves.

Another dear friend of mine at Harley-Davidson who has been so very helpful with this project and, frankly, anything I ask of him is Marty Rosenblum. Marty is the official historian for the Harley-Davidson Company. He is also a fine poet, musician, singer, and song-writer; he is the "Holy Ranger" and if you get to sample his work, you will enjoy it. Thank you, Martin Jack Rosenblum—may the Holy Ranger ride with the wind.

Another good friend of mine at Harley-Davidson is Art Gompper. Art has helped me many times through the years. When I started this project he was there to help again. Thank you, Art, for all your help and assistance on this project and in the past. I would also like to thank Steve Piehl, Paul James, Sue Jones, and the whole communications department at Harley-Davidson for their rapid and thorough assistance with my information needs regarding Riders Edge, among other factory programs that I wanted to be certain I had my facts straight on. Also, thanks go to Leslie Hudson from BRAG/Buell and Heidi Zogg and Melinda Kumm from H.O.G. for their help with both these wonderful riders' organizations.

Mark Langello is a good friend and a great photographer whom I have had the pleasure of working with on many magazine stories. It is both a pleasure and an honor to have some of Mark's images of me within this book.

I would like to send a big thank you to the AMA and the Motorcycle Hall of Fame Museum folks who sent in recipes and images and helped me get the word out about this book; they are too numerous to list but they know who they are.

Several personal friends, some riders and some who also work in the motorcycle industry, helped me get the call for recipes out, among them Susan Buck, Josh Placa, Scott Cochran, Mark Kalan, Joan Pearson, Scott Rodas, and Cecile Brion.

During the development of my recipes for this book many of my friends in Asheville, North Carolina, joined me for taste-testing dinners; the list is too long and I would surely miss someone's name. I would like to thank my good friend Kathleen Sioui, who helped me with several of those dinners.

The baked goods recipes submitted to this book required extra testing to ensure that they would work. Baking is both an art and science and while I am a good cook (if I say so myself), I am still learning about baking. I would like to thank my special friend Mary S. Ray, who is an artist at baking, for her help in testing those recipes.

I would like to thank all the wonderful people at The Harvard Common Press who in one way or another turned this project from my ideas and words into the fun book you are reading or cooking from. First, there is president and publisher, Bruce Shaw, who had the vision and made the commitment to publishing and marketing this book. Next, Liza Beth, office manager and business assistant, then the folks I worked closest with in the editorial and production department: Valerie Cimino, managing editor; Pam Hoenig, executive editor; Jodi Marchowsky, production editor; and Virginia Downes, production manager. Also the marketing and sales department for their efforts to bring this book to the widest possible distribution level: Christine Alaimo, director of sales and marketing; Betsy Young, director of sales development; Sunshine Erickson, marketing manager; Abbey Phalen, special sales manager; and Dana Garczewski, marketing assistant. Last but not least the publicity department: Skye Stewart, publicity manager; and Beatrice Wikander, publicity associate, who worked so hard to place this book in the public's eye. I appreciate everything each of you has done to advance this cookbook.

Although I just mentioned her above, I would like to send an especially warm thank you to Pam Hoenig, my editor. This is the second book Pam and I have worked on together; both have been a joy. A writer surrenders his or her words to the editor with the hope that what is returned will be improved. Writing is a very private and personal process, and an editor can encourage or stifle a writer. Pam has always encouraged me greatly; I can feel her faith in my work and me; this has set me free as a writer. When she returns my words, I always find my voice is not only still intact but clarified. She has shown a great respect for my work, and I respect and appreciate her work in turn. This book has brought to her desk many challenges, many voices to hear and protect, many recipes that needed a preservationist's gentle hands and a cook's eye too; she has done a fantastic job—I don't think I could have done it without her help. Thank you, Pam!

Last, I would like to thank all the people who have purchased this book and my previous two books, who have watched my TV show, and who have come to see me perform live. So many of you have expressed kind words of appreciation for my work; I want you all to know that I appreciate you greatly. You make my job the truly joyful and fun endeavor it is for me. *Thank you!*

PREFACE

One hundred years ago in a city called Milwaukee in a still young country called America, three young men started to build motorcycles in a 10 x 15-foot shed in the backyard of the Davidson house. Arthur and Walter Davidson and Bill Harley could have had no idea what their backyard project would evolve into a hundred years later. But they surely must have had a great sense of pride in their workmanship and a dedication to build something special. Working in their spare time after their full-time jobs and on weekends, they built that first motorcycle. Four years and 150 motorcycles later, the three, along with William A. Davidson, formed the Harley-Davidson Motor Company.

The early years of the twentieth century were a time when many young men were building new things and creating what would ultimately be the world we inherited. Motorcycles were being built in backyard sheds, basements, and workshops all over America, Henry Ford and others were building cars, and the Wright brothers were taking to the air. Man was about to start moving faster than ever before and the world was about to change in big ways. The force of change has proved to be the only constant from then to now, as few original companies born in that era of great invention have survived intact, yet the inventions are all doing just fine as parts of our daily

lives today. Of all the American motorcycle makers that started in those decades, only Harley-Davidson is still in business and has been making motorcycles continuously for the past hundred years. Other companies have come and gone and, in this current era of retro revival, some have been born again. To my knowledge Harley-Davidson is the only original American company from that era that produced a major durable product and is the sole survivor in their business category. But it takes more than just being a survivor to become the American icon that Harley-Davidson is.

It takes a sound, a feel, a look, a form of magic—and maybe even an attitude—which all combine to stir the soul. It is the attitude of faith and belief in one's own abilities; it is the attitude that says, I can overcome the odds. It is the pioneer spirit combined with hard work, American ingenuity, and the strength of a true survivor: it is perhaps one of the clearest examples in our time of the classic spirit of America.

Harley-Davidson motorcycles have been with us through the tremulous times of the past century when America has time and again affirmatively answered the proposition that Abraham Lincoln set forth at Gettysburg when he said, "testing whether that nation or any nation so conceived and so dedicated can long endure." Americans have gone to war with Harley-Davidson motorcycles as part of their arsenal. Our great leaders have been escorted in both the business of life and to a final resting place with Harley-Davidson motorcycles at their side. Americans from all walks of life, such as Malcolm Forbes, Jay Leno, Senator Ben Nighthorse Campbell, and probably your plumber or doctor or lawyer or the mayor of your town, have traveled to and from work aboard a Harley-Davidson motorcycle. These motorcycles have also carried us to honor our war heroes at events like Rolling Thunder each year in Washington, D.C., lest we forget. Those selfsame motorcycles also convey us to national parks, monuments, and many peaceful places where we rest our sometimes weary souls so that we can return to our jobs refreshed on Monday and continue to build this great nation. We as a nation and Harley-Davidson as a brand have endured and I believe shall continue to endure because that is our spirit. It is our American way.

Harley-Davidson motorcycles have appealed to me since I was a child. Perhaps the clearest childhood memories I have are of police officers mounted on Harleys. Yet the first motorcycle I personally lusted after was a friend's 1939 Knucklehead. This bike was chopped, chromed, and painted an eye-popping yellow. It was a classic chopper, the ultimate in cool. I remember how each chromed part had to be fitted, then sent away for chroming, then refitted and installed. It was not like today, where you can pick up a catalog, order a part, and know it will fit with little or no trouble. Things sure have changed, but my lust for a Harley-Davidson never went away.

Today I proudly ride a 1996 fuel-injected Road King Police Bike; in the end, you come back to what you are first drawn to. I also ride a 2000 Buell S3T Lightning since I love to dance through the mountains and valleys with my bike. For me the Motor Company's products have been instruments of landmark change in my life. They have in many ways set me free and they have enabled me to find a new beginning and a livelihood that I truly love. Along that roadway of change, I have had the pleasure of meeting many of the people who are part of the Harley-Davidson Motor Company. Through the years quite a few have become close friends of mine. We live hundreds of miles apart and usually only see each other when our paths intersect as we all crisscross this country attending and working at motorcycle rallies and events. Yet we share a strong common bond, the passion for riding our Harleys and the experiences we have shared doing that.

As the 100th Anniversary approached, I wanted to do something to say thank you and to pay tribute to Harley-Davidson, its people, and its motorcycles. This cookbook is that thank you. It is not a licensed product, but I did ask for and receive permission to use both Harley and HOG in the title—respect and gratitude go hand in hand. This is a community cookbook of the people who feel like I do about Harley-Davidson. It is in a sense a big birthday card. Over the past year I put the call out for recipes and personal stories about our collective love affair with Harley-Davidson motorcycles. In effect, I asked anyone who wanted to share this expression to sign this birthday card. The responses are here for you to enjoy. Happy 100th Birthday, Harley-Davidson!

INTRODUCTION:
A Tale of My
Hunger for the Road

O ver the years, a lot of people I have met at rallies and events have asked me how I got started doing what I do as Biker Billy: cooking, riding, writing, and performing. Here is the short version of the tale of my hunger for the road.

Many years ago I was deeply involved in an exciting career of owning and operating television production studios in Manhattan. This was not the career I had planned on, but the road of life had led me around several interesting turns. I had been intent on pursuing a career in the fine arts and am much more of a country boy at heart than a city kid, but there I was living and working in the big city.

My college years led me to Pratt Institute in Brooklyn, where I was working on a degree in printmaking. I could clearly see that even great artists have a tendency to starve a lot, and I was not a great artist or one for missing a meal. So I decided to find an art-related craft or profession that would both help my personal art career and provide a steady income. Deciding on photography, I signed up for a summer internship with a successful New York City photographer, figuring I would learn a lot about that field. Well, unbeknownst to me, he was just about to make the big move to directing TV commercials. So, after one or two photo jobs, we started to shoot TV commercials. I fell in love with the exciting process of filmmaking—the teamwork, the equipment, and, most of all, the people. After the hard work was done, to see it edited into a neat little film and to know all of the stuff that went into making it was just so cool to a 21-year-old kid, and it still is cool to me today.

After that summer, I returned to Pratt Institute and changed my major to filmmaking and, by the time my senior year was up, I discovered that I had even more credits to earn to finish my Bachelor of Fine Arts degree. I was always being told to keep it under my belt that I was in film school or no one would take me seriously on the job. I decided to "finish" my degree the old-fashioned way, with on-the-job training, so I left school and kept working in the field.

A decade later, I owned and operated a television production facility in Manhattan. While this was a great career in a great city, I had for a long time felt there was just something missing. One spring day I looked at my then partner and wife and asked, Can you do without me next week? I told her I needed to get away and think or I was going to go stir crazy. I wanted fresh air and some elbowroom, scenery that was dramatic yet peaceful, and friendly people. I wanted a place where my mind could wander. I decided on Maine.

I flew up to Maine and rented a big luxury car, tilted the seat back, and started to cruise up the coast. In the midst of my week of reflection and soul searching, it happened. First I heard them, then I saw them ride over the next ridge on two chopped Harleys with their hair flowing in the wind. I have on many occasions told folks that that moment was an epiphany for me. It truly was a religious experience—a reawakening of an inner self long buried in the hustle and bustle of a big-city career-focused life. It was as though a big light had shined into the deepest recesses to reveal the restless soul within; in so many ways I was reborn that day, or perhaps I truly began the process of discovering myself.

My childhood had been an interesting blend of the south Bronx and the mountains of eastern Tennessee, so I grew up with knowledge of both the city and the country. From an early age I developed a love for the road and traveling, since our family summer vacations were road trips from New York City to Grandma's farm in Tennessee. I looked forward to them like all children do. While I did very much

enjoy the time spent on Grandma's farm, it was the road trip I liked best.

These trips were mostly taken before the big interstates were completed along the route my family preferred. We stopped at all sorts of little places along the way and stayed in mom-and-pop motels. This was an America that is almost gone now, bypassed and forgotten by the big highways and look-alike chain businesses. It is an America I hunger for more with each passing year. I do believe that it is a part of what makes traveling by motorcycle so enjoyable to me: the winding roads and the more adventurous pace that allows for pausing at the little places along the way and savoring a vanishing America. It is a way of sampling our history firsthand, of honoring a bygone era when things were, if not better, well, they were different. It was a time when each place was just a bit different than the last, and more of a reflection of the local folks who proudly built it.

Deep within me, all those years living and working in the Big Apple, that hunger lay buried. Like so many New Yorkers, I had forsaken the ownership of wheels due to the obscene parking fees, taxes, and traffic. Subways, buses, and taxis moved my flesh around but left my soul unstirred, yet the wanderlust lay just under the surface.

This yearning had expressed itself in me at an early age. As soon as I was able to get a driver's license, I wanted a motorcycle. I had sampled friends' bikes and loved the rush of riding. My beloved mom, God rest her soul, would have no part of me riding a motorcycle at that time. She would not cosign the loan on a motorcycle, which, as a 17-year-old, I needed. As much as I resented it, she was right—I was too wild and thought myself indestructible. Many years later, when I was much more sensible and had learned to ride a motorcycle, she became a big fan of my bike and my choice to ride. She was a great lady and I do owe so much of what is good about me to her and her influence raising me all by herself after my father died when I was six.

It was at the ripe old age of 30 when I began to ride motorcycles and I began a process of rediscovering myself. It is funny how much we can forget about life while we are busy running the rat race. Riding has given me the chance to explore things forgotten and things yet to be discovered about this great country, life, and myself. The openness of the people who ride motorcycles has transformed me in many ways. Before I embarked on my personal adventure of discovering motorcycling, I was basically very shy—I know it is hard to believe if you have ever seen me on stage. But somehow being around people who share a common passion allowed me to open up more and more. It was at motorcycle club breakfast meetings that I really became comfortable speaking in front of groups of people. Heck, I was talking about the ride I had planned for them, where I had chosen for us to stop for a meal, and where we would end up for some fun at the end of the ride. I was sharing motorcycling fun and it was a blast.

Somewhere along the road I started to share one of my other hobbies with my riding buddies, that hobby being cooking. I grew up with lots of good old-fashioned home cooking, both in Mom's kitchen and at Grandma's farm. Mix in some New York City restaurants and, of course, a good sampling of interesting road food and you raise a kid who enjoys his food. Cooking was something I started to learn at an early age; my mom felt that I should be able to take care of myself. She was a very independent woman and she passed that spirit on to me. I also became a vegetarian while still in high school; how and why is too long a story to share here.

Being a vegetarian was what drove me to learn to cook, but not just because I could not find available meat-free choices. It evolved from mere subsistence into a hobby and eventually into a career. Back in the days when I ran the TV studios, the times I could cook were an enjoyable mini vacation from the high-pressure world I worked in. Cooking became one of the ways in which I expressed myself creatively, and I enjoyed sharing my creations.

Living in New York City I was exposed the world's great cuisines in many fabulous restaurants. I read a lot of menus, saw and smelled a lot of exotic dishes, and taught myself to cook a diverse collection of cuisines. After a while, though, I became somewhat bored. It was at this point that I started to experiment with hot peppers.

Oh, the joy of experimenting with hot peppers: burn, baby, burn. I did this before there were whole sections dedicated to fiery food cookbooks in bookstores. I learned about fiery foods the way I have learned many things—the hard way. The first time I found fresh habaneros, I nearly killed my ex-wife and myself. I took an innocent-looking habanero pepper and sliced off a small piece from the bottom of the pod, tasted it, and deemed it to be hot but not too hot, saying something like, These ain't so hot, what's all the fuss about? I proceeded to mince up the whole pod, seeds and all, and sprinkle it over two plates of tortilla chips and cheddar cheese. One bite revealed a

fire straight from the burning bowels of hell. She wisely left hers alone and made something else. I, being who I am, decided to pick off the pieces of habanero and eat some more. Well, after a few more cheesy chips, I was a walking Roman candle with flames coming out of my ears, eyes, nose, etc., and my lips had literally turned blue. I had just learned by firsthand research that capsaicin is truly a fat-soluble chemical. I survived my baptism by fire; thankfully we had some half-and-half in the fridge, which I had to just about soak my face in to cool off.

For many years I had rejected beans as part of my diet but shortly after the hot pepper bug bit, I started to experiment with them, which led directly to my foray into making chili. I eventually created my own complex recipe from individual spices, herbs, hot peppers, beans, and a slew of other fresh ingredients. I cooked and served this special recipe for my riding buddies and other friends on many occasions. So many of them kept saying that I should market this chili that I finally listened to them. I was reluctant since this was one of my escapes from work and I wanted to protect my peaceful endeavor.

I started to think about product names and came up with "Biker Billy's Chili." One day I was thinking about how to market my chili and I had an idea. There I was, owning and operating a TV production facility planning on launching a new product—why not combine my work in TV, my hobby of cooking, and my passion for motorcycling and produce a cooking show? I came up with the idea of a cable television cooking show called *Biker Billy Cooks with Fire* that was designed to appeal to both fiery food lovers and motorcycle riders. This was before the Food Network started and cooking shows became so popular. At the time, cable television was all about narrowcasting and finding extremely focused segments of the TV marketplace. I was looking to appeal to folks who would enjoy fiery foods and the biker lifestyle. I signed up for a 13-week series on the local cable system Manhattan Neighborhood Network and started to produce shows. It was quite a challenge at first to move from behind the cameras to in front of them. But since I was talking about two very important things, my passion for riding motorcycles and my hobby of cooking, it got easier each time. As a bonus, I got to air public service announcements about motorcycle safety and PSAs aimed at improving car driver awareness of motorcycles on the road.

About six weeks into airing the first shows, I started to get viewer mail. People wanted to receive copies of the recipes. The thing that surprised me the most was the variety of people who were writing in saying that they liked the show. I had only hoped for hotheads and bikers. I was getting mail from people from all walks of life, everyone from Catholic nuns, Methodist ministers, school teachers, lawyers, and doctors to little kids and parents writing saying that three generations would gather together to watch the show. I never imagined in my wildest dreams that so many people would enjoy watching me jump up and down, toss food around, scream and yell, and just have a good old time cooking up a storm. I went from being a very shy person who was happy to hide behind the camera to being able to go on *The Tonight Show with Jay Leno*, and I owe it to riding motorcycles and maybe a little to eating fiery foods. By 1995, I retired from the television facility business to pursue my new career as Biker Billy full time. Since then I have been all over this great country, from Daytona Beach, Florida, to the streets of Deadwood, South Dakota, from the Superdome in New Orleans to the opening of the Guggenheim Museum's Art of the Motorcycle exhibit in Las Vegas, and even to Harley's 95th Anniversary Celebration in Milwaukee, Wisconsin. My television show was made part of the 100 Years of the Motorcycle in Film, which was the companion exhibit to the Guggenheim Museum's Art of the Motorcycle exhibit in New York City.

In 1999 W. Atlee Burpee & Company of Warminster, Pennsylvania, honored me by naming a pepper plant after me, the Hot Pepper Biker Billy Hybrid, in recognition of my efforts to encourage people to garden and grow their own hot peppers and vegetables. George Ball, president and owner of Burpee, had the Biker Billy hybrid jalapeño bred to produce both a large flavorful pod and a powerful fire level, and it has received rave reviews from gardeners, the garden press, and fiery food aficionados across America. George Ball also commissioned the creation of the Burpee Biker Billy show bike, a 1999 Harley-Davidson Road King Classic that features, among other trick details, a special paint job that changes color as you walk around it and a real gold leaf Burpee logo from the late 1800s. The bike is also equipped with working flamethrowers, which I utilized at many events as part of my live cooking show. In recognition of the positive public awareness we created, the AMA bestowed George Ball and myself with their Most Valued Person Award and created a special Most

Valued Pepper Award for the Hot Pepper Biker Billy Hybrid. This was and still is truly a great honor for me and allowed me to share another of my private passions, gardening, with the public.

I continue to perform at Harley-Davidson dealership events, motorcycle rallies, indoor bike shows, and events large and small for audiences composed of the general public and my motorcycling family. I hope I get to see you at an event and share some of the fun of this new book and tour.

Eat to Ride and Ride to Eat

It so often seems that my motorcycles are instruments with a culinary purpose. I think that, besides having a visible speedometer, there is an invisible restaurantometer that guides them like an autopilot does a plane. I can hardly remember going on a group ride that did not start at a restaurant or at the very least did not feature some supply of yummy pre-ride munchies. Major runs always involve doughnuts and coffee, plus iced tea, lemonade, and/or water if it is in the hot season at the start sites. Having your body well fueled—and this does include good hydration—is just as, if not more, important than having your gas tank filled when you start a ride. But it goes way beyond that—bikes seem to be found parked around food joints much more often than you see them parked at gas stations.

There are breakfast runs, lunch rides, and dessert runs; heck, I think somewhere in this great country there must even be a midnight snack ride. Let's just face it; we really Eat to Ride and Ride to Eat. Food is such an important part of sharing good social times together that this makes total sense. But I also think riding a motorcycle is such a sensory experience that it heightens your awareness of your surroundings. This heightened state of awareness persists for some time after you stop riding, much like an image flashed before your eyes will stay in your vision. I have come to believe that this heightened sensory awareness is what makes good food so much more enjoyable after a ride.

One of the best ways to pick a restaurant is to look for one with bikes parked outside—the more bikes, the better the food. If you happen to see several police bikes parked out front (red and blue turned lights off, of course), then it must be a great place—after all, an officer who is going to spend all day in the saddle is not going to eat twice at a bad restaurant. One of the best Mexican meals I ever had at a restaurant was at a little place in New Mexico where I saw three Harley Police Bikes parked out front. I would say more on this topic but I have an American Bikers Aimed Toward Education (ABATE) meeting to ride to now—at a restaurant, of course.

Riders' Recipes: Keeping the Faith

This book contains many recipes that were shared by fellow Harley-Davidson enthusiasts and some close friends of mine. Each of those recipes represents a personal expression of culinary creativity, just like each Harley-Davidson motorcycle is a creative expression of the individual who owns and loves it. Some of these recipes have been handed down for generations unchanged, while others are deliberate acts of creation for this book.

It has been with a steadfast purpose that I have endeavored to leave the shared recipes as true to the original as possible. I have, of course, tried to make the directions as clear and precise as possible, often asking many questions of the recipe's author. But I have not made changes to the recipes, as is a habit, an addiction, a way of life, with my riding and modifying my personal motorcycles. We did rigorously test the baked goods; as my delightful editor correctly advised there is nothing worse than a flat muffin (well, maybe a flat tire on your bike). On the very few occasions when something needed adjustment, if possible I consulted the recipe's source for clarification to stay true to the original.

You might say, But Biker Billy, we want you to assure us that we will like all the recipes in here. Well, it's like custom motorcycles—no one likes every custom bike; that's why there are so many different expressions. What I can assure you, however, is that this book contains foods that your fellow Harley riders are very fond and proud of. In these pages you will find a virtual covered dish dinner prepared by Harley-Davidson enthusiasts from all over America. To sample these dishes as prepared by the wonderful folks who shared their personal favorite recipes, you would have to spend years and tens of thousands of miles crisscrossing this great land—not a bad thing to do, just not everyone is that lucky or has the time.

It has been my purpose with this book to share with you—the cook, the hungry diner, and the armchair connoisseur—a sampling of the flavorful foods of my chosen family and to bring to you some of the experiences, a taste of the adventures, and the feeling of family we share as aficionados of this great brand of motorcycle. A place has been set at our table for you, and you are welcome to join us. I suggest that you try these recipes as offered by their creators; once you have, then make them your own and customize them to suit your taste and the tastes of your friends and family. I have delivered them to you as their creators or caretakers gave them to me. Cook, eat, ride, enjoy, and know the meaning of "Eat to Ride and Ride to Eat." Alright!

RISE AND RIDE:
BREAKFAST

Breakfast is the first and, as it is said, the most important meal of the day. Most of us would not start a long ride with an empty gas tank on the Harley, yet a lot of people will skip breakfast to get an earlier start on the road. I have been known to ride a hundred or more miles before breakfast while touring the country on my Road King. Somehow that morning dose of fresh air and the rumble of my big twin motor builds a healthy appetite; indeed, I am usually starved by the time I belly up to the breakfast table. Yet when I am at home, I like to eat a good breakfast before I start my ride. Go figure, I guess the availability of a kitchen changes my morning appetite.

I also enjoy breakfast as dinner sometimes, since breakfast foods are often what can be called comfort foods. This chapter has some yummy breakfast dishes to fuel your ride, whether you choose to eat before you start riding or pack some breakfast to enjoy along the road at your favorite scenic pullout. Whenever or wherever you serve them, these recipes will surely please any hungry biker at your table. Try sharing them with your non-riding friends too and maybe you just might inspire them to take a Motorcycle Safety Foundation Rider Education Course (MSF-REC) like the Rider's Edge classes that many Harley-Davidson dealers now offer. Wouldn't it be great to share your passion for all things Harley with a friend while guiding them toward being a safe rider?

LISA PETERS'S RALLY CIRCUIT HONEY NUT GRANOLA

Here is a breakfast treat that you can pack in your saddlebags and take on the road for a tasty breakfast far from home. This recipe comes from Lisa Marie Kateri Peters, a Harley fan and regular on the rally circuit who hails from New Hampshire. Lisa says, "I am a licensed massage therapist and have a thriving office practice, as well as a reasonably decent following of touch junkies out on the motorcycle rally circuit. I love to take my massage chair out on the road and hit as many events as I can during the rally season. I love being out in the fresh air, working on people who are regular massage receivers and being able to introduce massage to people who are new to the idea. And I've yet to meet someone who couldn't use a great massage! Plus, I get to be outside enjoying the beautiful rumble of all those throaty Harley-Davidsons." Take it from me, she knows how to cook and heal road-weary backs. Try this tasty breakfast, then ride off to a rally for a great massage.

> **1 cup corn, sunflower, or canola oil**
>
> **1 cup honey**
>
> **5 cups old-fashioned rolled oats**
>
> **1 cup unprocessed sesame seeds**
>
> **1 cup wheat germ**
>
> **1 cup unsweetened shredded coconut**
>
> **1 cup nonfat instant milk**
>
> **1 cup soy granules (optional)**
>
> **1 cup sliced almonds**
>
> **1 cup walnut pieces**
>
> **1 cup shelled roasted pumpkin seeds (available at the health food store)**
>
> **1 cup golden raisins**

1. Preheat the oven to 275°F.

2. In a large mixing bowl, mix together the corn oil and honey. Add the rest of the ingredients, except the raisins, and mix until everything's coated with the honey mixture. Spread the mixture out over 2

ungreased baking sheets and bake for 30 minutes at 275°F, then reduce the oven temperature to 250°F and bake till light brown, stirring the mixture every 10 to 15 minutes so it browns all over.

3. Remove from the oven, let cool a bit, and stir in the raisins. Let cool completely, then store in an airtight container to keep it from getting stale.

MAKES 10 TO 12 CUPS

LISA'S DAY-LONG MUFFINS

These muffins are hearty enough to carry you through a long distance ride, according to Lisa Peters from Concord, New Hampshire, who shared her recipe with us. Bake them the day before you head out on an all-day ride. Enjoy them before you roll out in the morning and make sure you pack a few into your saddlebags for later, when the bike and your own tank need a refill.

> ½ cup (1 stick) butter, softened
>
> 1 cup packed brown sugar
>
> 2 large eggs, lightly beaten
>
> 2 tablespoons milk
>
> 1 tablespoon vanilla extract
>
> 2 cups all-purpose flour
>
> ½ teaspoon ground cinnamon
>
> ½ teaspoon ground nutmeg
>
> ½ teaspoon salt
>
> ½ teaspoon baking powder
>
> 2 cups mashed ripe bananas
>
> 1 cup semisweet chocolate chips
>
> ¾ cup chopped nuts (optional)

1. Preheat the oven to 350°F. Grease three 6-cup muffin tins.

2. In a medium-size mixing bowl, cream together the butter and brown sugar. Add the eggs and mix well. Add the milk and vanilla and blend thoroughly.

3. In a large mixing bowl, sift together the flour, cinnamon, nutmeg, salt, and baking powder. Add the brown sugar mixture and stir just until blended. Add the bananas and mix till smooth. Fold in the chocolate chips and nuts, if using.

4. Divide the batter among the muffin cups and bake until golden brown and a toothpick inserted in the middle comes out clean, 35 to 45 minutes.

MAKES ABOUT 18 MUFFINS

DEDE VECCHIO'S STURGIS FARMER'S OMELET

This road recipe is from DeDe Vecchio, a Harley rider from Asheville, North Carolina. Here is what DeDe has to say: "I learned this recipe in the Black Hills Motorcycle Classic down at the Graveyard in 1984. First fry up some potatoes and onions. Maybe a little bacon if you want. You can add peppers, of course, and anything that is on sale at the local grocery store. Then break eggs on top and cook and stir in the pan. It's all mixed up and it tastes real good. I rode from Florida to Alaska, then back down to Sturgis on a 1964 Panhead hard tail. Loved it." Damn, Florida to Alaska to Sturgis on a rigid Panhead, that is really riding, so if DeDe says it tastes real good, you can take her word for it. How many of you could ride that far on a rigid?

¼ cup (½ stick) butter

2 potatoes, peeled and diced

½ onion, diced

1 to 2 hot peppers, seeded and diced

Bacon (optional), cut into ½-inch pieces

6 to 7 large eggs, beaten

In a large frying pan melt the butter over medium heat. Add the potatoes and onions and fry until the potatoes are tender and browned. Add the hot peppers and bacon, if using, and cook until the peppers are tender and the bacon is crisp. Add the eggs and stir until they are firm. Serve up hot.

FEEDS 4 HUNGRY BIKERS OR 5 OL' LADIES

DENA SHEETS'S FIERY BREAKFAST BURRITOS

Here is another pack 'em in your saddlebag and ride breakfast treat. After you work up an appetite riding in the morning air, you can enjoy these at a scenic rest area. This recipe is from Dena Sheets, a Harley lady from Lead, South Dakota, who tells us, "These burritos are great to fix in the morning, go for a putt, and chow down in about an hour. Wrap them in tin foil, put them in the saddlebags, and eat in about an hour or two."

> **2 pounds pork roast, cooked in the slow cooker the night before (see Note)**
>
> **Twelve 10-inch flour tortillas**
>
> **12 large eggs, scrambled**
>
> **Two 4-ounce cans diced green chiles, drained**
>
> **Two 4-ounce cans diced jalapeños, drained**
>
> **12 ounces cheddar cheese, shredded**
>
> **Salsa**

1. Heat the shredded pork in a small amount of water till very hot. Heat the tortillas one at a time in the microwave according to the package directions.

2. Place some shredded pork, eggs, chiles, jalapeños, cheese, and salsa on each tortilla. Fold up and wrap in tin foil to keep warm or serve immediately.

MAKES 12 BURRITOS

N O T E Cook the pork with 2 teaspoons ground cumin, 2 tablespoons chopped garlic, 2 teaspoons chili powder, and salt and black pepper to taste. Once it's fork tender, shred the pork and refrigerate till morning.

RICH'S DINE AND DASH POTATOES

This quick and easy recipe is from Rich Machesney, who works with Wyatt Fuller creating special bikes and parts for Harley-Davidson. Rich calls Hickory, North Carolina, home and had this to say about his recipe: "For lack of a better name, I call them Dine and Dash Potatoes. Not to recall those days of getting a free meal once in a while, that's another story. I don't think I'd want to put it in writing."

6 to 8 medium-size potatoes, diced

1 small onion, diced

¼ cup (½ stick) butter, melted

2 tablespoons vegetable oil

1 tablespoon Mrs. Dash seasoning

1. Preheat the oven to 400°F.

2. Place the potatoes and onion in a baking dish and drizzle with the butter and oil. Sprinkle with the Mrs. Dash and bake for 45 minutes, stirring occasionally. They also come out great cooked on a grill in a foil bag.

MAKES 4 TO 6 SERVINGS

DARIA SCHOOLER'S ALTERED STATES PANCAKES

"My passion for motorcycling started after I lost 100 pounds and was able to start wearing leather. That landed me at the local Harley dealer quite a bit. It wasn't long before I started sitting on bikes and chose the Fat Boy. It got a new paint job, pipes, engine guard, and *lots* of chrome, including a tank cover with a Dreamcatcher engraved on it. The same design is etched into the windshield and is the bike's name on the plate frame. This bike was just the beginning. Now I have a 2001 Sportster 1200 and a 2002 red Screamin' Eagle Road King for short- and long-distance riding respectively. Nothing is more liberating to the soul than rolling down the road on a Harley. The sound of the machine, the wind, the smells in the air, and the feel of the bike rumbling on the pavement, taking you where you may never have been before, make every journey in life worthwhile. But all that riding makes one very hungry! Just recently I discovered my passion for cooking equals my passion for riding. In fact, I discovered both at about the same time, after turning forty! It's true, old dogs can definitely learn new tricks. My love for life is forever joined with my love for learning.

"My mom makes great pancakes and I asked her to share her recipe with me. To add variety and a flavor other than syrup to pancakes, I changed a few ingredients around from her basic recipe to liven things up. As with my Dreamcatcher, switching the paint and adding lots of special chrome to create a unique and beautiful bike, altering Mom's basic recipe has led to some awesome results. Basically, substitution of different ingredients for some or all of the milk quantity is the secret to custom Altered States Pancakes. Every pancake chef can come up with their own."

> 1¾ cups all-purpose flour
>
> 1 tablespoon baking powder
>
> ¼ teaspoon salt
>
> 2 teaspoons sugar
>
> 2 large eggs, separated (whip the egg whites until stiff peaks form)
>
> 1¾ cups milk (see page 9 for variations)
>
> ½ teaspoon vanilla extract
>
> ⅓ cup vegetable oil

1. In a large mixing bowl combine the dry ingredients. Add the egg yolks, milk, vanilla, and oil and beat with an electric mixer until smooth. Add the whipped egg whites by gently stirring them into the batter with a rubber spatula.

2. Ladle the pancake batter into a hot greased skillet over medium heat. Flip over when bubbles start to form on top. Remove from the pan when both sides are golden brown.

3. Top with butter or whatever you like and enjoy!

MAKES 15 PANCAKES

ALTERED STATES #1 For banana walnut pancakes, substitute for the milk 1 banana, peeled and liquefied in a blender, ½ cup black walnut liqueur, and ¾ cup heavy cream.

ALTERED STATES #2 For blueberry white chocolate pancakes, substitute one 12-ounce can evaporated milk and ¼ cup white chocolate liqueur for the milk and stir ¾ cup fresh blueberries, picked over for stems, into the batter.

Daria Schooler and her custom Fat Boy

KATHY AUSTIN'S NUTTY FRENCH TOAST

"This is a great twist to the traditional French toast," says Kathy Austin from Houston, Texas. "It has a nutty texture and lots of protein! Great for those cold mornings before heading out on the road!" Well, once you whip up a batch of these, you will be nuts about them too. What a great way to start the day before a winter's ride on your Harley.

2 large eggs

1 cup milk

Granulated sugar

Crushed nuts (almonds, pecans, cashews, etc.)

Ground cinnamon

Ground nutmeg

Sliced bread (white or wheat, the thicker the better)

Butter (for cooking and to put on after cooking)

Confectioners' sugar (optional)

Syrup (optional)

1. In a large shallow bowl, mix the eggs and milk together well. Add granulated sugar, crushed nuts, cinnamon, and nutmeg to your taste.

2. Heat a large nonstick skillet (Silverstone or Teflon) over medium heat and melt some butter to cover the bottom or coat with nonstick cooking spray.

3. Place several slices of bread in the egg mixture and coat on both sides, letting the excess drip off a bit.

4. Lay the bread in the skillet and cook on both sides until golden brown.

5. Serve with butter, sprinkle with confectioners' sugar, if desired, and serve with syrup, if desired.

MAKES 4 TO 6 SERVINGS

Kathy Austin's 1995 883 Sporty

DANGEROUS CURVES: DRINKS

O ne of the sweetest parts of riding my Harley is guiding it through curvy roads. What a rush it is to pilot a big twin around a tight curve on a country road and find out what lies around the bend. It's like dancing, the music of the motor and the rhythm of leaning in and out of turns. The only thing more exciting is to ride those same roads on my Buell. Heck, I could ride curvy roads all day long on the Buell, since that is where those bikes shine the most. But I digress, back to food and, in this case, drinks.

When I plan a trip, I will often look for roads on the map that snake across the countryside and provide the most curves per mile. While the place I am headed to is a big part of any trip, the adventure is always in the journey there. Just like a nice meal, where the dessert is the sweet ending but the real excitement comes in getting there. That excitement should start with the first thing you serve.

When I plan a dinner gathering, I like to start with something that will set the tone for the meal. Like any fine restaurant experience, the meals at my house often begin with a cocktail and some conversation. You know that after a long ride we like to do some "bench racing"—there's nothing like telling tall tales with your riding buddies to get an appetite revved-up.

After the meal is done, it is time to kick back with a cup of Joe or some other after-dinner beverage and recap the day's ride or plan the next big road trip. It is during times like these, hanging with my riding buddies, sharing drinks and food, that it becomes so clear that we are all part of a big Harley riding family.

Just like you care about your family, I care about my Harley riding family. I feel it is important to offer along with these recipes a few words of family wisdom—*don't drink and ride*. With that said, enjoy these recipes and the camaraderie of your friends.

BIKER PATRIOT UNCLE JOHN'S NASTY BLACK COFFEE

Here is a cup of Joe that will make your hair stand on end, if you are crazy enough to drink it. This recipe comes from Josh Placa's Uncle John. J. Joshua Placa is the editor of *Cruising Rider* magazine. Biking and brewing go back generations in his family, as do cast-iron stomachs. Josh is a Harley-riding buddy of mine who calls the Arizona desert home, so you know he is a fiery biker. Josh sent along this quote from his uncle: "Sometimes, when times were hard, you just had to use what was around. And if you were wrenching on a Panhead and got hungry, sometimes parts fell in the pot. Not bad for ya, added a little iron. Just had to remember to let all the heavy stuff settle to the bottom."

Since this recipe is as vintage as a '49 Panhead, I have left it "unrestored" so you can savor the original flavor and style; I think in antique bike terminology this recipe is what would be called "barn fresh." As Uncle John would say, "No milk allowed. Sugar is for sissies. Ya can add ¼ teaspoon cayenne pepper or one cinnamon stick [for weak stomachs] while brewing."

Raw coffee beans

Big, old-fashioned stained and chipped enamel coffee pot

Some water

Reach into the coffee sack and grab yourself a big handful of beans. Fill the pot about two thirds full with cold tap water. Crush the beans with your hand and throw them hard into the pot. Bring to a boil, then simmer over low heat for about 10 minutes. Enjoy.

MAKES 1 SERVING

JASON'S BURNING MARYS

My buddy Jason works part time as a bartender here in Asheville, North Carolina. He whipped this up at one of my recipe taste-testing parties to the delight of all in attendance. This hopped-up drink will add some burn to your next party. While Jason is a man of few words, he did make this one recommendation: "Don't drink these Burning Marys and ride"—good advice from a good friend.

¼ teaspoon black pepper

2 canned chipotle peppers packed in adobo sauce

2 teaspoons prepared horseradish

¼ teaspoon salt

Juice of 1 lime

One 46-ounce can tomato juice

Vodka (if you are not riding)

Celery stalks

1. In a blender, combine the black pepper, chipotles, horseradish, salt, lime juice, and 1 cup of the tomato juice. Process until no large pieces of pepper remain, 30 to 60 seconds. Add the remaining tomato juice and process for 30 seconds. Add vodka to taste and process for 30 seconds.

2. Serve in tall glasses over ice with celery stalks.

MAKES ABOUT 1½ QUARTS JASON'S BURNING MARYS,
ENOUGH FOR 8 TO 10 DRINKS

JOSH PLACA'S GRANDMA'S WILD EGGNOG

My buddy Josh has a collection of true recipes and he's tried every one. "I had to, that's all there was to eat." He credits his parents, Frank and Anna Placa, for his well-nourished upbringing, and Uncle John Pagano for a dash of roguish flavor. Josh spends a lot of his days riding his custom Softail in the Arizona desert. After a day baking in the sun, he tells me that "Grandma's nog will chill your

fried noggin, and after a few glasses of nog, Uncle John's coffee is actually real tasty and much needed."

12 large eggs

2 cups sugar

2 cups dark rum

2 cups brandy

2 tablespoons vanilla extract

1 quart whole milk

1 quart heavy cream

Ground nutmeg

1. The night before the nog will be served, separate the eggs. Store the whites in the icebox in a sealed container. In a large punch bowl combine the egg yolks, sugar, rum, brandy, and vanilla and beat well with a hand or electric beater. Cover tightly with plastic wrap and refrigerate overnight.

2. The next day, just before serving, add the milk and heavy cream and beat it together.

3. In a large mixing bowl, whip the egg whites until stiff peaks form. Gently fold the egg whites into the nog.

4. To serve, ladle into a punch glass and sprinkle nutmeg on top. Enjoy.

MAKES ABOUT 3 1/2 QUARTS

Josh Placa with a reproduction of Peter Fonda's Captain America bike

LYNN DWIGHT'S BRANDY OR RUM SLUSHY

This recipe comes from Lynn Dwight, who is a member of the Killer Creek H.O.G. Chapter based at Killer Creek Harley-Davidson in Roswell, Georgia. Lynn says these are "Great on really, really hot days . . . but watch it . . . they catch up with you quickly!!!!" I have done cooking shows at Killer Creek H-D and I can tell you they have some hot weather and hot bikes there. But best of all, they have great southern hospitality. As Lynn says, "Here's another that's great for entertaining ('cause I do sooooo much entertaining!)." So, if you are entertaining, share Lynn's slushy with your buddies after you collect the bike keys.

> 2½ cups brandy or rum
>
> ½ to 1 cup sugar, to your taste
>
> 1 large can frozen lemonade concentrate, thawed
>
> 1 large can frozen limeade concentrate, thawed
>
> 9 cups water
>
> Seltzer (see Note)

1. Mix the brandy, sugar, concentrates, and water in a large plastic juice container. Place in the freezer until it gets slushy.

2. To serve, pour into a glass and top off with some seltzer.

MAKES ABOUT 3 QUARTS

N O T E You can use seltzer, club soda, or any clear soda that you prefer.

Future Harley owner Michael Pagan (sixth from left) and his touring buddies

MICHAEL PAGAN'S HIGH OCTANE MARTINI

Here is a recipe that I couldn't pass by. Sometimes I do enjoy a good martini once the bikes are locked away for the night. I have been accused of liking them solely for the chance to eat more olives—could be true, especially if they are spicy olives. This recipe is from Michael Pagan of Morris Plains, New Jersey. Here is some of what Michael has to say about his recipe and riding: "I don't ride a Harley, but I do ride a V-twin, a Ducati! However, every one of my motorcycle touring buddies rides a Harley, and I love to swap rides (I'll do anything for a test ride)." Sounds like there is a Harley in Michael's future. Michael goes on to wisely advise, "This recipe is definitely *not* for before or during the ride. But after the ride, one of the great pleasures is to relax and chase away the cold of an early spring or late fall ride with one of these drinks." One last thing Michael said just goes to show that people who ride motorcycles know that it is all about the riding: "I ride with a bunch of guys (and one gal) who all ride Harleys. I'm the odd man out on my foreign bike, but I respect them and they respect me (mostly), and we all love the ride." Enjoy Michael's recipe, just please don't drink and ride.

3 ounces pepper vodka (see Note)

¼ ounce dry vermouth

1 or 2 jalapeño-stuffed olives

1. Place about a half dozen small ice cubes in a tall glass, preferably a bartender's mixing container (made out of metal). Pour in the vodka and vermouth and stir for at least half a minute. The longer you stir, the more water will mix into the drink, as the ice cubes melt. Stirring for less than half a minute results in a drink that is too powerful, with the alcohol overpowering the taste of the pepper.

2. Strain into a 4-ounce cocktail glass and drop in a jalapeño-stuffed olive. Any olive brine still dripping from the olive will add to the taste complexity of the drink. Drink while still cold and don't ride your bike until the next day.

MAKES 1 MARTINI

N O T E If you don't have a pepper vodka, such as Absolut Peppar, you can substitute regular vodka and add a couple of dashes of Tabasco sauce.

KICK-STARTERS:
APPETIZERS

How do you kick-start a party or dinner? You serve appetizers.
Yes, the food designed to get your appetite all fired up. And believe me, some of these appetizers will not only fire your appetite up,
they may just make you do a smoky burnout all the way into the next
county. When you get pulled over, just tell the highway patrol officer
that you were conducting a top secret Biker Billy recipe test burnout.
Then offer him or her a sample from your saddlebag, after that swear
them to secrecy, and maybe, just maybe, you won't get a ticket. Hey, it
never works for me, but it is always worth the try and these appetizers are healthier than donuts, so you are doing a public health service
and you may just make a new friend.

I love to create appetizer recipes and it seems a lot of my fellow
Harley riders feel the same. What is more wonderful to share with

friends when you gather to talk motorcycles, adventures, and the open road than tasty finger food? These yummy treats are always welcome at H.O.G. chapter gatherings, Harley-Davidson dealership open houses, and anywhere bikers gather. Here is your chance to become the Chef of the Future—just cook any or all of these appetizers and surprise your riding buddies. They will have a new respect for your talents and your good taste. Alright!

DIABOLIC EGGS

Ordinary deviled eggs just don't do it for me, kinda like riding a bicycle. So I took this tired old appetizer and did a rebuild on it. Just like an old Harley fresh from the restorer's shop, these eggs will take your breath away and give you new ride—a fast ride, that is, to get a cold drink of milk.

6 hard-boiled eggs, cooled and peeled

1 scallion, ends trimmed and minced

1 teaspoon dried cilantro

½ teaspoon ground cumin

1 teaspoon dried parsley

½ teaspoon black pepper

2 tablespoons ranch dressing

1 teaspoon spicy brown mustard

1 canned chipotle pepper packed in adobo sauce, minced

Salt

1. Cut the eggs in half lengthwise, place the yolks in a small mixing bowl, and set the whites aside. Add the scallion, cilantro, cumin, parsley, black pepper, ranch dressing, mustard, and chipotle to the egg yolks and mix well with a fork until smooth. Season with salt to taste.

2. Spoon the yolk mixture into the hollow part of each egg white; there should be enough yolk filling to form a small dome on top of each egg white. Serve cool, not cold, for the most flavorful presentation.

MAKES 12 DIABOLIC EGGS

HOT NUTTY GOAT CHEESE

This killer cheese will surprise your riding buddies. It has a great nutty flavor and the sun-dried tomatoes add a sweet note, then the fire kicks in. It makes a wicked spread or roll it into ¾- to 1-inch balls for a surprising addition to salads like Suicide Shift Salad (page 77).

> 4 ounces goat cheese, softened
>
> ¼ cup shelled salted pistachios, finely chopped
>
> 2 tablespoons pine nuts, finely chopped
>
> 4 oil-packed sun-dried tomatoes, minced
>
> ¼ teaspoon cayenne pepper
>
> ¼ teaspoon salt
>
> ¼ teaspoon black pepper

1. Put all the ingredients in a small mixing bowl and mix well with a fork until completely combined.

2. Cover with plastic wrap and refrigerate for 1 hour to let the flavors develop. Serve chilled.

MAKES ALMOST 1 CUP

BIKER TOOTHPICKS

Mere onion rings pale by comparison to these deep-fried devils. It is like comparing the sound and feel of an Schwinn 10-speed bicycle with baseball cards clothespinned to the forks to a Harley-Davidson Electra Glide Ultra Classic with Screamin' Eagle mufflers. Geez, Louise, there is just no comparison at all. The wonderful combination of red onions, bell peppers, and jalapeño slices deep-fried in this tasty batter is to die for. To make the whole experience complete, serve these Biker Toothpicks with Iron Horseradish Sauce for dipping. Then you are ready to rumble off into the culinary sunset in true Biker Billy style.

> 3 cups all-purpose flour
>
> 1½ teaspoons salt

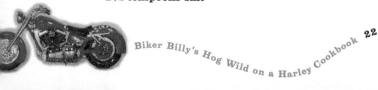

1½ teaspoons baking powder

1 teaspoon white pepper

½ teaspoon cayenne pepper

½ teaspoon ground cumin

2 cups water

2 jumbo eggs, beaten

2 tablespoons canola oil, plus extra for deep-frying

1 medium-size red bell pepper, seeded and cut into matchsticks

4 large jalapeños, seeded and cut into matchsticks

1 medium-size red onion, cut into matchsticks

Iron Horseradish Sauce (page 287)

1. In a large mixing bowl, whisk together the flour, salt, baking powder, white pepper, cayenne, and cumin. In a small mixing bowl, whisk together the water, eggs, and canola oil. Pour the water mixture into the flour mixture and whisk until a smooth batter forms.

2. Heat 3 to 4 inches of canola oil to 365°F in a deep pot or deep-fryer.

3. When the oil is hot enough, dip the vegetables in the batter and deep-fry until golden brown, 2 to 3 minutes. Do not crowd them while frying or the oil temperature will drop and you'll end up with greasy food. Use a slotted spoon to remove the vegetables from the oil, drain on paper towels, and serve hot with the horseradish sauce for dipping.

MAKES 4 TO 6 SERVINGS

LISA CARLINE'S HARLEY MAMMA JALAPEÑOS

Lisa Carline is a Harley rider from New Orleans and the owner/builder of a very sweet custom Harley. Lisa told me, "I am a certified chef from Louisiana. The two things that relax me most are riding and cooking. After eating a good meal, I hit the highway and get in the wind. Life just doesn't get any better than that." Lisa is so right. About her recipe, which is rightly named for her, she said, "These jalapeños are smooth tasting but will not set you ablaze. They contain the right blend of sweetness and pepper, giving it a perfect balance. Kind of like the relationship between me and my Harley; I ride every day and it keeps me balanced." A true Lady of Harley and a great chef too; try Lisa's recipe, then follow her lead and go for a ride on your Harley.

12 medium-size fresh jalapeños

One 8-ounce package cream cheese, softened

½ teaspoon vanilla extract

1 teaspoon hot sauce

1 teaspoon Worcestershire sauce

½ small onion, minced

12 strips hickory-smoked bacon

1. Preheat the oven to 350°F.

2. Wash and dry the jalapeños. Split them in half lengthwise and remove the seeds and white veins.

3. In a large mixing bowl, combine the cream cheese, vanilla, hot sauce, Worcestershire sauce, and onion and blend well. Fill the jalapeño halves with the cream cheese mixture until the cavity is full.

4. Cut the bacon strips in half crosswise. Wrap one strip of bacon around each jalapeño half. Place the jalapeños in a shallow baking pan in a single layer. Bake, uncovered, until the bacon turns brown, about 25 minutes. Drain off the grease and serve hot!

MAKES 8 SERVINGS

BOB KARCHER'S SHOP SNACKS

I met Bob Karcher in his hometown of Carlisle, Pennsylvania, at the 2002 Carlisle Summer Bike Fest. Later, Bob wrote me: "I would like to thank you for coming to Carlisle last week. Our love for Harleys extends not only to the bikes and rides themselves, but also to the political arena where our rights to ride may be threatened. American Bikers Aimed Toward Education (ABATE) of PA and other State Motorcycle Rights Organizations (SMROs) are where the real action is, and those who love it the most are those that sacrifice a few weekends or riding time to protect everybody's right to ride." About his recipe he said, "We have all been there. You plan for the big run the next day and your bike is still in boxes in the garage. Looks like an all-nighter. Your friends come over to help and this is something to feed them that is quick, requires no cooking time, and can be eaten while you work."

Generous amount of your favorite hot peppers

Three 3-ounce packages cream cheese, softened

2 tablespoons mayonnaise

Few shakes of garlic powder

5 large flour tortillas, warmed according to package directions

1. Dice the peppers and place them in a large mixing bowl with the cream cheese, mayonnaise, and garlic powder. Whip until smooth. Spread evenly over the tortilla shells, $\frac{1}{8}$ to $\frac{1}{4}$ inch thick. Roll the shells and put in the beer fridge for about half an hour.

2. Remove and cut each roll into 4 or 5 slices. Garnish with toothpicks or nails. Serve with beer.

SERVES A GARAGE FULL OF HUNGRY BIKE BUILDERS

SWEET POTATO FRITTERS

These spicy sweet fritters make potato latkes look like a pedal bike compared to a full-dressed Harley. Great all year long but especially welcome as a holiday appetizer. Try them at your next H.O.G. Christmas party.

4 canned chipotle peppers packed in adobo sauce, minced

2 tablespoons chopped garlic

⅓ cup packed light brown sugar

1 teaspoon salt

1 teaspoon white pepper

½ teaspoon ground nutmeg

½ teaspoon ground allspice

1 teaspoon ground ginger

½ teaspoon baking powder

3 jumbo eggs

1 cup all-purpose flour

4 cups peeled and shredded sweet potatoes

1 medium-size onion, coarsely chopped

¾ cup Craisins (dried cranberries; look for them near the raisins in your supermarket)

Olive oil for frying

1. Place the chipotles, garlic, brown sugar, salt, white pepper, nutmeg, allspice, ginger, baking powder, and eggs in a blender or food processor and process until no large pieces of chipotle remain, about 1 minute. Add the flour and process until smooth, about 1 minute.

2. Place the sweet potatoes, onion, and Craisins in a large mixing bowl and toss together well. Add the batter and mix well.

3. In a medium-size skillet, heat ¼ inch of olive oil over medium heat. Place 1 tablespoon of the sweet potato mixture in the hot oil and flatten gently with the back of the spoon. Repeat until the pan is full of fritters. Fry until the edges start to brown, 2 to 3 minutes. Turn and fry the other side until browned, another 2 to 3 minutes. Drain on paper towels and serve piping hot.

MAKES 10 TO 12 FRITTERS

FLAMETHROWER FRITTERS

These Indian-style fritters pack so much flavor that I just love to start a fancy Indian feast with them. They get your palate all warmed up for the flavor-intensive care of a curry or biriyani or any Indian-style dish you might be serving. These fritters are made with chickpea flour, which is ground-up dried chickpeas (garbanzo beans). This pale yellow flour adds a special flavor that really gives the fritters an authentic Indian flair. You will find chickpea flour in health food and specialty food stores or the organic food sections of upscale supermarkets.

Serve these fritters with the Biker Biriyani recipe from my first book, *Biker Billy Cooks with Fire*. Just don't put too many of these fritters on the table, since they will fill up your dinner guests before the main course arrives. They are also one of my favorite munchies to take to the garage when I am doing routine service on the Burpee Biker Billy Jalapeño show bike—you know, the one with those wicked flamethrowers. In fact, that is where I came up with the name for these tasty treats. Enjoy them—just don't burn the house down with the flames from your tongue.

1 cup chickpea flour

½ teaspoon baking powder

¼ teaspoon cayenne pepper

1 teaspoon salt

½ teaspoon white pepper

1 teaspoon ground cumin

1 tablespoon canola oil

½ cup water

1 bunch scallions, ends trimmed and cut into 1-inch pieces

1 shallot, quartered

Canola oil for frying

1. In a food processor, combine the chickpea flour, baking powder, cayenne, salt, white pepper, and cumin and pulse several times to mix. With the machine running, pour the oil through the feed tube, process for 30 seconds, and scrape the bowl down. With the machine running, pour the water through the feed tube, process for 30 seconds,

and scrape the bowl down. Process until a smooth batter forms. Add the scallions and shallot and pulse several times until well mixed. Transfer to a medium-size mixing bowl and allow to rest, covered, for 30 minutes in a warm place.

2. In a medium-size skillet, heat ½ inch of canola oil over medium heat and spoon 1 tablespoon of the batter per fritter into the oil. Fry until the edges begin to brown, 2 to 3 minutes. Turn over and fry until golden brown, 2 to 3 minutes. Drain on paper towels and serve warm.

MAKES 4 SERVINGS

RON JANICKI'S HOT ROD SAUSAGE ROLL PUFFS

This easy, fiery pork appetizer is from my friend Ron Janicki of Cumberland, Rhode Island. Says Ron, "Rhode Island has the best beaches in New England, and a hell of a lot of bikers to cruise around them. This is a ride-to-eat state and it is not uncommon to have a lot of bikers in your home. Twice Debbie and I have had the annual picnic for the Ocean State Chapter of H.O.G. in our backyard. It's great to have 100 people and bikes parked all over the place." Ron and I have shared a lot of food during open house events at Vanson Leathers in Fall River, Massachusetts. Vanson Leathers is the company that made my awesome Biker Billy jacket as seen on the cover of my last book, *Biker Billy's Freeway-a-Fire Cookbook*.

1 package Pepperidge Farm frozen puff pastry, thawed

One 1-pound package Jimmy Dean hot sausage, thawed

Cajun seasoning (optional)

1. Roll the puff pastry into a rectangle 15 x 9 inches and cut the rectangle into three strips, each 3 inches wide. Use the folds in the pastry as guides. Divide the sausage meat into thirds and roll each into a snake the length of the pastry. Place each roll of sausage along one edge of the pastry strip and sprinkle with seasoning (if you like it extra spicy). Roll the pastry around the sausage, wet the edges with cold water, and press to seal. Refrigerate the rolls for at least an hour.

Biker Billy's Hog Wild on a Harley Cookbook

2. Preheat the oven to 400°F.

3. Cut the sausage rolls into ½-inch-thick slices and put them on parchment paper-covered baking sheets. Bake until the pastry is puffed and golden brown, about 18 minutes.

4. Immediately sprinkle with more Cajun seasoning and serve.

MAKES 60 TO 70

Debbie Janicki on a 1997 Softail Custom and Ron Janicki on a 1995 Road King

RON'S MU SHU HOG

Ron says, "East meets West with this seductive treat that first is sweet, then finishes with the heat. You can roast this in an oven or in the indirect heat of the barbecue." Sweet and fiery is a killer combination that I enjoy surprising folks with; great minds do think alike, or at least great hungers do. Fire up that oven and get ready for some tasty hog treats.

> **1 to 2 pounds pork tenderloins, trimmed of any fat and silverskin**
>
> **One 1-inch piece fresh ginger, peeled and sliced**
>
> **2 scallions, ends trimmed and sliced**
>
> **½ to ¾ cup Kikkoman Teriyaki Marinade Sauce**
>
> **¾ to 1 cup hoisin sauce**

1. Put the pork, ginger, and scallions in a zippered-top plastic bag and pour in the teriyaki marinade sauce to cover the pork. Seal the bag and refrigerate for 24 to 48 hours.

2. Preheat the oven to 375°F.

3. Remove the pork from the marinade. Place the pork on a wire rack in a roasting pan and roast for 35 to 45 minutes. Baste the pork with the hoisin sauce and bake until an instant-read meat thermometer inserted in the thickest part registers 165°F, another 10 minutes.

4. Remove the pork from the pan, let it rest for 5 minutes to settle the juices, and cut into ¼-inch-thick slices. Heat up the remaining hoisin sauce to accompany the sliced pork.

MAKES 16 TO 32 SERVINGS AS AN APPETIZER
OR 4 TO 8 AS AN ENTRÉE

RON'S SPANISH PORK APPETIZER

Here is a recipe with a Latin flair straight from one of Ron's many adventures on his Harley; in Ron's words, "This will remind you of that drive through the Spanish Mission District, stopping by a tapas bar for some hog tenderloins." After you enjoy these hog tenderloins, you will be ready to mount your Hog and head out on your own Harley adventures.

FOR THE MARINADE

1 tablespoon Spanish paprika

3 cloves garlic, mashed into a paste

3 to 5 tablespoons extra virgin olive oil, or more, depending on how much pork you have

1 to 2 tablespoons fresh lemon juice

½ teaspoon dried thyme

½ teaspoon dried oregano

1 bay leaf, crushed

Salt and freshly ground black pepper

1 to 2 pounds pork tenderloins, trimmed of any fat and silverskin

Ron Janicki's Onion Marmalade (page 291)

Roasted red peppers

Sliced crusty bread

1. Combine the marinade ingredients in a small mixing bowl and stir well to blend. Put the pork in a zippered-top plastic bag and pour on the marinade, coating the pork evenly. Seal the bag and refrigerate for 24 to 48 hours, turning the pork several times.

2. Preheat the oven to 375°F.

3. Remove the pork from the marinade. Bring the marinade to a boil in a small saucepan. Set aside. Place the pork on a wire rack in a roasting pan and roast for 35 to 45 minutes. At this point, start basting the pork with the boiled marinade until an instant-read meat thermometer inserted into the thickest part registers 165°F, about another 10 minutes.

4. Remove the pork from the oven, let rest for 5 minutes to let the juices settle, and cut into ¼-inch-thick slices. Serve with onion marmalade, roasted red peppers, and sliced crusty bread.

MAKES 16 TO 32 SERVINGS AS AN APPETIZER
OR 4 TO 8 AS AN ENTRÉE

SPEED BUMPS:
DIPS AND SALSAS

O n the road there are often things that slow us down, whether we
want or need to slow down, like the traffic jam a half mile before your exit, especially if that exit is a "rest," gas, or dinner stop. In
some places, traffic engineers or local control freaks place speed
bumps to control traffic. Nothing like having to scrape the bottom of
the bike on a speed bump just to get into the supermarket parking lot.
Now, while you are in that supermarket you will want to have this
chapter open as your shopping list. The recipes in this chapter are all
delightful dishes that you will want to share with your H.O.G. buddies.
They will bring a new meaning to the term scraping the bottom. Yes,
your friends and you will be scraping the bottom of the serving bowl
to get the last tasty morsel of these party treats. In fact, one of the
recipes will find you actually eating the bottom of the bowl just to get

that last yummy taste. I won't slow you down anymore with my culinary traffic control, just dive into the first recipe like a Harley VR 1000 diving into the first turn at Daytona Beach International Speedway. From there you will roar off to the winner's podium after your riding buddies elect you Chapter Chef at your next H.O.G. meeting.

UNHOLY GUACAMOLE

A Mexican meal served without guacamole is like an unpainted motorcycle. No matter how well all the parts work together, it is unfinished. It would be a sin to serve Biker Billy–style Mexican food with some lame store-bought guacamole, sorta like calling a clone bike a Harley-Davidson. While there is some hot pepper in this guacamole, it is by no means fiery, just enough crushed red pepper to add a sparkle to the flavors, like a nice paint job on a custom bike.

2 ripe Hass avocados, peeled, pitted, and diced

Juice of ½ lemon

½ cup diced red onion

½ cup seeded and diced red bell pepper

½ cup canned corn kernels, drained

½ cup diced fresh tomato

½ teaspoon salt

½ teaspoon white pepper

½ teaspoon red pepper flakes

1. Place the avocado in a medium-size mixing bowl, sprinkle with the lemon juice, and stir well. Add the remaining ingredients and stir well.

2. Cover with plastic wrap and refrigerate for 1 hour to let the flavors develop. Serve chilled.

MAKES ABOUT 3 CUPS

JIM EDWARDS'S HOT GUACAMOLE FOR FRIENDS

T his recipe is from Jim Edwards of Darlington, South Carolina, who, besides being a rider, is a former MSF instructor, nurse anesthetist, and, his "favorite role," "Grampa to four beautiful grandkids." Jim knows that life is all about friends and family; he told me, "Riding with a group of friends or just you and your main squeeze to go out to lunch or supper is so enjoyable, especially trying out new places you've heard were really good." Jim has a special dedication for this recipe that I am sure will speak to you about our Harley family, as it spoke to me. In Jim's words, "This recipe is dedicated to Mark Pease of St. Joseph, Missouri. Mark was the consummate H-D man. His main ambition was to work for the H-D Company that built the bike he loved to ride. Mark realized that dream, but was struck down by cancer at forty-three. Mark would ride every day, even if there was snow on the ground, if the roads were dry. He was thought very well of by his fellow workers at the Kansas City H-D plant, where he worked. I only got to ride a little with my brother-in-law Mark, but he just touched a chord in the heart of everyone who met him. This one's for Mark." Godspeed, Mark.

> **1 to 2 habanero peppers, finely minced**
>
> **2 teaspoons minced garlic**
>
> **4 ripe avocados, peeled, pitted, and mashed**
>
> **1 tablespoon lime juice (fresh is best!)**
>
> **1 small onion, finely chopped**
>
> **½ cup medium hot chunky salsa**
>
> **1 tablespoon chopped fresh cilantro leaves**
>
> **Salt**

In a large mixing bowl, combine the habanero, garlic, avocado, lime juice, onion, salsa, and cilantro and mix well. Season with salt and serve with tortilla chips, corn chips, or whatever! Enjoy.

MAKES 4 CUPS

SPINACH SPEED BUMP DIP

There you are grazing at the snack table, speeding your way from one end to the other, piling your plate high with all sorts of goodies, then, wham, you have to slow down. Yes, there is a culinary speed bump in your path and it requires all your skill as a rider and a party goer to safely navigate it. This cheesy spinach combo is spiced just right and loaded with scallions and sun-dried tomatoes to add an

extra bump to the flavors. Just remember that the idea of a speed bump is to slow you down, not make you stop, so don't park yourself in front of this dip and start a snack table traffic jam. Make this dip and don't be surprised when your riding buddies start asking you to put speed bumps in their way again.

1 large loaf round bread

2 tablespoons extra virgin olive oil

1 bunch scallions, ends trimmed and cut into ¼-inch-thick slices

1 shallot, minced

½ teaspoon red pepper flakes

One 10-ounce package frozen spinach, thawed, drained, and squeezed dry

⅓ cup minced oil-packed sun-dried tomatoes, drained

2 tablespoons chopped garlic

½ teaspoon cayenne pepper

½ teaspoon dried chervil

1 teaspoon white pepper

1 teaspoon salt

½ cup half-and-half

One 8-ounce package cream cheese, softened and cut into 1-inch cubes

8 ounces Monterey Jack cheese, cut into ½-inch cubes

1. Cut a circular hole in the top of the loaf of bread, taking care to not cut through the bottom or sides. Pull out most of the center of the bread in bite-size pieces, leaving a hollow shell of crust with a thickness of ¼ to ½ inch. Set the bread shell and pieces aside.

2. Heat the olive oil in a large skillet over medium heat. Add the scallions, shallot, and red pepper and cook, stirring, until tender, 3 to 5 minutes. Add the spinach, sun-dried tomatoes, garlic, cayenne, chervil, white pepper, and salt and cook, stirring, for 5 minutes. Add the half-and-half, cream cheese, and Monterey Jack and stir just until the cheeses are completely melted.

3. Transfer the dip to the hollowed-out bread, place on a serving tray, surround with the bread pieces for dipping, and serve immediately.

MAKES 1 SPEED BUMP

LYNN VANDERVEST'S WILD FIRE H.O.G. CHAPTER CUCUMBER DIP

Lynn Vandervest, who is the owner of Vandervest Harley-Davidson in Peshtigo, Wisconsin, sent in this and the two dips that follow. Lynn's dealership is four years old and she told me, "Our H.O.G. Chapter is called the Wild Fire H.O.G. Chapter. Do you remember hearing about the Peshtigo Fire in your history books? Well, that is how we came up with our local H.O.G. Chapter name. We have a fun group of people in our chapter. I got voted as 'Ladies of Harley' director this year. We thought it would be fun to enter some of our favorite recipes in your book. Before owning the dealership, I ran a bar and grill for seventeen years. I had to entertain many groups and make food for weddings/parties. Here are some of my dips that people really like and are so simple to make. I also make these dips for our Open House Parties or events at the dealership."

If any of the other dips in this chapter set you on fire, this one will cool you down. Lynn says, "This is a great summertime dip. Use your garden fresh cucumbers, it's delicious!"

One 8-ounce package cream cheese, softened

2 tablespoons mayonnaise

½ teaspoon salt

2 tablespoons diced onion

1 cucumber, peeled, seeded, and diced

In a medium-size mixing bowl, combine the cream cheese, mayonnaise, and salt and mix well. Add the onion and cucumber and mix well. Don't use a mixer to do this. Cover with plastic wrap and refrigerate for 1 hour before serving. Serve with Frito Scoops.

MAKES ABOUT 2 CUPS

LYNN'S WILD FIRE H.O.G. CHAPTER BEER DIP

Okay, here is a sure-fire winner. Think Wisconsin and, yes, you think Harleys, cheese, and beer. Okay, don't mix bikes and beer, but cheese and beer, what could be better? I know there is something else big in Wisconsin, but I'll let Lynn tell you: "This dip will become a favorite to all. It's great for PACKER games!" Oh, yeah, the Green Bay Packers, they're pretty big in Wisconsin too.

> **Two 8-ounce packages cream cheese, softened**
>
> **1 package Hidden Valley The Original Ranch dip mix**
>
> **1 can beer**
>
> **One 8-ounce package shredded cheddar cheese**
>
> **One 16-ounce container French onion dip**

In a large mixing bowl, combine the cream cheese, ranch dip mix, and beer and beat until smooth. Fold in the cheddar cheese and onion dip. Cover with plastic wrap and refrigerate overnight. Serve with pretzels, Doritos, or Fritos.

MAKES ABOUT 4 CUPS

LYNN'S WILD FIRE H.O.G. CHAPTER LIVER PASTE

About this recipe Lynn says, "This is a very mild liver paste. Spread it on saltine or Ritz crackers, it's sure to be a hit."

> **¼ cup (½ stick) butter**
>
> **1 medium-size onion, sliced**
>
> **1 pound chicken livers, thawed if necessary**
>
> **Garlic salt**
>
> **Black pepper**
>
> **One 8-ounce package cheese cream, softened**

1. Melt the butter in a large saucepan over medium heat, add the onion and chicken livers, and simmer, covered, stirring occasionally, until the chicken livers are no longer pink, about 10 minutes. Sprinkle with garlic salt and black pepper to taste.

2. Allow to cool, then transfer to a blender, add the cream cheese, and process until smooth. Put in small containers and refrigerate overnight. Serve with crackers.

MAKES ABOUT 4 CUPS

JAHN TIGER'S FULL THROTTLE MEAT SAUCE AND DIP

This recipe comes from a good friend and fellow Buell rider, Jahn Tiger. Jahn is also responsible for keeping my Web site up and looking so good; he works at MMT Solutions in Parsippany, New Jersey. About his recipe, he said, "I decided to make some pasta sauce one day and just grabbed whatever I could find in the house. After I made it, my wife decided to use it as a dip because we had some guests over. The response was so great, I was asked to make it from then on. I ride a 1997 Buell M2 Cyclone and it's an extremely fun bike to ride. Just like I threw stuff together for the sauce, when I go riding I like to see where the next road takes me and I'll eventually figure out which direction I'm going. The results are great either way."

2 pounds ground beef

6 cloves garlic, chopped

1 medium-size onion, diced

1 medium-size ripe tomato, diced

½ cup finely chopped fresh oregano

¼ cup finely chopped fresh basil

1 tablespoon olive oil

¼ cup Lawry's seasoned salt

¼ cup Worcestershire sauce

1¾ cups tomato sauce

One 6-ounce can tomato paste

2 to 3 habanero peppers, finely chopped, or your favorite hot sauce

Shredded cheddar cheese (as much as you like)

1. In a large pot over high heat, break apart the meat and begin cooking it. Once the meat is mostly cooked, add the garlic, onion, tomato, oregano, basil, olive oil, Lawry's, and Worcestershire sauce. Mix everything together thoroughly and turn the heat down to medium-high. Continue to cook for about 5 more minutes. Now add the tomato sauce and paste (if you like your sauce a little thinner, leave the tomato paste out) and mix thoroughly. Let the sauce bubble up. Taste the sauce (careful, it will be hot) and add more spices for taste if necessary. Add the peppers or hot sauce and stir into the mixture. Turn the heat down to low or medium-low and let the sauce simmer for 20 to 30 minutes, stirring occasionally.

2. Remove from the heat, cover the top of the sauce with the cheese, and serve immediately. Great as a dip, over pasta, or on hot dogs or anything else you can think of.

MAKES 6 TO 8 CUPS SAUCE

Jahn Tiger and his 1997 Buell M2 Cyclone

DRUNKEN BEAN DIP

Seems like I can't go to a party without bringing this dip anymore; it just blows everyone away. I call it drunken bean dip because after everything is sautéed to perfection, I drown it in beer and let it stew until all the beer is gone. Yes, the beans in this dip have enough beer to be way over the legal limit. But don't worry, the only buzz you will get is from the chipotle peppers, since all the alcohol evaporates while it cooks. Enjoy the complex flavors of this dip and, if you decide to wash it down with a beer, leave the bike parked.

> ¼ cup extra virgin olive oil
>
> 2 medium-size onions, cut into matchsticks
>
> 3 canned chipotle peppers packed in adobo sauce, minced
>
> 3 tablespoons chopped garlic
>
> Two 15½-ounce cans light red kidney beans, rinsed and drained
>
> 1 teaspoon ground cumin
>
> 1 teaspoon ground coriander
>
> 1 tablespoon dried parsley
>
> 1 tablespoon dried cilantro
>
> 1 teaspoon salt
>
> 1 teaspoon black pepper
>
> 1 tablespoon liquid smoke
>
> 2 tablespoons dark molasses
>
> One 12-ounce bottle dark beer
>
> 2 cups shredded cheddar cheese
>
> Tortilla chips

1. Heat the olive oil in a large sauté pan over high heat. Add the onions and chipotles and cook, stirring, until browned, 3 to 5 minutes. Reduce the heat to medium, add the garlic, and cook, stirring, for 1 minute. Add the beans and cook, stirring a few times, until the beans begin to stick to the pan, 5 to 7 minutes. Add the cumin, coriander, parsley, cilantro, salt, black pepper, liquid smoke, molasses, and beer and bring to a boil. Reduce the heat to low and simmer until the liquid is almost gone, 20 to 30 minutes.

2. Add the cheddar cheese and stir until melted. Serve immediately.

MAKES ABOUT 1½ QUARTS

Biker Billy's Hog Wild on a Harley Cookbook

LINDA LEFFEL'S HOORAY FOR THE RED, WHITE, AND BLUE (DIP AND CHIPS)

This recipe is from Linda Leffel of San Diego, California, president of the San Diego Chapter of Women in the Wind, a group that strives to educate its members in motorcycle safety and maintenance, unite women motorcyclists with friends of common interests, and promote a positive image to the public of women on motorcycles. Linda told me this recipe is "hot, sweet, spicy, patriotic, and great fun at a party, just like me and my Harley!"

One 8-ounce package Philadelphia cream cheese (the "White")

½ bottle Bronco Bob's Roasted Raspberry Chipotle Sauce (the "Red"; can be found at Cost Plus)

1 bag blue corn tortilla chips (the "Blue")

1. Unwrap the cream cheese and put on a plate to soften at room temperature for half an hour before the party.

2. Pour the chipotle sauce all over the cream cheese. Surround with the chips and stick a few into the cream cheese to stand up like little flags.

MAKES 20 TO 30 SERVINGS

Linda Leffel on "Miss Liberty," her 2000 Harley-Davidson FXSTD (Deuce)

WYATT AND LOURDES FULLER'S "HOT MAMA'S" CHEESE DIP

Wyatt and Lourdes Fuller of Hickory, North Carolina, sent me this fiery dip recipe. Wyatt is a good friend who I have shared many a mile with riding Harleys. He is also an awesome bike builder who now works exclusively for Harley-Davidson creating special project bikes and designing custom parts and accessories. According to Wyatt and Lourdes, "This dip is great. Someone gave it to us a few years ago. You can't stop eating it and you'll like it cause it's hot! If you don't like it so hot, you can substitute mild Rotel tomatoes for the hot. Kids love it."

> **One 16-ounce package Jimmy Dean hot sausage**
>
> **Two 8-ounce cans Rotel extra hot diced tomatoes and chiles**
>
> **One 12-ounce can Hunt's diced tomatoes**
>
> **One 23-ounce package Velveeta cheese**

1. In a large skillet, cook the sausage and drain the fat from the pan.

2. Stir in the 3 cans of tomatoes with the sausage and cook for 5 minutes over medium heat.

3. Add the Velveeta, let the cheese melt, then stir and serve warm with tortilla chips.

MAKES A BIG BOWL

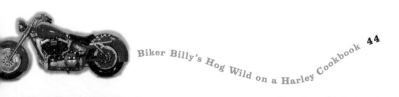

NANA'S FAMOUS HORSERADISH CHEESE SPREAD

Lynn Dwight, a member of the Killer Creek H.O.G. Chapter, based at Killer Creek Harley-Davidson in Roswell, Georgia, sent in her nana's recipe. Lynn, your nana gets all the credit for this tasty treat and you get my thanks for sharing it. Lynn also wants you to know that "guests will be surprised by the bite this dip has . . . My nana kept this simple recipe a secret for a long time. After she passed away, we laughed at the simplicity of the ingredients. If they like hot, spicy, they will love this!!! This recipe is much tastier than it sounds; do a taste test to see for yourself!!!!"

1 pound Velveeta cheese

½ cup mayonnaise

¼ teaspoon garlic salt

Dash of Worcestershire sauce

1 teaspoon dry mustard

One 5-ounce jar prepared horseradish (preferably Silver Springs brand)

1. In the top of a double boiler, combine all the ingredients and melt over medium heat, stirring as needed. Once completely melted, pour into crocks (such as the brown pottery style).

2. Let cool completely, cover with plastic wrap, and refrigerate. Serve with sesame breadsticks, sourdough pretzels, or something firm and crunchy.

MAKES ABOUT 3 CUPS

CHEESY DELIGHT DIP

This recipe is a personal-size dipping delight, just right for munching on while you read your H.O.G. chapter newsletter. Like a pocket race bike, this little treat will quickly speed away and only the memory will remain. But fear not, it is so easy and fast to make that you can whip up a batch before the checkered flag comes down. So, race into the kitchen and rev-up this cheesy delight.

 2 ounces cream cheese

 4 slices low-fat Swiss cheese

 2 to 3 dashes habanero pepper sauce

 $\frac{1}{8}$ teaspoon ground cumin

 $\frac{1}{8}$ teaspoon dried cilantro

 $\frac{1}{8}$ teaspoon salt

 $\frac{1}{8}$ teaspoon black pepper

In a medium-size microwaveable bowl, combine all the ingredients, heat in a microwave oven for 60 seconds at $\frac{1}{2}$ power, remove, and stir well. Return to the microwave, heat for 60 seconds at $\frac{1}{2}$ power, remove, and stir well. Serve with chips or crackers.

MAKES 2 SERVINGS

SHERRY'S SIZZLIN' SALSA

Sherry Phelps is a Ladies of Harley officer for Central Oklahoma #1 in Moore, Oklahoma. She is nicknamed "Pepper" because "I love the hot stuff" and she is a proud grandmother of two (Kody, three years, and Katlynn, eight months), so remember next time you see a motorcycle going down the road that someone's grandma could be aboard. Her fiery fresh salsa will be a welcome addition to any H.O.G. event. And you know it will be good since Sherry is "a true Chile Head from Albuquerque, though I am now living in Oklahoma. After a long ride, I like to eat something to warm up the body!" Way to go, Sherry, you know how to Eat Hot and Ride Safe!

Biker Billy's Hog Wild on a Harley Cookbook

2 to 3 cucumbers, peeled and seeded

5 Roma tomatoes

1 large yellow onion, peeled

3 garlic cloves, peeled

3 jalapeños

3 New Mexico peppers (use canned if fresh not available)

2 tablespoons chopped fresh cilantro leaves

Juice of 1 lemon

Salt

1. Finely chop all the ingredients. It may be easier to use a food processor and pulse until you get a crushed look to the salsa.

2. Stir in the lemon juice and season with salt. The hotter the salsa, the more salt you'll need to add. Cover with plastic wrap and refrigerate at least 1 hour to develop the flavors.

MAKES 6 TO 8 SERVINGS

Sherry and Larry Phelps in front of his 1997 Heritage Softail

GREEN FIRE
TOMATILLO SALSA

T art, tangy, and with just the right amount of fire, this fresh green salsa will turn your riding buddies green with envy. Like knowing the formula for building a high horsepower big twin, everyone will want your secret recipe. Just make them buy their own copy of this book so I can keep gas in my Road King.

This salsa is made with tomatillos, which look like green cherry tomatoes (to which they are distantly related, both being members of the nightshade family) with a parchment paper–like husk that slips off easily and a waxy residue that should be washed off before using. They have a tart flavor with a hint of lemon and undertones of cilantro. Tomatillos are an acquired taste and seem to appear in the markets erratically regardless of the season. While somewhat new in the U.S., they are a staple in Mexican dishes.

4 cups chopped fresh tomatillos

1 jalapeño, seeded and minced

1 serrano pepper, seeded and minced

1 medium-size onion, minced

2 tablespoons chopped garlic

1 tablespoon dried cilantro

1 teaspoon salt

½ teaspoon white pepper

Juice of ½ lime

Combine all the ingredients in a large mixing bowl, toss well to mix, cover with plastic wrap, and refrigerate for 1 hour to let the flavors develop. Serve chilled with corn tortilla chips.

MAKES ABOUT 1 QUART

SALLY GRACIA'S MAMA SALLY'S MANGO SALSA

Sally Gracia of Houston, Texas, sent me this recipe, saying, "I had a great little Sportster a few years ago. Never one to be satisfied with 'normal' or 'regular' things, but one that loves spicy Mexican foods, one day I decided to blend sweet with salty with tangy with spicy and came up with this great party salsa. The best part about this stuff is that all the ingredients fit into my saddlebags easily, so I can make it fresh once I get to the party. It goes best with some good Mexican beer, plenty of fresh limes, and real beer salt. I know it sounds a little strange, but try it—you'll like it!"

3 to 4 juicy red medium-size tomatoes, diced small

1 medium-size white onion, diced small

Salt to taste (beer salt with lime flavor if you can find it)

5 to 6 limes

2 firm, ripe mangos, peeled, seeded, and diced small

1 green bell pepper, seeded and diced small

2 jalapeños, seeded and diced small

1 bunch fresh cilantro, rinsed, stems removed, and leaves coarsely chopped

Place the tomatoes and onion in a serving bowl. Sprinkle with salt, squeeze a couple of fresh limes over the top, and toss well. Add the mangoes, bell pepper, and jalapeños. Repeat with the salt and lime juice. Add the cilantro and more salt and lime juice to taste. Mix well and let sit for a bit so the flavors can blend. Serve with Tostitos or as a condiment for fajitas. This is really good stuff! Oh, yeah, don't forget the cold beer.

MAKES A PARTY-SIZE BOWL

REST AREA:
BREADS

Bread's the staff of life, a staple, and, for me, a weakness in the battle of the bulge. Every time I think I am going to slim down so my bike will go faster (it is, after all, all in the power to weight ratio), I come across some yummy bread and, kaboom, I gain weight. But what would any meal be without bread? Incomplete, is the answer for me. Imagine the sandwich without bread—like a motorcycle without wheels, it just would not go anywhere.

Breads are often the first thing to arrive at the table when you're dining out. How many times have you sat at a restaurant and enjoyed the breads so much that by the time the main course arrives, you're not hungry anymore? The old saying that man cannot live by bread alone may be true, but while man can live without bread, life sure would be dull.

LISA PETERS'S BANANA BREAD

My friend Lisa Peters from Concord, New Hampshire, sent in this recipe for her banana bread. Besides being a Harley Lady, massage therapist par excellence, and great cook, she is also one heck of a baker. You'll go bananas over this killer bread.

1¾ cups all-purpose flour

1 teaspoon baking soda

½ teaspoon salt

½ teaspoon ground nutmeg

½ teaspoon ground cinnamon

½ teaspoon ground cloves (optional)

2 large eggs, beaten

1¼ to 1½ cups mashed ripe bananas

¾ cup chopped nuts

¼ cup finely chopped dried apricots (optional)

1. Preheat the oven to 350°F. Grease a 1½-quart loaf pan.

2. In a large mixing bowl combine the flour, baking soda, salt, nutmeg, cinnamon, and cloves, if using, and mix together well.

3. In a medium-size mixing bowl, combine the eggs and bananas together well. Pour the banana mixture into the flour mixture and mix well until a smooth batter forms. Fold in the nuts and apricots, if using.

4. Transfer the batter to the prepared loaf pan. Bake until golden brown and a toothpick inserted into center comes out clean, about 1 hour. Let cool for 10 minutes before taking out of the pan and putting on a cooling rack. Serve with butter or cream cheese.

MAKES 1 LOAF

IMOGENE'S BEST EVER BANANA BREAD

My friend Leslie Hudson sent me this recipe and explained its family origin. "My aunt, Sue Beichner, gave me this recipe. She received it from her sister-in-law, Imogene Beichner. It is delicious just out of the oven with real butter slathered on top." Leslie is one of the lucky folks who not only rides a Harley but also works for the Motor Company; I met her many years ago at A.D. Farrow's 85th anniversary celebration. "I have been in the motorcycle business since 1995, starting as the promotions coordinator at Farrow's Harley-Davidson/ Buell in Columbus, Ohio, 'the oldest continuously operating Harley-Davidson dealer in the world.' After working there for three years, I moved to Milwaukee, Wisconsin, to join the ranks of the corporate world at Harley-Davidson Motor Company. Working here has been a true pleasure for the last four years, first starting out in the Communications Department before taking on the role as manager of the Buell Riders Adventure Group. I am the editor of *FUELL* magazine, as well as the organizer for National Adventures (events) throughout the country and adviser for the local BRAG clubs across the United States.

"In this position, I have had the opportunity to ride on some of the nation's best roads, from the coast of California to the mountains in North Carolina, and a dozen scenic, curvy locations in between. My '97 M2 Cyclone just loves the twisty roads and so do I! I actually met my husband at a Buell event a few years ago. He had a '97 S3 Thunderbolt then, but now owns an '02 S3T Thunderbolt and rides it every day. I am sometimes able to ride a company vehicle, such as the '03 Firebolt XB9R, which is one of the most flickable bikes on the road today. To me, it doesn't matter what you ride, as long as you enjoy it and respect other people on the road."

¼ cup (½ stick) butter, softened

1 cup sugar

1 teaspoon vanilla extract

2 large eggs

1 cup mashed bananas (see Note)

1½ cups sifted all-purpose flour

1 teaspoon baking powder

1 teaspoon baking soda

1. Preheat the oven to 375°F. Grease a 9 x 5-inch loaf pan.

2. In a large mixing bowl with an electric mixer, cream the butter, then add the sugar and cream until smooth. Add the vanilla, then the eggs, beating after each addition. Add the bananas and mix on low to medium speed for just a minute or so (the batter should not be completely smooth).

3. In a medium-size mixing bowl, sift the dry ingredients together, then fold into the banana mixture. Again, do not beat until smooth, just until all the ingredients are mixed together. If you like nuts and/or chocolate chips, you can mix them in at this time.

4. Pour into the prepared pan and bake until a toothpick inserted in the center comes out clean (start checking at 35 minutes, but depending on your oven, it might need to stay in 45 to 50 minutes).

MAKES 1 LOAF

NOTE The key ingredient is the bananas. They should be soft and the skins mostly brown and black (but no mold!).

JALAPEÑO ZUCCHINI BREAD

Packed full with fresh zucchini and the goodness of whole wheat flour and wheat bran, this mildly fiery bread has the fresh green snap of jalapeño pepper. If a biker could live by bread alone, this would be the bread of choice.

1½ cups whole wheat flour

½ cup wheat bran

½ cup sugar

2 teaspoons baking powder

1 teaspoon ground cinnamon

¼ teaspoon cayenne pepper

1 teaspoon baking soda

1 cup buttermilk

3 jumbo eggs, beaten

1 jalapeño, seeded and minced

1½ cups shredded zucchini

1. Preheat the oven to 425°F. Grease a 1½-quart loaf pan.

2. In a large mixing bowl, combine the flour, wheat bran, sugar, baking powder, cinnamon, cayenne, and baking soda, whisking everything together.

3. In a medium-size mixing bowl, combine the buttermilk, eggs, and jalapeño, whisking everything together. Pour the egg mixture into the dry ingredients and stir together until all the flour is moist, but do not overmix. Fold in the zucchini.

4. Transfer the batter to the prepared loaf pan and bake until the top is golden brown and a toothpick inserted in the middle comes out clean, 35 to 40 minutes. Let cool 5 to 10 minutes before slicing.

MAKES 1 LOAF

CAGE-RATTLING CARROT BREAD

This carrot bread will have you rattling your cage for more. It's sweet but not too sweet, fiery yet not too fiery, and has enough carrot flavor to please a bunny rabbit. If you could get all the Cagers driving around to eat more carrots, maybe they would see the motorcycles and avoid hitting us. Well, it's an idea—why don't you test it out by baking some for the Cage drivers in your family.

2½ cups whole wheat flour

⅔ cup sugar

1 teaspoon baking powder

1 teaspoon baking soda

1 teaspoon ground cinnamon

¼ teaspoon cayenne pepper

¼ teaspoon ground allspice

½ teaspoon salt

3 jumbo eggs, beaten

½ cup vegetable oil

½ cup half-and-half

1 tablespoon honey

1 cup shredded carrots

½ cup chopped walnuts

½ cup **Craisins (dried cranberries; look for them where raisins are sold in your market)**

1. Preheat the oven to 350°F. Grease a 1½-quart loaf pan.

2. In a large mixing bowl, combine the flour, sugar, baking powder, baking soda, cinnamon, cayenne, allspice, and salt, whisking everything together.

3. In a medium-size mixing bowl, combine the eggs, oil, half-and-half, and honey, whisking everything together. Pour the egg mixture into the flour mixture and stir together until just combined; do not overmix. Fold in the carrots, walnuts, and Craisins.

4. Transfer the batter to the prepared loaf pan and bake until the top is golden brown and a toothpick inserted in the middle of the loaf comes out clean, 50 to 60 minutes. Let cool 5 to 10 minutes before slicing.

MAKES 1 LOAF

LISA'S SPINACH-FETA BREAD

Spinach and feta cheese go together like chrome on a Harley—they are a natural. This interesting recipe is easy to make and will surely please your riding buddies. The spiral of spinach, feta, and spices makes an attractive addition to any breadbasket. Bake up a loaf and enjoy this classic combo. Kudos go to Lisa Peters of Concord, New Hampshire, for this recipe.

One 1-pound loaf frozen bread dough

1 cup crumbled feta cheese

1/3 cup softened lowfat cream cheese

1/2 teaspoon dried oregano

1/4 teaspoon salt (optional)

One 14-ounce can artichoke hearts, drained and chopped

One 10-ounce package frozen chopped spinach, thawed, drained, and as much water as possible squeezed out

3 to 4 cloves garlic, to your taste, minced

1 large egg white

2 tablespoons freshly grated Parmesan cheese

1. Thaw the dough in the refrigerator for 12 hours. Coat a baking sheet with nonstick cooking spray.

2. Combine the feta, cream cheese, oregano, salt, if using, artichokes, spinach, garlic, and egg white in a large mixing bowl.

3. Roll the dough into a 16 x 10-inch rectangle on a lightly floured work surface. Spread the spinach mixture over the dough, leaving a 1/2-inch border on all sides. Begin with a long side and roll it up. Pinch the seam and ends together to seal. Place the roll seam side down on the prepared baking sheet. Cut diagonal slits into the top of the roll. Cover with a clean dishtowel and let rise in a warm place (about 85°F) until doubled in size, about 1 hour. Preheat the oven to 365°F.

4. Sprinkle the Parmesan evenly over the top of the loaf and bake for 45 minutes.

MAKES 1 LOAF

BEER BLASTER BREAD

I love the taste of beer so much that I keep advocating for beer to be considered its own food group. While drinking and riding is just plain stupid, cooking with beer is an act of genius. And baking with beer, well, once you smell this bread baking, you will know that they should award a Nobel Prize for beer breads.

1 cup whole wheat flour

1 cup all-purpose flour

½ cup wheat bran

3 tablespoons sugar

2 teaspoons baking powder

½ teaspoon baking soda

½ teaspoon salt

½ teaspoon ground cumin

2 jalapeños, seeded and minced

1 bunch scallions, ends trimmed and minced

One 12-ounce bottle dark beer

1 cup shredded mild cheddar cheese

1. Preheat the oven to 400°F. Grease a 1½-quart loaf pan.

2. In a large mixing bowl, combine both flours, the wheat bran, sugar, baking powder, baking soda, salt, and cumin, whisking everything together well.

3. In a medium-size mixing bowl, combine the jalapeños, scallions, and beer. Pour the beer mixture into the flour mixture and stir until just moistened; do not overmix. Fold in the cheddar cheese.

4. Transfer the batter to the prepared loaf pan. Bake until golden brown and a toothpick inserted into center comes out clean, 35 to 40 minutes. Let cool 5 to 10 minutes before slicing.

MAKES 1 LOAF

DIXIE RIDER'S SOUTHERN LACE CORNBREAD

Sylvia and Scott Cochran from Swainsboro, Georgia, sent in this classic southern recipe. Scott told me, "As associate editor for *Dixie Rider Motorcycle News*, Sylvia Cochran loves motorcycles. She is constantly wanting to ride somewhere, anywhere to escape from the mundane chores of office life. Her favorite rally is the Survivors Rally in Cherokee and her favorite foods are anything southern, although she does enjoy good Mexican food too!"

Both Scott and Sylvia, founders of *Dixie Rider Motorcycle News*, have fond memories of their grandmothers' lace cornbread. "In the South, there is a rule. You don't criticize someone's cornbread and that means comparing the cornbread in front of you to that which you ate in a previous meal. It is just as rude to say, 'Miss Scarlett, your cornbread is much better than Miss Julie's' as it is to say, 'Miss Scarlett, this cornbread is good, but it ain't near as good as Miss Julie's.' In the South, one should simply compliment cooks on their cornbread talents. It is acceptable to comment that this cornbread reminds you of your mother's or grandmother's.

"What makes this lace cornbread taste so good is that you get two different textures—crunchy and chewy. It's also good for making collard green or mustard green sandwiches. The best lace cornbread is made in a cast-iron skillet. If you don't have one, borrow one from a neighbor. If you can't borrow one, go out and buy one. It's worth the investment. Never wash a cast iron skillet in a dishwasher. It removes the temper and causes the skillet to rust. After hand washing your skillet, rub a tiny amount of cooking oil or lard all over to prevent it from rusting. Wash before use."

2 cups cornmeal

1½ cups hot water (maybe a little extra just in case)

1 teaspoon salt

Cooking oil

1. Mix the cornmeal, hot water, and salt together in a large mixing bowl into a thin consistency. The more water you use, the thinner your lace cornbread will be. There is a point where your cornbread will be too thin and not hold together. This is not good.

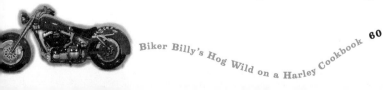

2. Pour about ⅛ inch oil in an 8-inch cast-iron skillet. Heat the oil but don't let it start to smoke. You can tell the oil is ready by letting a little water drip into the grease. It will sizzle and pop and "fry." Be very careful, as many a southern kitchen has suffered smoke damage from hot grease catching up when an inattentive cook became distracted while making lace cornbread. When the oil is right, pour about ¼ cup of your cornmeal-and-water mixture into the middle of the pan, letting it spread out to the sides. The trick is to have the middle thicker than the edges. As the mixture cooks, the water will evaporate from the thin edges and leave a "lace" appearance. The mixture must be just slightly suspended in the oil, otherwise it will stick to the pan and you will not be able to turn it over after 1 minute, or when you see the lace begin to form on the edges. Use as wide a metal spatula as you have and turn the mixture, taking care not to splash hot grease into the stove. After another minute, the mixture will be golden brown, about as thick in the middle as a nickel, and crunchy around the edges. Remove from the skillet. Add extra oil as needed after each is removed and reheat before adding the new batter.

MAKES 8 SERVINGS

CHIPOTLE CHEESE CORNBREAD

The almost sweet and decidedly smoky flavor of the chipotle pepper is one of my favorite fiery friends. Combine that chipotle fire with cheddar cheese, especially Wisconsin cheddar, and you have a biker culinary dream team. Mix those into a cornbread and, holy smokes, you have the bread worthy of any table where bikers gather. This bread might just be the perfect companion for chili, so test it out with the recipes in the Bridge Freezes Before Road: Chili chapter (page 143).

> 1¼ cups cornmeal
>
> ¾ cup all-purpose flour
>
> 2 teaspoons baking powder
>
> ½ teaspoon baking soda
>
> ½ teaspoon salt
>
> 3 canned chipotle peppers packed in adobo sauce, minced
>
> 2 jumbo eggs, beaten
>
> 1⅓ cups buttermilk
>
> ¼ cup dark molasses
>
> 2 tablespoons canola oil
>
> 1 cup shredded cheddar cheese

1. Preheat the oven to 400°F. Grease a 1½-quart loaf pan.

2. In a large mixing bowl, combine the cornmeal, flour, baking powder, baking soda, and salt, whisking everything together well.

3. In a medium-size mixing bowl, combine the chipotles, eggs, buttermilk, molasses, and oil, whisking together well. Pour the wet mixture into the flour mixture and stir until just moistened; do not overmix. Fold in the cheddar cheese.

4. Transfer the batter to the prepared loaf pan. Bake until golden brown and a toothpick inserted into the center comes out clean, 20 to 25 minutes. Let cool 5 to 10 minutes before slicing.

MAKES 1 LOAF

LISA'S SWEET POTATO BISCUITS

If you read my last book, *Biker Billy's Freeway-a-Fire Cookbook*, you will know that I am a biscuit lover. I am not the only one, either. If you love biscuits, you will enjoy this recipe from my Harley-riding buddy Lisa Peters from Concord, New Hampshire.

2 cups all-purpose flour

⅓ cup yellow cornmeal

2½ teaspoons baking powder

½ teaspoon salt

⅓ cup chilled butter, cut into small pieces

1 cup peeled and mashed cooked sweet potato

½ cup fat-free milk

2 tablespoons honey

1. Preheat the oven to 400°F.

2. Lightly spoon the flour into dry measuring cup and level with a knife. Place in a medium-size mixing bowl, add the cornmeal, baking powder, and salt and mix together well. Cut in the butter with a pastry blender or a couple of butter knives till the mixture looks like a coarse meal. Add the sweet potato, milk, and honey and stir until just combined.

3. Turn the dough onto a heavily floured work surface and knead lightly only 5 times, otherwise the dough will get tough. Pat the dough into a 9-inch square and cut into 16 squares.

4. Place the biscuits on a baking sheet. Bake until golden brown, about 20 minutes. Serve hot from the oven with butter or honey. Both are good too!

MAKES 16 BISCUITS

MOWING AHEAD:
SALADS

That highway warning sign "Mowing Ahead" says a lot to a motorcycle rider. It tells us to watch out for the workers and their machines; it says look out—the road ahead could be covered with slippery grass clippings. It also says that up ahead we will be awash in the sweet smell of fresh-cut grass. We who ride know the intense joys of passing through all the scents of the natural world as we cruise the highways and byways of this great country. The millions of miles of fabulous back roads in America pass through some of the most productive farmlands in the whole world. Yes, we are the bread basket of the world, but we are also the source of some of the tastiest fresh produce too. There is nothing like salad fixings picked fresh and prepared the same day. I love to stop at farm stands while I am cruising on my Road King or carving up the back roads with my Buell S3T. Loading up the ample saddlebags with great salad goodies, I ride home, a man with a mission. That mission is cooking—okay, not actually cooking, but wielding that big knife and slicing and dicing my way into salad heaven.

This chapter is filled with some delicious salads, dressings, and accoutrements. It is all here for you to enjoy. The great bonus is that salads are good for you, besides tasting good. I have found that, especially in the summer, salads make the perfect rider's meal, as they provide slowly released long-lasting energy that keeps me alert and well fueled on the road. How perfect is nature to provide these great foods in the peak of freshness at the peak of our riding season? I wonder, does this miracle mean that God rides a Harley? While you ponder those questions, ride out to your local farm stand and do your part to support the American farmer. Then head home and chop your way into salad paradise.

RUMBLING RANCH DRESSING

This is a quick and easy salad dressing that has just the right level of fire to make any salad come alive.

1 cup sour cream

1 cup buttermilk

½ cup plain yogurt

1 tablespoon dried parsley

1 tablespoon garlic powder

1 teaspoon onion powder

1 teaspoon dried cilantro

1 tablespoon dried chives

½ teaspoon dillweed

½ teaspoon dried oregano

¼ teaspoon cayenne pepper

1½ teaspoons salt

1½ teaspoons white pepper

1 tablespoon fresh lemon juice

1 tablespoon cider vinegar

¼ cup freshly grated Parmesan cheese

2 tablespoons grated Asiago cheese

In a blender, combine all the ingredients and pulse several times to blend. Refrigerate for at least 1 hour before serving to let the flavors develop. This will keep for 3 to 5 days in the refrigerator.

MAKES ABOUT 3 CUPS

ATOMIC BALSAMIC DRESSING

This dressing will nuke any salad into oblivion. It is thick and clings well to a fresh green salad. Try it in Suicide Shift Salad (page 77) or use it as a marinade.

⅓ cup minced red onion

⅓ cup oil-packed sun-dried tomatoes, drained and minced

½ teaspoon red pepper flakes

½ teaspoon salt

½ teaspoon black pepper

½ cup balsamic vinegar

¼ cup extra virgin olive oil

Combine all the ingredients in a blender or food processor and process until smooth, about 1 minute. This will hold 3 to 5 days in the refrigerator.

MAKES ALMOST 1½ CUPS

SUN-DRIED TOMATO DRESSING

Fresh garden tomatoes are one of the true delights of any salad. After you have had tomatoes fresh from the garden, the store-bought ones taste and feel like plastic. Since I really like to have tomatoes in my salads, I developed this dressing using sun-dried tomatoes so I could enjoy the great sunny taste of tomatoes long after my garden is wearing its winter coat. While it is not a replacement for garden-fresh tomatoes, it will delight you nonetheless. Like hearing the sound of a big twin winding through the gears in the distance is no substitute for riding, it still stirs the soul of a Harley rider.

12 sun-dried tomatoes

1 dried de Arbol pepper, stemmed

¼ cup boiling water

¼ cup extra virgin olive oil

1/4 cup balsamic vinegar

1 tablespoon dried basil

1 tablespoon chopped garlic

1/2 teaspoon salt

1/2 teaspoon black pepper

1. In a small mixing bowl, combine the sun-dried tomatoes, de Arbol pepper, and boiling water. Set aside and allow to cool.

2. Transfer the sun-dried tomatoes and de Arbol pepper and their soaking liquid to a blender or food processor, add the olive oil, vinegar, basil, garlic, salt, and black pepper, and process until smooth, about 1 minute. This will keep in the refrigerator for 3 to 5 days.

MAKES ALMOST 1 CUP

HOT HARLEY HONEY-MUSTARD VINAIGRETTE

Like a hot Harley honey makes a Harley rider take notice, this dressing will make your salads a head turner. Sweet and sharp, with just enough vinegar to give it a snap, it is sure to please. Show it some respect, like you do your Harley honey, and introduce it to your friends. They will know you as a person of good taste.

1/4 cup extra virgin olive oil

1/4 cup plus 1 tablespoon honey

1/4 cup brown mustard

2 tablespoons cider vinegar

2 tablespoons fresh lemon juice

1 teaspoon salt

1 teaspoon white pepper

1/4 teaspoon cayenne pepper

Combine all the ingredients in a blender or food processor and process until smooth, about 1 minute. Refrigerate for 1 hour to let the flavors develop. This will keep for 3 to 5 days in the refrigerator.

MAKES ALMOST 1 CUP

SIDECAR SOY-GINGER SALAD DRESSING

Like adding a sidecar to an Electra Glide Ultra Classic changes the whole dynamic of the ride, this simple dressing transforms any salad, adding a unique flavor to your fixin's. I use this when I am preparing an oriental feast, since it brings a classic Western salad into the theme of the rest of the meal.

> **2 tablespoons peeled and chopped fresh ginger**
>
> **2 tablespoons chopped garlic**
>
> **1 small shallot, coarsely chopped**
>
> **¼ cup rice vinegar**
>
> **1 tablespoon soy sauce**
>
> **½ teaspoon salt**
>
> **½ teaspoon white pepper**
>
> **½ teaspoon red pepper flakes**
>
> **½ cup olive oil**

Combine all the ingredients in a blender or food processor and process until smooth, about 1 minute. Refrigerate for 1 hour to let the flavors develop. This will keep for 3 to 5 days in the refrigerator.

MAKES ALMOST 1 CUP

CROUTONS À LA DIABLO

I love these big crunchy croutons on my salads. They are bigger than the weenie little ones from the supermarket and therefore don't get soggy as fast. I use them in Suicide Shift Salad (page 77). They are also great in soups.

> **4 cups French bread cut into ¾-inch cubes**
>
> **Seasoned oil from Grilled Veggies à la Diablo (page 73)**

1. Preheat the oven to 350°F.

2. Place the bread cubes in a large mixing bowl. Drizzle the seasoned oil over the bread cubes while tossing them. Toss well until all the seasoned oil is absorbed.

3. Spread the bread cubes in a single layer on a baking sheet and bake until golden brown, turning once during baking to brown on all sides, about 15 minutes. Remove from the oven and allow to cool. These will keep in a zippered-top plastic bag for several days.

MAKES 4 CUPS

MICHAEL PAGAN'S VMD
EGG SALAD

Michael Pagan from Morris Plains, New Jersey, sent in this recipe after I selected him as a volunteer cooking assistant at one of my shows during the American Motorcycle Association's (AMA) Vintage Motorcycle Days (VMD) 2002. Says Michael, "I call this recipe 'VMD Egg Salad' because it came to me while riding back to New Jersey from a mid-Ohio racetrack after the AMA Vintage Motorcycle Days event. I had been 'volunteered' as a Biker Billy taste tester and Billy had insisted that I taste test a little orange habanero pepper. Ouch!" Okay, I did offer it, but he ate it of his own free will.

2 large hard-boiled eggs, peeled

1 canned chipotle pepper in adobo sauce, plus 1 teaspoon of the sauce

2 to 3 tablespoons sour cream, to your taste

1 tablespoon chopped fresh chives

1 teaspoon ground cumin

1 teaspoon fresh lime juice

1 tablespoon chopped fresh cilantro leaves

Salt and pepper to taste

1. Remove the yolks from the eggs and set aside the whites. Finely chop the chipotle pepper (a mini food processor helps). In a small bowl, mix the yolks and all the other ingredients except the whites.

Smush (a technical cooking term) the ingredients together with a fork until smoothly blended. Make sure the chipotle is evenly distributed into the mix or you'll end up with hot spots.

2. Once the ingredients are fully mixed, chop the egg whites into tiny bits and mix them in with the rest of the ingredients.

3. Spread the egg mix on a slice of bread, sprinkle a little cilantro on top, top off with another piece of bread. Voilà! VMD Egg Salad sandwich.

MAKES 1 SERVING

GRILLED VEGGIES À LA DIABLO

I use this seasoned oil for brushing on vegetables before and during grilling them. It adds a nice level of heat and brings out the flavors of the veggies. After grilling, I allow the vegetables to cool and use them as a special garnish on salads in other recipes. I enjoy grilling zucchini, eggplant, summer squash, tomatoes, and onions—try your favorites and enjoy the fire. I also use this oil to make Croutons à la Diablo (page 70).

½ cup extra virgin olive oil

½ teaspoon red pepper flakes

1 tablespoon dried basil

1 tablespoon chopped garlic

½ teaspoon salt

½ teaspoon white pepper

Vegetables for grilling

1. In a small heatproof bowl, combine the olive oil, red pepper, basil, garlic, salt, and white pepper and stir well. Heat in a microwave oven on medium power or in a small saucepan over medium heat until warm; stir well.

2. Brush the flavored oil on both sides of vegetables before grilling and each time you turn them on the grill.

MAKES 1/2 CUP SEASONED OIL

DAL SMILIE'S POTATO, POTATO, POTATO SALAD, A.K.A. GER'S POTATO SALAD

Here is a recipe from one of my buddies, Dal Smilie, vice chairman at the American Motorcyclist Association. I am a life member of the AMA because they are so important to defending and preserving our freedom to ride. If you know anything about freedom, you know that the fight to keep it is an ongoing process. If you ride a Harley, then you know the value of our American freedoms and will want to protect them, so join the AMA.

Dal wanted to dedicate this recipe to the AMA Hall of Fame Museum, which preserves our riding history, and he also wanted his mother-in-law, Geraldine Glatz, who is a southsider from Chicago, to get credit too, since it is her recipe. This is what Dal had to say about this tasty salad: "My mother-in-law has a killer recipe for potato salad. How excited can you get about potato salad? This reminds one a little of German potato salad, but better. You can eat it cold or hot but you may eat it rather than the rest of the meal." Dal also told me that the sauce for this can be used for cole slaw or other salads. Move over burgers and dogs; this potato salad is all you will want to eat at your next H.O.G. picnic.

> **2 cups mayonnaise or salad dressing (light or nonfat is fine)**
>
> **1 cup sugar**
>
> **½ cup white vinegar**
>
> **6 large potatoes, boiled in water to cover until tender, drained, and sliced**
>
> **6 hard-boiled eggs, peeled and sliced**
>
> **¾ pound bacon, diced, cooked until crisp, and drained on paper towels**
>
> **1 onion, diced and sautéed in a little of the bacon grease till soft and clear**
>
> **3 stalks celery, diced**
>
> **2 sweet pickles, diced**
>
> **Garlic powder**
>
> **Salt**
>
> **Black pepper**
>
> **Chopped fresh dill**

1. In a medium-size mixing bowl, combine the mayonnaise, sugar, and vinegar, whisk together well, and set aside.

2. In large mixing bowl, combine the potatoes, eggs, bacon, onion, celery, and pickles, tossing them together well. Add the sauce and toss to coat well (you might have some left over, depending on how saucy you like it and how large the potatoes are). Add garlic powder, salt,

pepper, and dill to your own personal taste. Cover with plastic wrap and refrigerate for several hours before serving.

MAKES ABOUT 12 SERVINGS

SPIKE'S HORSERADISH POTATO SALAD

"Owning a Harley has been a dream of mine for as long as I can remember. When the day came that I actually ordered my Harley, I was told that I would have to wait several months before I would take actual delivery. During those months of waiting in anticipation of the joy it would bring me, I visited the Milwaukee and York plants and contacted Waugh Harley-Davidson in Orange, Virginia, the dealer I ordered it from, asking them over and over, when will it be here, when is it going to come in. My Heritage Softail was delivered on my birthday in 1996. The first time I started it up and rode down my driveway onto the open road, I felt, without a doubt, that all my expectations had been fulfilled. It is now several years since I bought that first Harley (I now ride an Ultra with a side hack and have a 100th Anniversary Fat Boy on order) and I still get the same satisfying feeling every time I start up and head out on the open road." Larry (Spike) King, who is a pharmacist from Culpeper, Virginia, shared his story of Harley happiness, as well as this zesty potato salad recipe.

7 to 10 medium-size red potatoes, skins left on

1 cup mayonnaise (lowfat or fat free is fine)

½ cup milk

2 teaspoons prepared horseradish

2 stalks celery, coarsely chopped

4 large dill pickles, coarsely chopped

4 scallions, ends trimmed and coarsely chopped

Salt to taste

White pepper to taste

1. Place the potatoes in a large saucepan, cover with water, bring to a boil, and let boil until tender, 25 to 30 minutes. Drain the potatoes and, when cool enough to handle, dice with the skin on.

2. In a large bowl, stir together the mayonnaise, milk, and horse-radish. Add the potatoes, celery, pickles, and scallions and toss gently until everything is covered with mayonnaise. Sprinkle with salt and white pepper to taste. Cover and chill before serving.

MAKES 4 TO 6 SERVINGS

TOMATO SALAD À LA DIABLO

This salad is a perfect way to enjoy the fresh tomatoes, cucumbers, and basil from your garden or from a farm stand. I find it makes a great start to an Italian feast or a light after-ride snack. So, next time you ride that big Harley past a farm stand, remember this recipe; you might just want to turn around and fill your saddlebags with some salad fixings.

> 4 medium-size ripe tomatoes, cut into ¾-inch cubes
>
> 8 ounces fresh mozzarella cheese, cut into ¾-inch cubes
>
> 1 cup peeled and seeded cucumber cut into ¾-inch cubes
>
> 1 tablespoon tightly packed coarsely chopped fresh basil leaves
>
> 2 tablespoons seasoned oil from Grilled Veggies à la Diablo (page 73)
>
> Croutons à la Diablo (page 70)

1. In a large mixing bowl, combine the tomatoes, mozzarella, cucumber, basil, and seasoned oil. Toss well to mix and refrigerate, covered with plastic wrap, for 1 hour.

2. Serve with the croutons.

MAKES 4 TO 6 SERVINGS

SUICIDE SHIFT SALAD

This is a salad that will impress your riding buddies almost as much as a new custom paint job on your Harley. If you prepare the four recipes I have fused into this salad, you can make at least 4 to 6 servings, depending on the size of salads. The directions below are for making each plate or serving.

> 1 recipe Hot Nutty Goat Cheese (page 22)
>
> 1 head red leaf lettuce, torn into bite-size pieces
>
> 1 medium-size yellow bell pepper, seeded and cut into matchsticks
>
> 1 cup baby carrots, cut into matchsticks
>
> 1 recipe Righteous Red Potatoes (page 241)
>
> 1 recipe Croutons à la Diablo (page 70)
>
> Atomic Balsamic Dressing (page 68)

1. Roll the goat cheese into ³/₄-inch balls and set aside.

2. Arrange a bed of lettuce on each serving plate. Add some yellow pepper and carrot matchsticks. Add some Righteous Red Potatoes pieces, 2 or 3 of the goat cheese balls, and some croutons. Serve with the dressing drizzled on top.

MAKES 1 SERVING

JENNIFER LEVAN'S KILLER CORN SALAD

"I have loved motorcycles since I was a little girl! When my husband, David, and I opened Battlefield Harley-Davidson/ Buell of Gettysburg, Pennsylvania, in June 2000, it was truly a dream come true. We are blessed with an incredible staff that shares our philosophy to provide our customers with friendly and knowledgeable service because we all love what we do!

"Prior to becoming a dealer, I spent twenty years planning and catering events in Philadelphia and the tri-state area. I love to have events at our dealership, because it's fun! We have over a 100 events throughout the year, including annual signature events like the

Easter Egg Hunt (we hide 10,000 eggs), the Buell Is Cool Extravaganza in April, and the Corn Roast in October.

"Our birthday party in June is a two-day event (one day would not be enough to thank everyone who has supported us), with great food and entertainment such as Big Brother and the Holding Co., Leon Russell, and, of course, our friend Biker Billy!

"I hope you enjoy this recipe for Killer Corn Salad! It's fast, easy, looks good, and everybody always raves about it!"

Two 16-ounce cans corn kernels, drained

One 15½-ounce can black beans, drained and rinsed really well

1 large white onion, diced

1 large red onion, diced

2 green bell peppers, seeded and diced

4 jalapeños, seeded and thinly sliced

2 large roasted red peppers, diced

3 large ripe tomatoes, diced

1 large bunch fresh cilantro, rinsed really well, stems removed, and leaves finely chopped

Salt and pepper to taste

Juice of 2 lemons

1. In a large glass or ceramic mixing bowl, combine all the ingredients, except the lemon juice, and mix well. Cover with plastic wrap and chill for at least a half hour.

2. Right before serving, stir in the lemon juice.

MAKES ABOUT 18 BIKER-SIZE PORTIONS

CRUCIFIED CUCUMBER SALAD

Sinful and simple, this salad will just blow you away like a hot rod big twin. The twin cylinder punch of the de Arbol and jalapeño make a nice combo. The jalapeño is the milder of the two but reaches my palate first, then de Arbol comes on second with a rounder, hotter punch. Enough said—try it!

3 tablespoons rice vinegar

5 teaspoons sugar

1 tablespoon dried cilantro

2 medium-size cucumbers, peeled, seeded, and cut into
¼ x 2-inch strips

3 tablespoons canola oil

3 dried de Arbol peppers, stemmed and crushed

1 jalapeño, seeded and minced

½ teaspoon salt

½ teaspoon white pepper

1. In a small bowl, combine the vinegar, sugar, and cilantro and stir well to mix. Place the cucumbers in a medium-size mixing bowl, pour the vinegar mixture over them, and toss well to coat. Cover and refrigerate for 30 minutes.

2. In a small sauté pan over medium heat, heat the canola oil. Add the de Arbol, jalapeño, salt, and white pepper and cook, stirring, for 2 to 3 minutes. Pour the oil mixture over the cucumbers, toss well, and serve immediately.

MAKES 4 TO 6 SERVINGS

JANE SMILIE'S I DON'T WANT A PICKLE—JUST A HIGH-PERFORMANCE CUCUMBER

My friend Dal Smilie, the vice chairman of the AMA board of directors and former long-time chairman of the board of the AMA's Hall of Fame Museum, sent in his wife Jane's recipe in honor of the AMA and the AMA's Hall of Fame Museum.

Says Jane, who Dal calls "an all-around motorcyclist and great cook," "Cucumber salads are as much a part of summer Midwest nights as fireflies and Harley-Davidson. These have been personally modified for higher performance, personalized just like your Harley. The addition of the jalapeño wakes up this little dish and makes it fun, but don't make it so hot your buddies will be offended."

½ **cup vinegar**

½ **cup water**

½ **cup sugar**

Green or purple onions or leeks cut up as you like, to your taste

Peeled and sliced cucumbers

Chopped jalapeño pepper—add to whatever "stage" of enhanced performance you like

1. Place the vinegar, water, and sugar in a large saucepan and bring to a boil. Add the onions or leeks, cucumbers, and jalapeño.

2. Transfer to a container and let marinate in the fridge for a while before serving.

MAKES 8 SERVINGS

MEAN 3-BEAN SALAD

This spicy yet sweet salad has a nice fire, thanks to the de Arbol peppers. Serve this on your favorite salad greens, since there is enough dressing in this salad to make it both a salad and a dressing.

1 cup trimmed fresh green beans cut into 1-inch lengths

One 15½-ounce can chickpeas, drained and rinsed

One 15½-ounce can dark red kidney beans, drained and rinsed

3 scallions, ends trimmed and cut into 1-inch lengths

3 dried de Arbol peppers, stemmed and crushed

½ cup balsamic vinegar

2 tablespoons extra virgin olive oil

1 tablespoon chopped garlic

½ teaspoon dillweed

2 tablespoons honey

½ teaspoon salt

½ teaspoon white pepper

Salad greens

1. Steam the green beans until crispy tender, about 10 minutes, rinse under cold running water to stop the cooking, and allow to drain. Combine the green beans, chickpeas, kidney beans, and scallions in a large mixing bowl and toss together.

2. In a blender, combine the de Arbol peppers, vinegar, olive oil, garlic, dill, honey, salt, and white pepper and process until smooth, about 1 minute. Pour the dressing over the beans and toss well to coat. Cover with plastic wrap and refrigerate for 1 hour.

3. Serve on a bed of salad greens.

MAKES 6 TO 8 SERVINGS

LOURDES FULLER'S CLUCK DELICIOUS CHICKEN SALAD

Wyatt and Lourdes Fuller of Hickory, North Carolina, sent me this salad recipe, a favorite around their house. Wyatt and his hard-working crew enjoy this salad on lunch breaks at the shop where they create killer custom bikes and components for Harley-Davidson. Try this when you're customizing your own Harley.

2 cups chopped cooked chicken

1 cup peeled and cubed cooked potatoes

One 16-ounce can mixed vegetables, drained

1 small onion, chopped

3 celery stalks, chopped

3 small apples, cored and chopped

Mayonnaise to taste

Salt and pepper to taste

1. In a large mixing bowl, mix together all the ingredients.
2. Chill for about 1 hour and serve.

MAKES 4 SERVINGS

SLIPPERY PAVEMENT: SOUPS

I think I have clocked more miles of riding in the rain than the Michelin man and I do look a whole lot better wearing my Harley-Davidson rain suit, that is, if I say so myself. I love to see those road signs that say "Pavement Slippery When Wet." Duh, anyone who has hammered cross country on the Eisenhower Interstate System knows that wet roads are slippery. Riding in the rain is not really fun, but if you ride a motorcycle, sure as the sun rises in the East, you will get rained on. In the summer, even if you get your rain gear on before the downpour, you will still get soaked within the suit—not much you can do about that. In the colder months, the rain suit may help keep you warmer as well as drier, yet old man winter will make sure you know it is his season. During those winter months, riding in the rain can chill you inside and out. There is a raw naked cold that just surrounds your bones and stays with you. As a seasoned rider knows, sometimes all the insulating warm gear just does no good if there is no heat left in you to hold in. It is at that point that I begin to dream of a hot, steaming bowl of soup and a chair by the fireplace. Yes, soup is a godsend to a wet, weary wintertime rider. Like that big canned soup company keeps saying, "Soup is good food," yet, as easy as canned soup can be, it is just a poor second cousin to fresh homemade soup. When you own a Harley-Davidson motorcycle, you know that it is not truly yours until you customize it. We all start off with one of the sweet designs that come out of Milwaukee and then begin to make them our own expressions of America, freedom, and our love of the open road. For me, food is just the same. This chapter has some heartwarming soups that will nourish and comfort any weary rider. I suggest that you customize them to make them your own.

GREASEBERG'S KILLER CONCH CHOWDER

Lanny "Greaseberg" Greenberg of Jackson, Mississippi, told me, "I've been eatin' all my life and ridin' since I could afford to buy my first bike ('69). I grew up riding in the Miami/Ft. Lauderdale area. When it came time to stop for some grub, nothing was more satisfying than a hot, spicy bowl of conch chowder, some hearty bread, and a cold brew, especially when you could enjoy such a repast in a good ole waterfront dive, where there were always hot babes and cool bikes. If your local seafood market doesn't stock conch, they can usually order it for you."

1 pound conch steaks, finely chopped (a food processor works best for this)

1 tablespoon fresh lime juice

½ teaspoon salt

2 strips bacon, cut into ¼-inch pieces

1 large potato, cut into ¼-inch cubes

1 onion, chopped

2 stalks celery, chopped

2 carrots, cut into ¼-inch cubes

2 or 3 Roma tomatoes, diced

4 cloves garlic, minced

One 14-ounce can chicken broth

Two 8-ounce cans tomato sauce

½ cup white wine

1 tablespoon Worcestershire sauce

½ teaspoon dried thyme

Black pepper

Tabasco sauce

1. Place the chopped conch in a medium-size mixing bowl with the lime juice and salt. Mix well by hand and let marinate for half an hour.

2. In a large pot or Dutch oven, cook the bacon over low heat to release the fat, then raise the heat to medium. Add the potato and cook, stirring, for 2 minutes. Add the onion, celery, and carrots

and cook, stirring, for 1 minute. Add the conch and cook for 2 minutes. Add the tomatoes and garlic and cook 1 minute more. Add the chicken broth, tomato sauce, wine, Worcestershire sauce, and thyme, bring to a boil, then reduce the heat to low and simmer for 30 minutes, adding salt, pepper, and Tabasco to taste.

3. Serve with toasted French bread, and don't forget the cold beer.

MAKES 4 OR MORE SERVINGS

SASHA'S MANHATTAN BIKER BABE CLAM CHOWDER

Sasha Mullins is an NYC Biker Babe. She is a Harley-riding lady from the big city who writes for motorcycle magazines and is also a great musician and songwriter. Sasha sent in her Auntie Fran Winkelman's killer soup recipe. If you want a real adventure, ride your Harley on the mean streets of the Big Apple. New York City is where I learned to ride and you just gotta respect anyone who rides there. When I asked Sasha about being a Lady Harley Rider in NYC, she said, "I gotta roarrrrr my motorcycle hard to the core and steal some serious asphalt when I slice though traffic in Manhattan on my 'Tigerlily' of a scooter."

6 strips bacon, diced

1 cup chopped onions

3 large potatoes, peeled and diced

1 stalk celery, diced

3 carrots, diced

½ teaspoon salt

1 to 2 dozen chowder clams, shucked, liquor reserved, and chopped, or one 8-ounce bottle clam juice and two 8-ounce cans chopped or minced clams

One 16-ounce can whole tomatoes, chopped

½ teaspoon dried thyme, crumbled

1. Fry the bacon until almost crisp in a kettle, remove from the pot using a slotted spoon, and set aside to drain on paper towels.

2. Stir the onion into the drippings and cook, stirring, until soft. Add the potatoes, celery, carrots, salt, and reserved clam liquor or clam juice. Simmer, covered, until the vegetables are tender, about 15 minutes. Stir in the clams, tomatoes with their juice, thyme, and the cooked bacon; simmer 15 minutes longer. A small amount of water may be added if the soup is too thick.

MAKES 6 TO 8 SERVINGS

*Sasha Mullins on her 1999
Harley-Davidson Sportster,
affectionately named "Tigerlily"*

PULSATING PUMPKIN SOUP

Everyone associates pumpkin with pie and the holidays. While this is a great holiday soup, it is a welcome treat all year long. In fact, it is so hearty that it is a one-dish meal. I especially enjoy this after a cold ride—it will gently warm you and satisfy your hunger. Try it and you will feel your palate pulsating just like your bike's motor.

3 ½ cups canned pumpkin puree

2 cups vegetable broth

1 cup heavy cream

2 tablespoons onion powder

1 teaspoon garlic powder

¼ teaspoon cayenne pepper

½ teaspoon ground cinnamon

¼ teaspoon ground nutmeg

½ teaspoon ground allspice

1 tablespoon dried parsley

1 teaspoon dried cilantro

½ teaspoon salt

¼ teaspoon white pepper

One 9-ounce package cheese tortellini

1. Combine all the ingredients, except the tortellini, in a large saucepan. Stir well to mix, place over medium heat, and cook for 20 to 25 minutes, stirring often.

2. While the soup cooks, bring a pot of salted water to a boil, add the tortellini, and cook until *al dente*. Drain.

3. To serve, place several tortellini in each bowl and ladle the soup over them. If there are leftovers, store the tortellini and soup separately so the tortellini remain firm.

MAKES 6 TO 8 SERVINGS

MEGA MOTO MUSHROOM SOUP

Warm and comforting with a rich mushroom flavor and a nice fire, this thick, creamy soup will warm you after a long, cold ride. It will also get you ready for a biker-style feast.

2 tablespoons extra virgin olive oil

4 scallions, ends trimmed and minced

1 shallot, minced

2 tablespoons chopped garlic

2 canned chipotle peppers packed in adobo sauce, minced

8 ounces mushrooms, sliced

2 medium-size red potatoes, peeled and diced

1 teaspoon dillweed

½ teaspoon ground savory

1 teaspoon salt

1 teaspoon black pepper

1½ cups water

1 cup half-and-half

1 tablespoon red wine

1. In a large soup pot, heat the olive oil over medium heat. Add the scallions, shallot, garlic, and chipotles and cook, stirring, until they begin to brown, 5 to 7 minutes. Add the mushrooms and cook, stirring, until they begin to sweat, 5 to 7 minutes. Add the potatoes and cook, stirring, until they are tender, 5 to 7 minutes. Add the dill, savory, salt, black pepper, and ½ cup of the water, stir well, scraping up any browned bits from the bottom of the pot, and remove from the heat. Allow to cool for 5 minutes.

2. Transfer to a food processor and process for 20 seconds. Add the remaining 1 cup water, the half-and-half, and wine and process until smooth, about 1 minute.

3. Return to the soup pot over low heat, simmer, stirring often, until heated through, about 10 minutes, and keep warm until ready to serve.

MAKES 4 TO 6 SERVINGS

JENNIFER TERRY'S GARDEN GAZPACHO

This fresh garden soup is from Jennifer Terry of Gettysburg, Pennsylvania, who says, "I came up with the recipe trying to use everything in my garden. Gardening and going for long rides are my favorite pastimes." Lots of Harley riders also enjoy gardening and we all love the joy of riding through the beauty and splendor of nature.

> **1 medium-size orange bell pepper, seeded and diced**
>
> **1 medium-size red bell pepper, seeded and diced**
>
> **1 jalapeño, seeded and diced**
>
> **1 cucumber, peeled, seeded, and diced**
>
> **1 medium-size zucchini, seeded and diced**
>
> **2 medium-size ripe tomatoes, chopped**
>
> **1 small onion, diced**
>
> **1½ cups V-8 vegetable juice**
>
> **Salt and pepper to taste**
>
> **Sour cream for garnish**
>
> **Sprigs fresh cilantro for garnish**

1. Mix all the ingredients, except the garnishes, together in a large mixing bowl. Transfer half of the mixture to a food processor and pulse 4 or 5 times. Return to the bowl and stir.

2. Cover with plastic wrap and chill about 1 hour. Serve in chilled bowls, garnished with a dollop of sour cream and a cilantro sprig.

MAKES 6 SERVINGS

GREEN FIRE ZUCCHINI SOUP

This is a rich, creamy green soup—yes, a green soup. It will bring summertime into your winter. The tender flavor of the zucchini contrasts well with the green fire of the jalapeño and the fresh snap of the scallions. The celery seeds add a sweet fragrance that makes the whole house warmer. Finally, I find the cayenne pepper adds a

warm glow that balances the creamy richness of the buttermilk, egg yolk, and Parmesan cheese—heck, I am getting hungry just writing about this. Try it next time you're feeling the winter blues.

2 tablespoons extra virgin olive oil

1 medium-size jalapeño, seeded and minced

1 bunch scallions, ends trimmed and minced

1/2 cup water

1 teaspoon celery seeds

1/4 teaspoon cayenne pepper

1/2 teaspoon dried basil

1/2 teaspoon white pepper

1 teaspoon salt

4 cups shredded zucchini

2 cups buttermilk

1 jumbo egg yolk

1 tablespoon cornstarch

1/4 cup freshly grated Parmesan cheese

1. In a large soup pot, heat the olive oil over medium heat. Add the jalapeño and scallions and cook, stirring, until tender, 3 to 5 minutes. Add the water, celery seeds, cayenne, basil, white pepper, and salt and stir well. Add the zucchini and simmer until tender, 7 to 10 minutes.

2. While the zucchini is simmering, combine 1/2 cup of the buttermilk, the egg yolk, and cornstarch in a small mixing bowl and whisk together well.

3. Transfer the zucchini mixture to a food processor and process until smooth, about 1 minute. Return to the soup pot over medium heat. Add the remaining 1 1/2 cups buttermilk and stir well. Add the buttermilk-egg mixture, stirring constantly, then reduce the heat to low and simmer until the soup thickens, about 10 minutes. Do not let it come to a boil, or the soup will curdle. Stir in the Parmesan cheese and serve immediately.

MAKES 4 SERVINGS

BLACK LEATHER EGGPLANT CHICKPEA SOUP

I love Italian foods. They are so comfortable, much like a well-worn black leather jacket. This soup is no exception. It is a light garden-fresh soup, yet so comforting. This is one soup I enjoy all year long.

1 medium-size eggplant, left unpeeled and cut into ¼-inch dice

Salt

One 15½-ounce can chickpeas, drained and rinsed

½ teaspoon red pepper flakes

2 tablespoons cider vinegar

2 tablespoons extra virgin olive oil

1 medium-size onion, diced

2 tablespoons chopped garlic

5 plum tomatoes, peeled and diced

½ teaspoon white pepper

1 tablespoon dried parsley

¼ cup tightly packed minced fresh basil leaves

4 cups water

¼ cup dry white wine

1. Place the eggplant in a colander in the sink, sprinkle with salt, stir, and allow to drain for 20 minutes. Rinse, then press any excess liquid out of the eggplant.

2. Combine the chickpeas, red pepper flakes, and vinegar in a medium-size mixing bowl and allow to marinate for 15 minutes.

3. Heat the olive oil in a medium-size soup pot over medium heat. Add the onion and cook, stirring, until browned, 5 to 7 minutes. Add the garlic and cook, stirring, until it begins to color, about 1 minute. Add the chickpeas and their marinade and simmer until the liquid is gone, 3 to 5 minutes. Add the eggplant and cook, stirring, until tender, 5 to 7 minutes. Add the tomatoes, ½ teaspoon salt, the white pepper, parsley, basil, water, and white wine, stir well, and let simmer until the soup begins to thicken and the vegetables are tender, 25 to 30 minutes. Serve warm.

MAKES 6 TO 8 SERVINGS

MILWAUKEE PROUD BEER AND CHEESE SOUP

O h, my gosh, beer and cheese, I must be in Wisconsin. Wait, what
is that thundering sound I hear, is it a Twin Cam 88 running
wide open down Juneau Avenue? No, it is the sound of cayenne pepper
pounding in my ears. If you are feeling homesick for Juneau Avenue,
make a pot of this soup and pull out your copy of the Motor Company's Parts and Accessories catalog and dream of chrome from back
home at the factory.

¼ cup water

3 tablespoons cornstarch

2 tablespoons butter

1 medium-size onion, minced

2 tablespoons chopped garlic

One 12-ounce can dark beer

2 cups vegetable broth

½ teaspoon cayenne pepper

1½ teaspoons salt

1 teaspoon white pepper

1 teaspoon ground cumin

½ teaspoon ground savory

2 cups half-and-half

2 cups shredded mild cheddar cheese

1. In a small bowl, combine the water and cornstarch, stir well, and
set aside.

2. Melt the butter in a medium-size soup pot over medium heat. Add
the onion and cook, stirring, until it begins to brown, 5 to 7 minutes.
Add the garlic and cook, stirring, just until it begins to color, about 1
minute. Add the beer, vegetable broth, cayenne, salt, white pepper,
cumin, and savory, bring to a boil, and reduce the heat to low. Slowly
pour in the half-and-half, stirring constantly. Add the cheddar cheese
and stir until melted. Add the cornstarch mixture and stir well. Let
simmer until the soup thickens, stirring often, 5 to 7 minutes. Serve
immediately.

MAKES 6 TO 8 SERVINGS

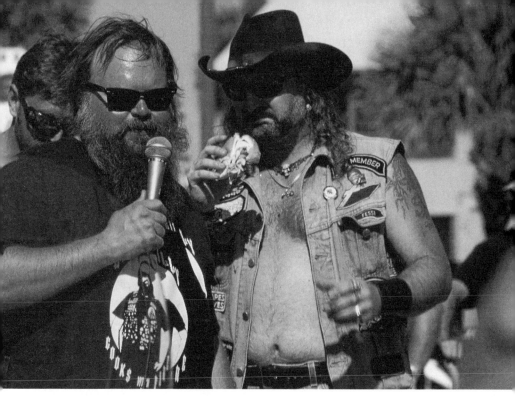

CONSTRUCTION ZONE: WRAPS, FAJITAS, AND MORE

One time I was riding through the Atlantic provinces of Canada and rounded a bend to find myself in the midst of a construction zone. There had been no warning signs at all. Even signs in French (which I don't read) would have been nice. Well, that road was just gone, kaput, simply blown into pieces, and big pieces at that. After I picked my way through that mini war zone like a trials rider using an 800-pound dresser, I developed a great appreciation for all those orange warning signs back home in America.

Building things is a big part of the American dream. We have built the most wonderful system of highways and byways, allowing us to freely travel in safety and with ease. Many of us dream of one day building that special house, one with a big honking huge garage with all the power tools and a small living place attached. In that dream garage we will build that special scooter—our own expression of the Milwaukee dream—yes, it is every biker's dream to build a custom motorcycle. Some of you have reached that dream and are already thinking of the next bike, and the next bike, an endless dream of steel, chrome, and killer paint jobs. Well, sometimes you have to eat between all that dreaming and building. At such times, why not enjoy foods that will allow you to express your building lust? This chapter is filled with build-it-yourself food, so roll up your sleeves and start building a custom biker meal. When you are done eating, it is back to the garage to spin them wrenches—gotta get that new scoot finished before Bike Week.

ROB TONNESEN'S ORTEGA HIGHWAY WRAPS

Rob Tonnesen is an avid biker and MSF instructor, as well as a professional skydiver, who says, "I have little time for meals that require me to spend hours preparing them. This is just the ticket after a long day outdoors." Rob lives in that motorcycle playland called southern California and what a life it must be there. He told me, "After a day of storming a thirty-mile stretch of the Ortega Highway, between the 5 and Lake Elsinore in southern California, I like to relax with my friends and eat something that is good, easy, and satisfying." That's the life, storming the hills and valleys on your Harley, then chowing down with your buddies.

One 10-count package 10-inch flour tortillas

Lowfat garlic mayonnaise

Shredded cheese (such as kasseri/Jack/mozzarella mix)

Vegetarian salami, sliced

Fresh arugula

Funky tortilla chips

Spread each tortilla with some mayonnaise, sprinkle with a handful of cheese, and microwave for 25 to 30 seconds. Then place a layer of vegetarian salami over the cheese, add a layer of arugula, and wrap them up. Cut in half and serve with tortilla chips.

MAKES 10 WRAPS

INFERNO TACOS

As hot as a chapter from Dante's *Inferno*, these tacos will set you ablaze. After you eat these spicy devils, the wimpy ones from your local drive-through joint will taste like taco hell. So why lose a Mexican stand-off by purchasing wimpy gringo tacos? Just cook the Inferno Tacos and win!

For a fabulous Mexican fiesta, serve these tacos with Screaming Yellow Rice (page 246) and Unholy Guacamole (page 35). If you would like to make them vegetarian style, increase the olive oil to $\frac{1}{4}$ cup and substitute 4 cups thawed frozen textured vegetable protein (TVP) crumbles in place of the beef.

2 tablespoons extra virgin olive oil

4 cups lean ground beef

4 canned chipotle peppers packed in adobo sauce, minced

1 medium-size onion, diced

$\frac{1}{2}$ cup diced baby carrots, diced

$\frac{1}{2}$ cup seeded and red bell pepper

1 tablespoon dried cilantro

1 tablespoon dried parsley

1 teaspoon garlic powder

1 teaspoon onion powder

1 teaspoon ground cumin

1 teaspoon ground coriander

$\frac{1}{2}$ teaspoon salt

1 teaspoon black pepper

1 tablespoon liquid smoke

One 14$\frac{1}{2}$-ounce can diced tomatoes with green chiles

1 cup beer

12 to 18 taco shells

Shredded lettuce

Diced tomatoes

Chopped onions

Shredded cheddar cheese

1. Heat the olive oil in a large skillet over medium heat. Add the ground beef and cook until no longer pink, about 5 minutes. Add the chipotles, onion, and carrots and cook, stirring, until the beef and onion are browned, 7 to 10 minutes. Add the bell pepper, cilantro, parsley, garlic powder, onion powder, cumin, coriander, salt, black pepper, liquid smoke, tomatoes, and beer, stir well, and let simmer until the liquid is almost gone, 15 to 20 minutes. Remove from the heat.

2. Warm the taco shells according to the package directions. Place a few spoonfuls of the taco filling in each shell. Add some lettuce, tomatoes, onions, and cheese and serve immediately.

MAKES 12 TO 18 TACOS

BLACK LEATHER TOSTADAS

What a well-dressed dish this is. Is there any more perfect riding wear than black leather? Well, of course not, and these tostadas are dressed in black—black beans à la Biker Billy, that is.

¼ cup extra virgin olive oil

2 medium-size onions, cut into matchsticks

2 to 4 canned chipotle peppers packed in adobo sauce, to your taste, minced

¼ cup chopped garlic

Two 15½-ounce cans black beans, drained and rinsed

1 tablespoon ground cumin

1 teaspoon ground coriander

2 tablespoons dried cilantro

1 teaspoon salt

1 tablespoon black pepper

1 tablespoon liquid smoke

1 tablespoon dark molasses

1 cup dark beer

¼ cup bourbon

Corn tortillas, warmed or lightly fried

Shredded lettuce

Diced tomatoes

Shredded cheddar cheese

Hot Rod Red Pepper Sauce (page 289) or Killer Queso Sauce (page 288), optional

1. Heat the olive oil in a large skillet over high heat. Add the onions and chipotles and cook, stirring, until the onion is browned, 5 to 7

minutes. Add the garlic and cook, stirring, until it just begins to color, about 1 minute. Add the black beans, cumin, coriander, cilantro, salt, black pepper, liquid smoke, molasses, beer, and bourbon, bring to a boil, reduce the heat to low, and simmer until the liquid is almost gone, 10 to 15 minutes.

2. Place a scoop of the bean mixture on a tortilla and top with some lettuce, tomatoes, and cheese. If you want, add a shot of Hot Rod Red Chile Sauce or Killer Queso Sauce. Serve immediately.

MAKES ABOUT 24 TOSTADAS

SPINACH CORN ENCHILADAS

These rich, creamy enchiladas are a favorite when my buddies ride over for dinner. Seems I can never make enough of them. Serve them with Green Fire Tomatillo Salsa (page 48) for a Mexican feast.

¼ cup extra virgin olive oil

2 medium-size onions, cut into matchsticks

2 jalapeños, seeded and minced

¼ cup chopped garlic

One 10-ounce package frozen spinach, thawed, drained, and squeezed dry

One 10-ounce package frozen corn, thawed and drained

1 tablespoon ground cumin

1 teaspoon ground coriander

1 teaspoon salt

1 teaspoon white pepper

1 cup half-and-half

8 ounces Monterey Jack cheese, shredded

Corn tortillas, warmed or lightly fried

Hot Rod Red Pepper Sauce (page 289)

Shredded cheddar cheese

1. Heat the olive oil in a large skillet over high heat. Add the onions and jalapeños and cook, stirring, until the onions are browned, 5 to 7 minutes. Add the garlic and cook, stirring, until it just begins to color, about 1 minute. Add the spinach, corn, cumin, coriander, salt, white pepper, and half-and-half, bring to a boil, reduce the heat to low, add the Monterey Jack cheese, and stir well. Simmer until the sauce thickens, 5 to 10 minutes.

2. Preheat the oven to 350°F.

3. Place a spoonful of the filling on a tortilla, roll up, and place in a baking dish. Ladle some Hot Rod Red Pepper Sauce on top and repeat until all the enchiladas are rolled and in the dish. Sprinkle the cheddar cheese on top and bake until the cheese is melted. Serve warm.

MAKES ABOUT 24 ENCHILADAS

KEITH WINN'S FLAMIN' FAJITAS

Here is a fun recipe for your custom food-building delight that Keith Winn from Plantation, Florida, sent me. "I am a Road Captain with the Ft. Lauderdale H.O.G. Chapter. My custom red Harley Wide Glide, adorned in Harley flames, exemplifies my style of life and food—hot! I believe in safety with style in riding and, being a vegetarian, safety with style in eating as well." Says Keith about this recipe, "Roll your own! No, I'm not talking about that other stuff, just the easiest, healthiest, and quickest fajitas you've ever tasted. This recipe doesn't take a lot of time, so after dinner, you can get back in the saddle for that evening spin."

¼ cup canola oil

4 large red onions, cut into 2-inch-long strips

2 large green or red bell peppers, seeded and cut into 2-inch-long strips

One 1-pound package "chicken" style seitan, cut into strips

1½ tablespoons chili powder

¾ tablespoon ground cumin

¼ pound cheddar cheese or tofu cheese, shredded

1 small jar medium or hot salsa

1 small jar hot sliced jalapeños

Sour cream (optional)

Guacamole (optional)

One 10-count package 10-inch flour or whole wheat tortillas, warmed

1. Heat 2 tablespoons of the oil in a large skillet over medium heat for 2 minutes. Add the onions and cook, stirring, for 3 minutes. Add the bell peppers and cook, stirring, for 5 minutes. Add the seitan, chili powder, cumin, and the remaining 2 tablespoons oil and cook, stirring, until the seitan is hot, about 3 minutes.

2. Place the skillet on a hot plate or trivet at the table. Place the cheese, salsa, jalapeños, sour cream, and guacamole in individual bowls, place the hot tortillas in a napkin-lined basket, and let everyone roll their own. Serve with spicy Mexican rice.

MAKES 4 SERVINGS

Keith Winn and his 2000 Dyna Wide Glide

VROOM VROOM MUSHROOM FAJITAS

These mushroom fajitas are so tasty, they are gone as fast as a top fuel Harley drag bike leaves the line at the green light. Serve some Green Fire Tomatillo Salsa (page 48) on the side to give this recipe its own green light.

¼ cup extra virgin olive oil

1 medium-size onion, cut into matchsticks

2 canned chipotle peppers packed in adobo sauce, minced

1 cup carrot matchsticks

1 medium-size red bell pepper, seeded and cut into matchsticks

1 medium-size zucchini, cut into matchsticks

Two 14-ounce packages mushrooms, sliced

¼ cup chopped garlic

1 teaspoon ground savory

1 teaspoon ground cumin

1 teaspoon dried cilantro

1½ teaspoons salt

½ teaspoon white pepper

Flour tortillas, warmed or lightly fried

Shredded cheddar cheese (optional)

Killer Queso Sauce (page 288; optional)

Sour cream (optional)

1. Heat the olive oil in a large skillet over medium heat. Add the onion, chipotles, and carrots and cook, stirring, until the onion begins to brown, 5 to 7 minutes. Add the bell pepper, zucchini, mushrooms, garlic, savory, cumin, cilantro, salt, and white pepper and cook, stirring, until the mushrooms have darkened and are tender, 5 to 7 minutes.

2. Ladle a spoonful of the filling on a tortilla and top with any of the optional sides. Serve immediately.

MAKES 6 TO 8 SERVINGS

PASSING ZONE: PASTAS

Wind your way through any of the scenic byways or national parks and forests and you will come upon one of those rolling roadblocks, a.k.a. an RV. While I can see the joys and comforts of bringing everything including the kitchen sink along when you travel, these lumbering monsters are no fun to ride behind, especially when you have a line of cars piling up behind you. All it takes is a moment of sightseeing bliss on the part of a car or RV driver to miss seeing the little motorcycle between them and the next vehicle to turn you into a sandwich. Maybe that is why they invented passing zones, just for the safety of motorcyclists. Okay, wishful thinking on my part, but none-theless passing zones are a boon to motorcyclists trapped behind slow-moving vehicles.

While passing RVs is a given when you are riding, there is one thing that I know almost every rider will not pass and that is a hearty pasta dish. Oh, that magic combination of flour, oil, water, and sometimes eggs—PASTA. It comes in almost as many shapes as there are styles of custom Harleys. Pasta dishes run the gamut of culinary traditions from Chinese to Italian to eastern European—stuffed or fancy shaped draped in simple sauces to extravagant concoctions fit for a king—a Road King, that is. Pasta is one of those food groups that is almost always welcome, just like a passing zone is when you are crawling uphill behind a rolling roadblock while riding your Harley on a beautiful twisty road. So pass the RV and then when you reach the ride's end, sit down for supper and pass the pasta. I am sure your riding buddies will appreciate your passing them some of these tasty recipes.

RON AND DEBBIE JANICKI'S SOFTAIL SHRIMP FETTUCCINE

Here is a great recipe from two of my Harley friends in Massachusetts. The love for riding is a family affair within our Harley community, but where and when each of us comes to know we must ride is different. Listen to what Ron has to say about his experience: "I am not sure when the motorcycle bug hit me, but it now appears that I was born with it. Shortly after I purchased my first bike, a used 250cc BSA, an old photo of my father turned up. Back around 1932 Dad owned a 1929 Harley JD. He said, 'It could drive up a lamp post' and 'outrun any car.' My next bike was a new 1971 BSA Lightning, which was with me for a few years. The professional life did away with the bikes for some time. The bug returned in 1992 with a new Dyna Glide Custom. Then my wife, Debbie, got her first bike, a new 1994 Sportster 1200. Then came my 1995 Road King. Then Debbie's 1997 Softail Custom. Over the years, we have been involved in many motorcycle activities, especially with Ocean State H.O.G." See, it just gets in your blood and the whole family wants to be involved. Try this recipe named for Debbie's '97 Softail Custom and start your own family tradition.

> 2 tablespoons margarine
>
> 2 cloves garlic, crushed
>
> 2 shallots or scallions, diced
>
> 1½ teaspoons dried thyme
>
> 2¼ teaspoons seasoned salt
>
> 1 pound medium-size shrimp, shelled and deveined
>
> 3 large ripe tomatoes, diced
>
> ½ cup white wine
>
> 1 pound fettuccine or angel hair pasta, cooked *al dente* according to package directions, drained, and kept warm

1. Melt the margarine in a large skillet over medium heat. Add the garlic, shallots, thyme, seasoned salt, and shrimp and cook, stirring, for 2 minutes. Add the tomatoes and wine, reduce the heat to low, and simmer 3 to 4 minutes.

2. Ladle the sauce over the pasta and serve immediately.

MAKES 6 TO 8 SERVINGS

ANGELIC FRA DIABLO WITH SHRIMP

The four types of hot peppers used in this recipe combine to make a devilishly delicious fire. The complexity of the heat and the heartiness of the portobello mushroom create a sauce that is sinfully satisfying. Add the succulent shrimp, ladle it over a bed of angel hair pasta, and you have a divine dish.

1 pasilla pepper, seeded and torn into small pieces

1 dried New Mexico pepper, seeded and torn into small pieces

1 dried de Arbol pepper, stemmed and crushed

2 canned chipotle peppers packed in adobo sauce

¼ cup boiling water

¼ cup extra virgin olive oil

2 medium-size onions, coarsely chopped

10 cloves garlic, coarsely chopped

2 shallots, minced

2 large portobello mushrooms, stems discarded and caps cut into ½-inch squares

1 red bell pepper, seeded and cut into ½-inch squares

One 28-ounce can peeled whole tomatoes, coarsely chopped, with their juices

¼ cup dried basil

1 tablespoon dried oregano

½ teaspoon salt

1 teaspoon black pepper

1 pound shrimp, peeled and deveined

1 pound angel hair pasta

1. Place the pasilla, New Mexico, de Arbol, and chipotle peppers in a small mixing bowl and cover with the boiling water. Allow to cool to room temperature. Transfer the peppers and soaking water to a blender or a food processor and process until no large pieces of pepper remain, about 1 minute.

2. Fill a large pot with salted water and bring to a boil.

3. Heat the olive oil in a large skillet over medium heat. Add the onions and cook, stirring, until tender, 5 to 7 minutes. Add the garlic and shallots and cook, stirring, until the onions begin to brown, 5 to 7 minutes. Add the pureed peppers, mushrooms, and bell pepper and cook, stirring, until the mushrooms are tender, 5 to 7 minutes. Add the tomatoes, basil, oregano, salt, and black pepper, stir well, and simmer until the sauce just thickens, 8 to 10 minutes. Add the shrimp, stir well, and simmer until they are pink, 5 to 7 minutes.

4. While the shrimp are simmering, cook the pasta in the boiling water until *al dente*. Drain and rinse with hot water to remove excess starch. Allow the pasta to drain thoroughly.

5. Place the pasta in a large serving bowl. Cover with the sauce, toss well, and serve immediately.

MAKES 4 TO 6 SERVINGS

RUTH'S SMOKIN' SALMON AND CORN PASTA

Here is a recipe from "Mama Ruth" from the Motorcycle Hall of Fame Museum. She says: "I'm a fan of original condition old Harleys. Their classic lines, two-tone paint schemes, interesting little badges in art deco design, leather seats with patina, a little oil encrusted on the engine for character and some aroma, that's good stuff for me. Out in the wind, riding the back roads on a vintage Harley, you work up an appetite. I hope other riders enjoy my smoked salmon and corn pasta sauce."

⅓ cup milk

½ cup heavy cream

⅓ cup softened cream cheese

1 small clove garlic, minced

1 teaspoon chopped fresh chives

1 teaspoon chopped fresh basil

1 teaspoon chopped fresh parsley

18 ounces fresh linguine, cooked according to package directions

2 cups cooked fresh corn kernels (removed from 4 ears), drained

1 cup smoked salmon broken into ½-inch pieces

1. Combine the milk, cream, and cream cheese in a medium-size heavy saucepan over low heat. Add the garlic, chives, basil, and parsley and stir together well. Do NOT let it come to a boil.

2. Drain the pasta well and place in a large serving bowl. Add the corn and salmon to the cream sauce and stir together. Immediately pour the finished sauce over the pasta, toss to coat well, and serve at once.

MAKES 4 SERVINGS

PAINFUL PESTO

The only real pain with this pesto pasta dish is when you miss getting the last serving. I always love to make this after I return from a ride on my Buell, especially when I show an Italian sport bike rider how fast is done American style. This dish is as fast to make as a ride to the market on a Buell White Lightning; just have the pasta ready at the same time the sauce is finished and you win the race to dinner.

3 tablespoons dried basil

3 tablespoons boiling water

½ cup extra virgin olive oil

3 tablespoons chopped garlic

½ teaspoon red pepper flakes

½ teaspoon white pepper

½ teaspoon salt

½ cup shelled unsalted pistachios, coarsely chopped

3 tablespoons pine nuts, coarsely chopped

½ cup freshly grated Parmesan cheese

¼ cup shredded Asiago cheese

1 pound tri-color fusilli pasta, cooked *al dente* according to package directions, drained, and kept warm

1. Combine the basil and boiling water in a small heatproof bowl, stir well, and set aside to cool to room temperature.

2. In a small saucepan, heat the olive oil over medium heat. Add the garlic and cook, stirring, just until it begins to color, about 1 minute. Add the crushed red pepper, white pepper, salt, pistachios, and pine nuts and cook, stirring, for 1 minute. Reduce the heat to low, add the basil and its soaking liquid, stir well, and simmer for 2 minutes. Add the cheeses, stir well, and remove from the heat.

3. Pour over the hot pasta, toss well to cover with the sauce, and serve immediately.

MAKES 6 TO 8 SERVINGS

LESLIE HUDSON'S "PERFETTO" PESTO SAUCE

This recipe comes from my friend Leslie who is the manager of the Buell Riders Adventure Group. Leslie is one of the people who introduced me to riding Buells; now she'll introduce you to her recipe: "My husband and I make this usually once every week or so in the summer, when we have an abundance of fresh basil in the garden. It is easy to make and really tasty after a long day of riding our Buell motorcycles. The key to this recipe is to use the best ingredients. For the olive oil, I like these Italian brands: Saico Castelvetrano and Antica Italiana. They are more full-bodied than regular extra virgin olive oils. Also, dried basil will not work. I tried it once, and I have one word for that concoction—yuck! You can use minced garlic from a jar, but it just doesn't taste as good. Get a good garlic press and use fresh cloves (make sure to take the skin off them). You'll never go back to the jarred stuff. The cheese is probably the most important ingredient (maybe I feel this way because I've lived in Wisconsin for four years). Parmigiano-Reggiano is the only way to go in our house when we make this. Try it and you'll see why. It may be a bit difficult to find in your area, and it isn't the least expensive type of Parmesan cheese out there, but it is well worth it. I have to go to a local Italian grocer for it. If you can't find it, you can use regular Parmesan, but keep your eye out for the PR when you're shopping."

>   ¾ cup extra virgin olive oil
>
>   30 to 40 fresh basil leaves, cleaned and dried
>
>   3 medium-size cloves garlic, peeled
>
>   ¾ cup pine nuts
>
>   1½ to 2 cups freshly grated Parmigiano-Reggiano cheese, to your taste

1. Mix in a blender on high speed, add the ingredients one at a time in the order listed. The consistency should be like mustard. If it is too thick, add more oil. If it is too thin, add more cheese. You can adjust any of these ingredients to taste. For example, if you blend it all together and think it still needs more cheese (as I usually do), then add a bit more. Or maybe you're a garlic lover—add another clove . . . you get the idea.

2. Spread over hot pasta (I love farfalle) and top with more grated cheese.

MAKES 3 TO 4 SERVINGS

BEAU AND VICKI PACHECO'S SPAGHETTI CARBONARA

This recipe comes from dear friends of mine, Beau and Vicki Pacheco. Beau wrote me saying, "There is food, and there is food. My motto, after all, has always been: Eat, Ride, or Get Out of the Way. In my checkered career, I have ridden thousands of miles around the globe searching for good food. Sometimes I found it, lots of times I didn't, and many times I was surprised by the divergence of food quality to environment. The best tacos I ever had were at a roadside stand outside of Tijuana where the lady was cooking the carnitas on a flat grill over charcoal. They cost a quarter and I would have paid ten bucks each for them. Conversely, I've had swill's second cousin served at fancy schmancy restaurants in Monte Carlo overlooking the marina where Aristotle Onassis's boat tugged at her moorings.

"On one particular trip in 1985, I started from Denver and rode all the way down to Corpus Christi, Texas, and back to Denver searching for the perfect burrito. I found it, too, and, wouldn't you know it, that perfect burrito lived only three miles away from my home. But then, the journey's the thing, and the search was sublime.

"If we are to talk about motorcycles and food, then we should remain as dedicated as possible and only talk about food in the context of riding. Road food can turn out to be what you will tolerate while on the road and your schedule. There have been days on the road when I couldn't spend the time to sit down and eat, and consumed only what I could find in the gas station. Sometimes, you have enough time to sit down, and you can stop at franchise burger joints, and eat interchangeable bland fare: no great food or bad food. Or, you can stop to eat at private mom and pop hash houses and risk the occasional bad meal, along with the possibility of enjoying the occasional spectacular meal. There are some ladies out there who can turn out a meatloaf fit to dazzle the most persnickety gourmet.

"However, when the day's ride is done, it's time for a little luxury after the hardship of the road. Everyone, however, has their favorite meal and mine is spaghetti carbonara. I have ordered that dish all over the world, and even the worst plate of it was heavenly. The taste of the sauce captures me. When the whipped cream meets the bacon grease, and the eggs snuggle in for a threesome, only to fall disgracefully in love with the garlic . . . *La vita è molto buona!!* Life is very very good.

"The best spaghetti carbonara I've had is to be found at: Tre Moschettieri (Three Musketeers), Via S. Nicola da Tolentino, in Rome, Italy; the Hilton in Padova, Italy; Anna's in Daytona Beach; and Caffe il Farro in Newport Beach, California.

"The only wine that I'll have with carbonara is Chianti. I prefer a classico if it's offered. Since this is a rather heavy meal, I usually round it off with a good cigar. A dinner like this deserves the best and I light up a Padron Anniversario with a glass of tawny port afterward. This, my friends, is perfection.

"When the ride ends at home, then it's best eaten at home. My wife, Vicki, has become an expert at creating carbonara and her recipe, to my taste, is perfect. She is my best riding bud and my culinary soulmate. *Goda il suo carbonara!*" Enjoy your carbonara.

½ **pound sliced bacon**

2 **cups whipping cream**

2 **large eggs, beaten**

¼ **cup crushed garlic**

Salt and pepper to taste

½ **pound thin spaghetti, cooked according to package instructions, drained, and kept warm**

1 **cup freshly grated Parmesan cheese**

1. In a large skillet, fry the bacon until crisp, then drain on paper towels, reserving the bacon grease (measure it out), and crumble.

2. Pour the whipping cream, 6 to 8 tablespoons of the bacon grease (or more to taste), and the eggs into the skillet. Stir over medium heat until the mixture thickens. Thickness is important here; it can be the difference between memorable carbonara and just so-so pasta. Grainy sauce is the bane of all true carbonara lovers. The sauce should be creamy and smooth. Although we use whipping cream, the

sauce should *not* be as thick as strawberry topping. Once the sauce is perfect, add the garlic and season with salt and pepper to taste.

3. Pour your lovely cholesterol concoction over cooked spaghetti. Sprinkle the crumbled bacon and grated Parmesan on top.

If your dinner is an elegant affair and the carbonara is to be mixed and served at the table, once your sauce is poured over the spaghetti, crack a fresh egg over the sauce and mix it in thoroughly. Over this, place ultra-thin slices of Parmesan. Carbonara is sometimes served with peas or some other vegetable. This is heresy. Never let a vegetable touch your spaghetti.

MAKES 2 SERVINGS

Beau and Vicki Pacheco and their
Harley-Davidson Electra Glide Classic

PANHEAD PENNE WITH ZUCCHINI

Summertime has many great things to offer a Harley rider—long days with lots of sunshine, vacation time to spend touring on your bike, loads of weekend runs, and big rallies to attend. Summertime is also when your garden or local farm stand has lots of fresh produce just waiting for you to enjoy. One of my personal favorites is zucchini. This light, fresh dish makes good use of all that fresh zucchini, while the jalapeño gives it a nice fire and the orange bell pepper adds that special splash of color for eye appeal. This will make a great lunch for all your H.O.G. buddies when they gather at your garage for some summertime fun and bike maintenance.

¼ cup extra virgin olive oil

1 jalapeño, seeded and thinly sliced

1 medium-size onion, cut into matchsticks

3 medium-size zucchini, cut into matchsticks

1 orange bell pepper, seeded and cut into matchsticks

2 tablespoons chopped garlic

2 tablespoons dried basil

1 teaspoon dried oregano

1 teaspoon salt

1 teaspoon black pepper

1 pound penne, cooked *al dente* according to package directions, drained, and kept warm

½ cup grated Romano cheese

1. Heat the olive oil in a medium-size skillet over medium heat. Add the jalapeño and onion and cook, stirring, until tender, 3 to 5 minutes. Add the zucchini, bell pepper, garlic, basil, oregano, salt, and black pepper and cook, stirring, until the onion begins to brown, 5 to 7 minutes.

2. Toss with the hot pasta, sprinkle with the Romano cheese, and serve immediately.

MAKES 6 TO 8 SERVINGS

TOM LINDSAY'S BLAZIN' BOWTIES

Here is a recipe from a long-time friend and Harley rider. Tom was Americade's announcer, a.k.a. "The Voice of Americade," from 1991–1999 and currently works for the American Motorcyclist Association (AMA) as public information director. Tom was always on hand when I did shows at Americade. It's great to have friends there to help—it's the biker way. Besides, Tom did confess to enjoying the samples of what I cooked. I hope you enjoy Tom's recipe—good food, good friends, and good motorcycles, ah the good life, a.k.a. the Harley Lifestyle.

1 pound bowtie pasta

2 ancho peppers

2 heads garlic

1 bunch scallions, ends trimmed

1 cup sun-dried tomatoes (not packed in oil)

3 tablespoons extra virgin olive oil

1 to 2 teaspoons chipotle sauce (Tom uses Coyote Cucina brand), to your taste

Freshly ground black pepper

1 cup freshly grated Parmesan cheese

1. Cook the pasta according to the package directions. While the water is heating and the pasta is cooking, soak the anchos in hot water to cover. Peel and mince the garlic. Chop the scallions. Slice and chop the tomatoes. Drain the anchos, remove the stems and seeds, slice, then chop.

2. When the pasta is cooked, drain and set aside. Put the olive oil in the pasta pot and, over low heat, cook the garlic, scallions, anchos, and tomatoes over low heat, stirring constantly. Add the chipotle sauce and season with black pepper. Cook only long enough to soften the scallions and tomatoes (don't brown the garlic or it'll become bitter). Add the pasta to the mixture and mix thoroughly. Remove from the heat, add the cheese, and mix again.

MAKES 4 TO 6 SERVINGS

CAVATELLI FROM HELL

This pasta dish features a creamy cheese sauce laced with chipotle fire. The smoky flavor of the chipotle peppers blends so well with the sautéed onions and garlic to create a warm base for the cheese sauce. Draped over broccoli and pasta, it is a heartwarming meal to enjoy after a long ride on your Hog.

¼ cup extra virgin olive oil

2 canned chipotle peppers packed in adobo sauce, minced

1 medium-size onion, cut into matchsticks

2 tablespoons chopped garlic

1 bunch broccoli, cut into bite-size florets

1 teaspoon dried basil

¼ teaspoon dried oregano

½ teaspoon salt

½ teaspoon white pepper

1 cup half-and-half

½ cup freshly grated Parmesan cheese

One 8-ounce package cavatelli or tortellini, cooked *al dente* according to package directions, drained, and kept warm

Heat the olive oil in a large skillet over medium heat. Add the chipotles and onion and cook, stirring, until the onion begins to brown, 5 to 7 minutes. Reduce the heat to low, add the garlic, and cook, stirring, for 2 to 3 minutes. Add the broccoli and cook, stirring, until the florets begin to turn dark green, 5 to 7 minutes. Add the basil, oregano, salt, white pepper, and half-and-half, stir well, and simmer for 2 to 3 minutes. Add the Parmesan and stir well. Add the pasta, stir well to coat with the sauce and heat through, and serve immediately.

MAKES 4 TO 6 SERVINGS

AFTER-BURNER PASTA SAUCE

This fresh pasta sauce is the perfect companion for Eggplant Exhaust Pipes (page 174), like flamethrowers are a perfect addition to the exhaust pipes on the Burpee Biker Billy show bike. Speaking of Burpee, this sauce features the Biker Billy hybrid jalapeño and three other hot peppers for a complex fire. The oregano and basil lend a fresh-from-the-garden taste and the orange bell pepper adds color. Try it on your favorite pasta and feel the burn.

1 dried chipotle pepper, stemmed

1 dried de Arbol pepper, stemmed

1 dried New Mexico pepper, stemmed and seeded

½ cup boiling water

3 tablespoons extra virgin olive oil

1 Burpee Biker Billy jalapeño, minced

2 medium-size onions, diced

1½ cups sliced mushrooms

1 orange bell pepper, seeded and diced

3 tablespoons chopped garlic

1 tablespoon minced fresh oregano leaves

⅓ cup fresh basil leaves, minced

1 teaspoon salt

1 teaspoon freshly ground black pepper

One 28-ounce can peeled whole tomatoes, coarsely chopped, with their juices

1. Place the chipotle, de Arbol, and New Mexico peppers in a small bowl and cover with the boiling water. Allow to cool to room temperature. Puree the rehydrated peppers and soaking water in a blender or a food processor equipped with a chopping blade until no large pieces of pepper remain, about 1 minute.

2. Heat the olive oil in a large skillet over medium heat. Add the jalapeño, onions, and mushrooms, stir well to coat with the oil, and cook, stirring, until the onions are golden brown, 5 to 7 minutes. Add the hot pepper puree, bell pepper, garlic, oregano, basil, salt, black pepper, and tomatoes, bring to a boil, reduce the heat to medium-low, and simmer until the sauce just thickens, 8 to 10 minutes.

MAKES ABOUT 5 CUPS

CHARLES MACK'S TACO PASTA

Charles Mack from Limerick, Pennsylvania, sent in this recipe, saying, "Well, my mother was Italian and I was brought up on good, spicy, fattening Italian food. I could probably eat pasta every day, but my waist couldn't tolerate that. The only thing better than a good ride is a good meal afterward. I don't care how long you have your Harley, every once in a while you still have to open up that garage door and just look at it like you did when you first bought it. My love for riding puts spice into my life. I have been riding for over 30 years now, and there's nothing better for relieving stress than getting on the back of my bike and just riding, with no destination in mind. I enjoy that same 'spice' in the foods that I eat, using lots of garlic and hot peppers. I always enjoyed making tacos and one day I came up with this recipe and I have been passing it on ever since."

> **1 pound ground beef or turkey**
>
> **Two 14½-ounce cans diced tomatoes**
>
> **2 to 4 chiles, to your taste, diced**
>
> **One 8-ounce can sliced black olives, drained**
>
> **One 8-ounce can taco sauce**
>
> **One 16-ounce jar of your favorite spaghetti sauce**
>
> **1 pound of your favorite pasta, cooked according to package instructions, drained, and kept warm**
>
> **1 loaf garlic bread**

1. In a large skillet over medium-high heat, cook the ground beef or turkey, breaking any pieces apart. When fully cooked, add the tomatoes, chiles, olives, and taco sauce. Let this simmer for 10 to 15 minutes to cook off some of the liquid. Add the spaghetti sauce and simmer for another 10 to 15 minutes, uncovered.

2. Put the cooked pasta in a large bowl and pour the taco pasta sauce over it. Serve with garlic bread and a good Chianti, if desired.

MAKES 4 TO 6 SERVINGS

PENNE WITH CRANKCASE VODKA SAUCE

While a pink Harley may look good with a beautiful Harley Lady astride it, it ain't a color I would paint my bike. And you can be sure that Biker Billy ain't gonna cook no pink vodka sauce either. However, if a fiery cream sauce blushes because I made it hot and wild, I would know it was like a compliment that pleases a lady and makes her blush. So, make that Harley Lady in your life blush, tell her how beautiful she looks in her riding gear, then serve her some of this dish and get her all cranked up. Where you go from there is the stuff of biker dreams.

3 ounces sun-dried tomatoes, minced

1 cup boiling water

¼ cup extra virgin olive oil

1 leek (white and green parts), trimmed, rinsed well, and cut into ½-inch-thick slices

1 medium-size onion, cut into matchsticks

3 tablespoons chopped garlic

5 canned chipotle peppers packed in adobo sauce, minced

1 tablespoon dried basil, minced

1 teaspoon dried oregano

1 teaspoon salt

1 teaspoon white pepper

2 cups half-and-half

¼ cup vodka

1 pound penne, cooked *al dente* according to package directions, drained, and kept warm

1. In a small heatproof bowl, combine the sun-dried tomatoes and boiling water. Set aside and allow to cool to room temperature.

2. Heat the olive oil in a large skillet over medium heat. Add the leek and onion and cook, stirring, until tender, 7 to 10 minutes. Add the garlic, chipotles, sun-dried tomatoes and their soaking water, basil, oregano, salt, and white pepper and cook, stirring a few times, until all the liquid is gone, 7 to 10 minutes.

3. Transfer to a food processor, add the half-and-half, and process until smooth, 1 to 2 minutes. Return to the skillet, add the vodka, stir well, and heat through over medium heat.

4. Place the pasta in a large serving bowl, pour over the sauce, toss well, and serve immediately.

MAKES 4 TO 6 SERVINGS

RON AND DEBBIE JANICKI'S VEGETABLE LASAGNA

Here is another great recipe from the Janicki family. Speaking of the family motorcycles, Ron's 1995 Road King and Debbie's 1997 Softail Custom, Ron said, "These two motorcycles and all the people and activities that go with them have become a major portion of our social life. We are living the American Dream—riding and eating our way around the USA on two beautiful Harleys." What more is there to say?

One 15-ounce container nonfat ricotta cheese

One 10-ounce package frozen chopped spinach, thawed, cooked according to package directions, drained, and squeezed dry

1¼ cups freshly grated Parmesan cheese

Salt

Pepper

Garlic powder

2% milk, as needed

2 small zucchini, thinly sliced, lightly steamed, and chopped

1 pound eggplant, peeled, thinly sliced, brushed with canola oil, broiled till lightly brown, and chopped

2 jars roasted red peppers, drained and chopped

1 cup artichoke hearts (not packed in oil), drained, chopped, and tossed with lemon juice

2 small cans sliced mushrooms, drained and chopped

1 pound lasagne noodles

3 jars sauce (I like tomato and basil and marinara with burgundy and use 2 jars of sauce when making the lasagna and heat up the third jar to serve on top of the lasagna)

8 ounces nonfat mozzarella cheese, shredded

1. In a medium-size mixing bowl, combine the ricotta, spinach, and 1 cup of the Parmesan, season to taste with salt, pepper, and garlic powder, and add as much milk as you need to moisten it a bit.

2. In a large mixing bowl, combine all the vegetables.

3. Bring a large pot of salted water to a boil. Add the lasagna noodles and cook until *al dente*. Drain and rinse well to keep the noodles from sticking to each other.

4. Preheat the oven to 350°F. Grease the bottom of 9 x 13-inch lasagna pan. Spread some of the sauce over the bottom of the pan, then add a layer of noodles, slightly overlapping them. Layer over that, in order, half of the ricotta cheese filling, half of the mozzarella, half of the vegetable mixture, and some sauce. Start with another layer of noodles and repeat the layers. Add a final layer of noodles, top with the remaining sauce, and sprinkle with the remaining Parmesan.

5. Bake, covered with a sheet of aluminum foil, for 30 minutes. Remove the foil cover and bake for another 15 minutes.

MAKES 10 TO 12 SERVINGS

PEANUT TANK THAI NOODLES

I love Thai food and can't get enough of it once I get a hankering for those fiery sauces laced with peanuts. Like riding once you learn the pleasures of roaring down the road on a Harley-Davidson big twin, nothing else compares. Try this tasty Thai-inspired noodle dish and you will hear the thunder in your ears—thunder from the peppers, that is. If it is not hot enough to kick-start your taste buds, replace the de Arbol peppers with cayenne peppers or, for that big inch stroker motor experience, try some habaneros.

¾ cup water

1 tablespoon cornstarch

¼ cup canola oil

2 dried de Arbol peppers, stemmed and crushed

2 tablespoons peeled and minced fresh ginger

2 tablespoons chopped garlic

3 scallions, ends trimmed and minced

¼ cup light soy sauce

¼ cup light teriyaki sauce

¼ cup chunky peanut butter

1 teaspoon white pepper

1 tablespoon dried chives

8 ounces buckwheat noodles, cooked *al dente* according to package directions, drained, and kept warm

1. In a small bowl, combine the water and cornstarch, stir well, and set aside.

2. Heat the canola oil in a small skillet over medium heat. Add the de Arbol pepper, ginger, garlic, and scallions and cook, stirring, until the scallions begin to brown, 5 to 7 minutes. Add the soy sauce, teriyaki sauce, peanut butter, white pepper, and chives, stir well until the peanut butter melts, and reduce the heat to low. Add the cornstarch mixture and simmer until the sauce thickens, about 5 minutes, stirring often.

3. Place the noodles in a medium-size serving bowl, pour the sauce over, toss well to coat, and serve immediately.

MAKES 4 TO 6 SERVINGS

HIGHWAY PAD THAI

Some of my riding buddies and I share an appreciation for Thai food. We have been known to plan rides around visiting a newly discovered Thai restaurant. I came up with this recipe after a visit to a small place in the Pocono Mountains of Pennsylvania.

2 tablespoons rice vinegar

2 tablespoons water

2 tablespoons light soy sauce

2 tablespoons light teriyaki sauce

½ teaspoon salt

1 tablespoon sugar

2 tablespoons chunky peanut butter

¼ cup canola oil

2 dried de Arbol peppers, stemmed and crushed

1 pound extra firm bean curd, drained and cut into ½-inch cubes

3 jumbo eggs, beaten

1 Hungarian wax pepper, seeded and minced

1 bunch scallions, ends trimmed and cut into ½-inch-thick slices

2 tablespoons chopped garlic

2 tablespoons peeled and minced fresh ginger

1 small zucchini, ends trimmed and cut into matchsticks

One 9-ounce package rice pad thai noodles, cooked according to package directions and drained

1 cup alfalfa sprouts, rinsed

½ cup dry-roasted peanuts, coarsely chopped

1. In a small bowl combine the vinegar, water, soy sauce, teriyaki sauce, salt, sugar, and peanut butter. Stir well to combine and set aside.

2. Heat 2 tablespoons of the canola oil in a large wok over a high heat. Add the de Arbol peppers and stir well to coat. Add the bean curd and stir-fry until browned, 5 to 7 minutes. Move the bean curd up the sides of the wok, pour the eggs into the center of the wok, and stir-fry the eggs with the bean curd until the eggs are firm. Break into bite-size pieces and remove from the wok.

3. Add the remaining 2 tablespoons oil to the wok and allow to heat for 30 to 60 seconds. Add the Hungarian pepper, scallions, garlic, ginger, and zucchini and stir-fry until the zucchini is just beginning to get tender, 2 to 3 minutes. Return the bean curd and eggs to the wok, add the noodles, and stir-fry for 1 to 2 minutes. Add the sauce mixture, toss well to coat, and heat the sauce for 1 to 2 minutes. Add the alfalfa sprouts and peanuts, toss well, and serve immediately.

MAKES 6 TO 8 SERVINGS

CHRISTINE FLEISSNER'S GARLICKY MACARONI AND CHEESE

Christine Fleissner of Milwaukee, Wisconsin, sent in this killer recipe. Here she speaks of Harleys and her recipe: "I love riding on the back of the Harley-Davidson, where I am free to enjoy the sights and smells of the ride. My favorite time to ride is in late May, when the lilacs are blooming and the smell as you ride past is fantastic! I love experimenting with different recipes and my husband loves being experimented on. I have loved macaroni and cheese since I was a child. This recipe is easy and quick to make. It is really cheesy (the cheesier the better). You can experiment with different kinds of cheese for a different flavor. I like to use pasta wheels when I make it to remind me of our Harley-Davidson."

> **1 pound pasta (wheels for bikers)**
>
> **10 to 15 cloves garlic, minced**
>
> **2 tablespoons olive oil**
>
> **3 cups milk**
>
> **½ teaspoon salt**
>
> **½ teaspoon black pepper**
>
> **3 cups shredded cheddar cheese**
>
> **1 cup shredded provolone cheese**
>
> **1 cup freshly grated Parmesan cheese**

1. Preheat the oven to 375°F.

2. Cook the pasta *al dente* according to the package directions. Drain well, rinsing some of the starch off the pasta.

3. In a medium-size saucepan over medium heat, heat the olive oil. Add the garlic and cook, stirring, just until it begins to color, about 1 minute. Add the milk and bring to a boil. Remove from the heat, add the salt, pepper, and cheeses and stir until the cheeses have melted slightly. Add the cooked pasta and coat with the cheese sauce.

4. Pour the cheese and pasta into a greased 2-quart baking dish and bake until lightly browned on top, about 45 minutes.

MAKES 4 TO 6 SERVINGS

MATT HARRINGTON'S SAC-ARONI AND CHEESE

Matt Harrington of Buffalo, New York, sent me this recipe and said, "I have been involved with H-D motorcycles for the last six years of my short life. There is nothing better than the speed and style of a Harley. I had the pleasure of meeting Biker Billy at the IX Center in Cleveland a few years ago. I bought his book *Biker Billy Cooks with Fire* and have been blazing in the kitchen ever since." Matt went on to say about his recipe, "There is nothing better than home-made mac and cheese. This recipe is almost as easy as what you can prepare from the box stuff. The *huge* difference is that this is 100 percent better. I always make this stuff when we have friends and family visit from out of town and they absolutely love it."

2 tablespoons butter

2 tablespoons flour

2 cups milk

Salt and pepper, to taste

3 cups shredded sharp cheddar cheese

1 pound elbow macaroni, cooked *al dente* **and drained**

Dry bread crumbs

1. Preheat the oven to 350°F.

2. In a deep skillet, melt the butter over medium heat. Add the flour to make a roux and cook, stirring to remove any lumps. Pour in the milk and cook until the mixture is thick and smooth. Season with salt and pepper. Stir in 2 1/2 cups of the cheddar and continue to cook until melted. Add the cooked macaroni and stir.

3. Transfer the mixture to a 2-quart casserole dish. Bake for 20 minutes. Remove the casserole from the oven, top with the remaining 1/2 cup cheese and the bread crumbs. Bake for an additional 5 minutes, until hot and bubbly.

MAKES 6 TO 8 SERVINGS

BIG WHEELS TURNING: SAVORY PIES

"**A** big wheel keep on turnin', Proud Mary keeps on burnin'." I am sure you know that great driving song Ike and Tina Turner made famous. I am often inspired by music. There are so many great road songs that make me just want to roll that big Harley-Davidson Road King out of my garage and ride; as the song says, I would be "rollin', rollin', rollin'" down the roadway. Since I am not a singer, I translate my inspiration from music and riding into creating recipes. So in a way I am always cookin', cookin', cookin' in the kitchen. One of the fun foods I like to cook up when I get a creative itch that needs scratching is pie. Speaking of scratching, I tried at one point to make the piecrusts from scratch. While it can be done and it does taste great, I discovered that it takes time that could be better spent riding my Harley. So you will find that I use packaged piecrust mix in these recipes, since I want you to have more time to ride too. Pies are such great fun to make and to serve.

There is something festive and yet comforting about a dinner pie that speaks of home and the safety and comfort of familiar faces and places. While I love to travel and adventure on my Harley, I do enjoy returning home, seeing my family and friends. I am sure you feel the same. There is something special about the balance of road time and home time. Perhaps it is that each makes you appreciate the other.

Sample these recipes and share them with your Harley family; they will make any meal feel like a homecoming. Plus those pies sitting on the table looking for all the world like big wheels will make you think about riding that big Harley. I guess it is no small wonder that most of the pie recipes I have created over the years make two pies, like the two wheels on my Road King. Sliced pies even remind me of spoked wheels. Okay, I don't know about you, but I am hungry now for both a ride and a slice of pie in precisely that order. Eat Hot and Ride Safe!

KOSCO H-D'S CHICKEN POTPIE

Kosco Harley began in 1988 in Pompton Plains, New Jersey, and expanded in 1996 to its present seven-acre facility in Kinnelon. They have a great H.O.G. chapter and many of the members are long-time friends of mine. Lou Kosco sent me this family recipe he wanted to share, and he wants you to know that you are welcome to "stop by for a hot cup of coffee and good conversation with fellow bikers and the friendly people at Kosco Harley-Davidson–Buell."

> **1½ cups shredded or diced cooked chicken**
>
> **1½ cups frozen or fresh mixed vegetables**
>
> **Two 10¾-ounce cans condensed cream of chicken soup**
>
> **2 cups Bisquick**
>
> **1 cup milk**
>
> **2 large eggs**

1. Preheat the oven to 400°F.

2. Mix the chicken, vegetables, and soup together in an ungreased 13 x 9-inch baking dish. In a large mixing bowl, combine the Bisquick, milk, and eggs, mixing together until blended, then pour evenly over the chicken mixture.

3. Bake until golden brown, about 30 minutes.

MAKES 6 SERVINGS

MACHINE-GUN PIE

When you bite into this pie, You'll hear the rat-tat-tat of machine-gun fire, which sounds just like a straight-piped Hog racing up an alley. It is a favorite of mine when I want something Italian but not pasta. This recipe is a variation on a classic ratatouille baked into a pie that will make veggie lovers' usual pizzas look anemic.

½ cup sun-dried tomatoes

½ cup boiling water

¼ cup extra virgin olive oil

1 medium-size onion, cut into matchsticks

4 canned chipotle peppers packed in adobo sauce, minced

2 tablespoons chopped garlic

1 medium-size eggplant, cut into 1-inch cubes

2 medium-size zucchini, halved lengthwise and cut into 1-inch slices

3 cups small brown mushrooms, cut in half

1 medium-size yellow bell pepper, seeded and cut into 1-inch squares

One 28-ounce can peeled whole tomatoes, quartered, with their juices

2 tablespoons dried parsley

2 tablespoons dried basil

1 teaspoon dried oregano

1½ teaspoons salt

1 teaspoon black pepper

1 box piecrust mix, prepared for two 9-inch deep-dish pies

4 cups shredded mozzarella cheese

1. Place the sun-dried tomatoes in a small heatproof bowl and cover with the boiling water. Allow to cool to room temperature. Remove the tomatoes from the water, reserving the liquid. Coarsely chop the tomatoes and return to the liquid.

2. Heat the olive oil in a large skillet over high heat. Add the onion and chipotles, stir well to coat with oil, and cook, stirring, until the onions begin to brown, 5 to 7 minutes. Reduce the heat to medium, add the garlic, eggplant, zucchini, mushrooms, and bell pepper, and cook, stirring a few times, until the vegetables are just tender, 5 to 7 minutes. Raise the heat to high, add the sun-dried tomatoes with their liquid, the peeled tomatoes, parsley, basil, oregano, salt, and black pepper, and cook, stirring a few times, until the sauce just thickens, 5 to 7 minutes. Remove from the heat and allow to cool to room temperature.

3. Preheat the oven to 450°F. Divide the filling between the two piecrusts. Cover the top of each evenly with the mozzarella. Bake until the cheese and crusts are golden brown, 12 to 15 minutes. Remove from the oven and serve immediately.

MAKES TWO 9-INCH PIES

LEEKY CAULIFLOWER PIE

Every time I serve this, someone says, "I never eat cauliflower, but I love this." Somewhere between a gratin and a quiche, this pie is always a welcome surprise, kinda like going into your garage and finding an original condition Panhead leaking on your clean floor. Okay, so you don't like an oil stain, but you're damn happy to have the bike.

¼ cup (½ stick) butter

1 bay leaf

3 medium-size leeks (white and green parts), trimmed, rinsed well, and cut into ¼-inch-thick slices

1 medium-size shallot, minced

1 medium-size onion, minced

2 tablespoons all-purpose flour

½ teaspoon cayenne pepper

½ teaspoon ground thyme

½ teaspoon ground savory

½ teaspoon ground nutmeg

1 teaspoon salt

½ teaspoon white pepper

1½ cups half-and-half

1 box piecrust mix, prepared for two 9-inch pies

1 medium-size cauliflower, cut into bite-size florets and steamed until tender

1 cup freshly grated Parmesan cheese

½ cup shredded Asiago cheese

1. In a large skillet, melt 3 tablespoons of the butter over medium heat. Add the bay leaf, leeks, shallot, and onion, stir well to coat with butter, and cook, stirring, until the leeks are tender, 10 to 12 minutes.

2. Combine the flour, cayenne, thyme, savory, nutmeg, salt, and white pepper in a small bowl and whisk together. Clear the center of the skillet and melt the remaining 1 tablespoon butter there. Add the flour-and-spice blend and whisk it into the melted butter. Stir well into the leek mixture and cook, stirring, until you can smell a toasty spice aroma rise from the pan, 2 to 4 minutes. Slowly add the half-and-half while stirring. Simmer, stirring often, until the sauce thickens, 4 to 6 minutes. Remove from the heat and allow to cool to room temperature.

3. Preheat the oven to 450°F. Divide the cauliflower between the two piecrusts and cover with the leek mixture. Remove the bay leaf. Sprinkle each evenly with both the cheeses. Bake until the cheeses and crusts are golden brown, 12 to 15 minutes. Remove from the oven and serve immediately.

MAKES TWO 9-INCH PIES

CHRISTINE FLEISSNER'S CHICKPEA QUICHE

Here is another recipe from Christine Fleissner of Milwaukee, Wisconsin. If you enjoyed her Garlicky Macaroni and Cheese (page 126), you will like this one too. About this recipe Christine told me, "This recipe is very versatile. The basic recipe can be combined with almost any vegetable and different cheeses. Broccoli or asparagus is a great substitute for the chickpeas and can be combined with cheddar or mozzarella cheeses. Stopping at a farmer's market or farmer's stand to pick up fresh ingredients while out for a ride adds to the fun of this dish!"

> 1 box piecrust mix, prepared for one 9-inch pie
>
> 2 cups shredded provolone cheese
>
> One 19-ounce can chickpeas, drained
>
> 10 cloves garlic, thinly sliced

2 large eggs

⅓ cup skim milk

¼ teaspoon salt

½ teaspoon black pepper

1 tablespoon crushed dried rosemary

1. Preheat the oven to 400°F.

2. Roll out the piecrust and place in a greased 9-inch pie pan. Bake until lightly browned, 10 to 15 minutes. Remove from the oven and let cool for about 10 minutes. Leave the oven on.

3. Layer 1 cup of the cheese over the bottom of the crust. Add the chickpeas in an even layer on top of the cheese. Arrange the garlic slices evenly over the chickpeas.

4. In a medium-size mixing bowl, whisk the eggs together well. Add the milk, salt, and pepper and stir until well combined. Pour the egg mixture into the crust. Sprinkle the top evenly with the crushed rosemary and the remaining 1 cup cheese. Bake until set and browned, about 30 minutes. Let rest a few minutes before slicing.

MAKES ONE 9-INCH QUICHE

Dick and Christine Fleissner with their 1997
Harley-Davidson Sportster 1200 Custom

PAINFUL PESTO PIE

I have for years wanted to make a pie that had pasta as part of the filling. I guess I like both piecrust and pasta a lot; just like my Harleys, two is better than one. As a result, I developed this rich, sinful dish, which makes a great side dish but is substantial enough to be a one-dish meal.

> **1 box piecrust mix, prepared for two 9-inch deep-dish pies**
>
> **1 recipe Painful Pesto (page 111)**
>
> **1 cup shredded mozzarella cheese**
>
> **1 recipe Grilled Veggies à la Diablo (page 73)**

1. Preheat the oven to 450°F. Divide the pesto between the two piecrusts. Sprinkle evenly with the mozzarella, then garnish with the grilled veggies.

2. Bake until the cheese and crusts are golden brown, 12 to 15 minutes. Remove from the oven and serve warm.

MAKES TWO 9-INCH PIES

EXHAUST PIPE PIE

G rilled veggies look so appealing and when you use my Diablo Marinade, they taste every bit as good as they look. I find that the flavors of grilled veggies combine really well with mild, creamy cheeses. This pie is a tasty blending of the two and the structure of a pie makes the perfect presentation. The finished product looks like it took more work than it actually does, which allows you time to polish the chrome on your bike before dinner. Your buddies will wonder how you manage to cook and keep the scoot so shiny. Let them just keep wondering, heck, a biker is entitled to some secrets, right?

> **Marinade from Grilled Veggies à la Diablo (page 73)**
>
> **1 medium-size eggplant, cut into ¼-inch-thick rounds**
>
> **2 medium-size yellow squashes, cut into ¼-inch-thick rounds**
>
> **1 large red onion, cut into ¼-inch-thick slices**

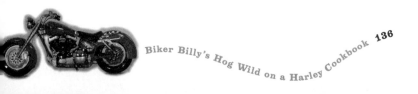

1 red bell pepper, seeded and cut open into one large piece

One 15-ounce container ricotta cheese

2 tablespoons dried basil

1 teaspoon dried oregano

1 teaspoon cayenne pepper

1 teaspoon salt

1 teaspoon white pepper

1 box piecrust mix, prepared for two 9-inch deep-dish pies

2 cups shredded mozzarella cheese

1. Preheat the oven to 375°F. Preheat your gas or electric grill or build a medium-hot charcoal fire.

2. Brush the marinade on both sides of the vegetables before grilling and each time you turn them on the grill. Grill until tender and browned, then allow to cool to room temperature.

3. In a medium-size mixing bowl, combine the ricotta, basil, oregano, cayenne, salt, and white pepper and mix well.

4. Divide the grilled eggplant between the two piecrusts, forming a layer on the bottom of each. Divide the ricotta mixture between the piecrusts, forming a layer on top of the eggplant. Divide the grilled yellow squash and red onion between the two piecrusts, forming a layer on top of the ricotta mixture. Divide the mozzarella between both pies, covering the squash and onions. Cut the grilled red bell pepper into long strips and garnish the top in a tic-tac-toe pattern.

5. Bake until the crust and cheese are golden brown, 30 to 40 minutes. Serve warm.

MAKES TWO 9-INCH PIES

SAMUEL FAIRCHILD'S PIZZA POT PIE

Samuel Fairchild of Bowie, Texas, sent this recipe and told me, "My first ride on a Harley was on the back of my uncle's '52 Harley. I didn't get my own until I was in my late thirties, so I've been making up for lost time. My wife took me to Deal Harley-Davidson in

Fayetteville, North Carolina, and told me to pick out the one I wanted!!!!!! So, I picked out a brand spankin' new 1990 FXSTC in a burnt cherry color. We have been all over the United States on it. Our most memorable ride was when we were living in Colorado Springs, Colorado, and we went to the first Four Corners Rally. When we left Colorado Springs, it was snowing heavily. We had to go through some very cold weather. After a while of riding, I noticed a vibration in my bike. It was shaking almost violently. It felt like a high-speed wobble. I slowed but the vibration-shaking was worse. I stopped on the side of the road with the engine running and the vibration was steady. I turned off the engine and the vibration/shaking was even worse. I realized it was my wife on the back seat. She was shivering so bad that it made my bike shake. She didn't want to say anything to me about it because she didn't want to be a wuss and didn't want to cause me to have to stop for the night. Well, we got a hotel room and she stayed in the tub with hot water running for over two hours before she finally warmed up. We enjoyed the first Four Corners Rally tremendously and we will never forget that ride!!!!

"This recipe is great for after a long, cold ride when you need to warm up the fingers and toes. A friend of mine made a similar dish for me ages ago. He said it came from the 'Old Country' (Italy) with some variations thrown in. I made my own variations to warm it up a bit. Hope you like it!!!!"

    1 pound ground beef (80% lean or more)

    ½ Vidalia onion (or whatever kind you prefer), diced

    6 jalapeños, thinly sliced

    ½ cup sliced fresh mushrooms (or drained canned)

    1½ cups spaghetti sauce

    12 ounces mozzarella cheese, sliced ⅛ inch thick

    1½ cups sour cream

    1 can crescent rolls dough

    2 tablespoons butter or margarine

    2 ounces Parmesan cheese, grated

1. In a large skillet over medium-high heat, brown the ground beef, breaking up any large clumps. Drain the fat from the pan and place over medium heat. Stir in the onion, then stir in the jalapeños and

cook, stirring, for a few minutes. Add the mushrooms and stir. Add the spaghetti sauce and heat until it bubbles.

2. Transfer the mixture into a 9-inch casserole dish. Take the sliced mozzarella and place it on top, making sure it reaches all the way to the edges of the dish so that none of the ingredients seeps through. Stir the sour cream and spoon over the mozzarella until it is completely covered.

3. Open the can of crescent rolls and flatten each roll individually. Place them over the sour cream, pinching them against the side of the dish. Slice pats of butter and place them evenly on the top of the crescent roll topping. Sprinkle the Parmesan evenly over the topping.

4. Place in a preheated 350°F oven and bake until the topping is golden brown, 18 to 22 minutes. Remove from the oven and allow to sit for approximately 5 minutes (if you can wait that long). Cut and serve with a metal spatula.

Caution: It will be very hot and very irresistible . . . have plenty of beer to cool your mouth!!!

MAKES 6 SERVINGS

Samuel Fairchild and his granddaughter Chrissy on his 1990 FXSTC, still going strong after more than 100,000 miles

LEATHER AND CHROME PIE

Spinach and feta cheese seem to belong together, like black leather and chrome. I have played around with different ways of combining the two over the years and I am always pleased to find a new way to combine these two favorite flavors. This simple pie is just right, like a custom Harley built with a clear concept and executed with no unnecessary extras. Just a clean, sweet design that says I know what I am, take me or leave me, but don't think of changing me.

2 tablespoons extra virgin olive oil

1 medium-size onion, cut into matchsticks

2 tablespoons chopped garlic

½ cup oil-packed sun-dried tomatoes, drained and minced

2 canned chipotle peppers packed in adobo sauce, minced

One 10-ounce package frozen chopped spinach, thawed and squeezed dry

½ cup black olives, drained, pitted, and sliced

½ cup water

3 jumbo eggs, beaten

1 cup half-and-half

1 teaspoon ground cumin

8 ounces feta cheese, crumbled

½ teaspoon ground nutmeg

1 box piecrust mix, prepared for two 9-inch deep-dish pies

1. Heat the olive oil in a large skillet over high heat. Add the onion and cook, stirring, until golden brown, 5 to 7 minutes. Reduce the heat to medium, add the garlic, sun-dried tomatoes, and chipotles, and cook, stirring, until the garlic begins to brown, 1 to 2 minutes. Add the spinach, black olives, and water and simmer until the liquid is gone, 5 to 7 minutes. Remove from the heat and allow to cool to room temperature.

2. Preheat the oven to 375°F.

3. In a medium-size mixing bowl, combine the eggs, half-and-half, cumin, feta, and nutmeg and mix well. Add this mixture to the

spinach mixture in the skillet once it's cooled down a bit and stir well to combine. Divide between the piecrusts.

4. Bake until the crust and filling are golden brown, 35 to 45 minutes. Serve warm.

MAKES TWO 9-INCH PIES

POTATO POTATO CORN PIE, A.K.A. MISFIRE QUICHE

Talk about a hearty meal—this pie has all the stick-to-your ribs satisfaction you need to ride your Hog all day. It is a blending of some wonderful comfort foods, flavorful herbs, and spices, plus a nice fire from the combo of jalapeños and cayenne. You might even miss the fire, since the potatoes, corn, eggs, half-and-half, and cheese can absorb a lot of heat, which is why I call it Misfire Quiche.

2 tablespoons butter

1 medium-size onion, cut into matchsticks

3 medium-size red potatoes, cut into ¾-inch cubes

2 jalapeños, seeded and minced

2 tablespoons chopped garlic

One 16-ounce can sweet corn, drained

3 jumbo eggs, beaten

1 cup half-and-half

1 tablespoon sweet paprika

¼ teaspoon cayenne pepper

1 tablespoon dried chives

1 teaspoon salt

1 teaspoon white pepper

3 cups shredded mild cheddar cheese

1 package piecrust mix, prepared for two 9-inch deep-dish pies

1. Melt the butter in a large skillet over medium heat. Add the onion, potatoes, and jalapeños and cook, stirring, until the potatoes are tender, 10 to 15 minutes. Add the garlic and corn and cook, stirring,

until the garlic begins to brown, about 3 minutes. Remove from the heat and allow to cool to room temperature.

2. Preheat the oven to 375°F.

3. In a medium-size mixing bowl, combine the eggs, half-and-half, paprika, cayenne, chives, salt, and white pepper and whisk together well. Add the egg mixture to the potato mixture and stir well. Add the cheese and stir well. Divide the filling between the two piecrusts.

4. Bake until the filling and crusts are golden brown, 45 to 50 minutes. Let cool for 5 to 10 minutes before slicing.

MAKES TWO 9-INCH PIES

BRIDGE FREEZES
BEFORE ROAD:
CHILI

lthough I had been cooking for decades before my career in cooking officially began, it started with one recipe—my chili. For years I had been making chili, always experimenting with the recipe. Like most chili cooks, I started with some packaged spice called chili powder and improved on it. Then I went solo and started from the ground up using individual spices. Over time, my chili evolved into a complex recipe that included several types of hot peppers and a carefully balanced combination of herbs, spices, and secret ingredients. I would cook this chili at different gatherings ranging from camping at the Americade Rally in Lake George, New York, to parties at the TV studios I owned and operated in Manhattan. My friends kept telling me I should package and market my chili, so I took a course at the New School on the specialty food marketplace and came up with a name for my chili—not surprisingly, "Biker Billy's Chili." Then one day I had an idea: I would create my own television cooking show to promote my chili. I called the show *Biker Billy Cooks with Fire* and less than a year later, a literary agent approached me with an offer from William Morrow and Company, Inc., to write a cookbook. It was too good to refuse; I accepted and wrote my first book, *Biker Billy Cooks with Fire*.

Over the years, many of you have asked for my secret chili recipe; well, guess what, it is still secret. That's right, folks, it's not in this book, but there are some other fantastic chili recipes from Harley riders around this great nation. So if you are lucky and attend an event where I cook my chili, enjoy it and until then, enjoy the chili recipes in this chapter.

WYATT BARBEE'S H-D CHILI

Wyatt Barbee of Dahlonega, Georgia, is a member of the Killer Creek H.O.G. Chapter based at Killer Creek Harley-Davidson in Roswell, Georgia. Wyatt said, "I have been making this for years but only recently been serving it at biker parties and rallies. Each time, it sells out and everyone asks me for the recipe." Wonder if this means that bikers like chili? Go hog wild and cook Wyatt's chili for your H.O.G. buddies.

1 onion, chopped

1 pound ground top round (use chili meat from grocer for best results)

¼ pound bacon, cut into ½-inch pieces

½ cup seeded and chopped green bell pepper (do not use food processor)

½ cup chopped celery (do not use food processor)

4 teaspoons red wine

Dash of Worcestershire sauce

1 teaspoon powdered chicken bouillon

½ teaspoon sugar

1 teaspoon chili powder

1 bay leaf, crushed

¼ teaspoon dried oregano

¼ teaspoon ground ginger

⅛ teaspoon cumin seeds

⅛ teaspoon paprika

⅛ teaspoon black pepper

⅛ teaspoon white pepper

One 10-ounce can Rotel tomatoes (hot or extra hot)

One 15-ounce can unseasoned tomato sauce

One 16-ounce can Bush's Chili Magic (any variety), undrained

1 teaspoon sambal oelek (ground fresh chile paste, found in Asian groceries)

1. In a large skillet over low heat, cook the onion, stirring, for 5 minutes. Add the chili meat and cook over low to medium heat until all the pink is gone.

2. Meanwhile, in a medium-size skillet over medium-high heat, cook the bacon, stirring, until brown to crispy, then remove using a slotted spoon and let drain on paper towels. Chop it into little pieces, add to the chili meat and onion, and stir. Add the bell pepper and celery and stir for 5 minutes. Add the wine and Worcestershire sauce and stir for 1 minute. Add the bouillon, sugar, and spices and stir for 1 minute. Stir in the Rotel, then the tomato sauce, then the chili beans, then the sambal oelek. Let simmer for 30 minutes and serve.

MAKES 8 SERVINGS

N O T E If doubling the recipe, double all the ingredients, except use one 15-ounce can and one 8-ounce can tomato sauce, and one 10-ounce can extra hot Rotel tomatoes (don't use 2 cans of Rotel tomatoes unless you omit the sambal oelek).

BRUCE PETERSON'S EMERGENCY CHILI

Bruce Peterson of Hot Springs Village, Arizona, shared this recipe and some of his riding history with me. "I've ridden since I was a kid. Bought and sold more bikes than I can count. I've had Triumphs, Nortons, Hondas, Suzukis, and Kawasakis. I was a traffic cop for a while and got paid to ride for a couple of years. Bought our '79 Low Rider with 9,000 miles and ride it daily. Been all over the southeastern eleven states without a major breakdown. Blew into Florida on the coattails of Hurricane Barry in the summer of 2001 and stayed in the Surf High Inn in Panama City Beach. The motel manager helped us push the bike into an unused room to protect it during the storm. Great folks!" Bruce went on to tell me, "Riding a Harley will make you fat! When the gang comes over to go for a ride, our destination is nearly always some place to eat. No better thing to do with friends, and no better way to do it."

Last, Bruce relates this interesting bit of biker wisdom on life and emergency cooking: "Here's the 'skinny.' You and yer ol' lady just went a couple o' rounds about leavin' the toilet seat up and she went back home to her mother again. That's okay, though, 'cause it gives you a couple days to kick back and polish some chrome. Just then 'Scooter' calls and says he's bringin' the crew over for some chow ('cause he knows how good yer cook is). Watcha gonna do? You can't get the neighbor chick to come over again 'cause of what happened the last time you seen her, besides her husband is home this time. You can't serve hot dogs from 'Wieners N'More' again 'cause the guys would recognize the wrappers for sure this time. Well, here you go. This is fast and simple. If you can read the weight requirements on a 16-inch tire, you can make this chili!"

Just remember to take your tongue out of your cheek before you try Bruce's Emergency Chili.

1 pound lean ground beef

1 medium-size onion, chopped or sliced real thin

¼ teaspoon garlic powder

One 8-ounce can unseasoned tomato sauce

One 15-ounce can Mexican-style stewed tomatoes

One 15½-ounce can red beans

1 large bag corn chips

½ case yer favorite beer

I have left Bruce's instructions as he presented them; follow them at your own risk.

Put the ground beef, the chopped onion, and the garlic powder in that ol' hubcap you call a skillet (you should use the one off a DeSoto 'cause you will need plenty of room for all the ingredients) and cook it over medium heat 'til the meat is brown and the onion is clear or transparent. While the meat is cookin', open the tomato sauce, the Mexican stewed tomatoes, the red beans, and set them aside for now. Put the knife away that you opened the cans with and suck down a beer while you stir the hamburger and onion. Drain the grease off into a can. (If you strain it through a sock or something to get the big lumps out, you can lube the wheel bearings on yer ol' lady's grocery wagon with it. Note: For real bad bearings, use regular ground beef.)

After the meat and onions are drained, add the tomato sauce, stewed tomatoes, and the beans to the hubcap. DO NOT DRAIN the tomatoes or the beans. Add the 'juices' to the chili. That gives it a nice consistency. Once the mixture is heated through, reduce the heat and open a couple beers. Simmer the chili for about 20 minutes. If you cook it too hot, it may get thick, you know, dry out. You can add about a half a can of water and return to a slow boil. When no one is lookin', pour half the corn chips into an empty Grape Nuts cereal box and put the box on the table. No one will touch it and this will ensure there are still chips for the meal after the cooking is done and most of the beer is gone. (Note: If you suspect that some of your guests may have indulged in an "herb burning" ceremony prior to their arrival, hide the Grape Nuts.)

Pour a few chips in the bottom of a bowl and scoop some chili in on top. Serve whatever beer is left to your bros, after all, they are your guests. The number of eaters is determined by the number of bowls and spoons you may have, however, at our house it serves four.

Suggestions: I like to sprinkle a little shredded cheddar cheese on the top before serving. You may also like to experiment with Rotel tomatoes with green chiles in place of the Mexican stewed tomatoes. Both are delicious.

MAKES 4 SERVINGS

Bruce Peterson on his 1979 Low Rider

LONG'S WESTERN-STYLE BEEF 'N' BEANS

Here is a hearty recipe from Thomas A. Long, a project engineer in the Harley-Davidson York purchasing department. Thomas wrote, "I am sending you my famous Western-Style Beef 'n' Beans recipe. I put this in a Crock-Pot and take it to work whenever we have an office party—everyone loves it."

3 pounds ground beef

2 medium-size onions, chopped

2 stalks celery, chopped

2 teaspoons beef bouillon granules

2/3 cup boiling water

Two 28-ounce cans baked beans with molasses

1½ cups ketchup

¼ cup prepared mustard

3 cloves garlic, minced

1½ teaspoons salt

½ teaspoon pepper

½ pound sliced bacon (I use pepper bacon), fried until crisp, drained on paper towels, and crumbled

1. Preheat the oven to 375°F.

2. In a Dutch oven over medium heat, cook the beef, onions, and celery together until the meat is no longer pink and the vegetables are tender; drain. Dissolve the bouillon in the boiling water, then stir into the beef mixture. Add the beans, ketchup, mustard, garlic, salt, and pepper and mix well. Cover and bake until bubbly, 60 to 70 minutes; stir a few times.

3. Top with the crumbled bacon.

MAKES 12 SERVINGS

BRAD PETERSON'S FAMISHED BIKER CHILI

Here is a recipe from a friend of mine who works for Drag Specialties. Brad has one of those fun jobs, showing bikers what they can do to customize their bikes. Along with the recipe Brad sent this note: "It was a tough choice on which recipe to send, but I fell back on one of my personal favorites. I like it best after a spring or fall ride. The air is cool and crisp and you are ready for some chili. The recipe is for a single batch, though I am usually tripling or quadrupling it. This chili is great with any kind of sandwich! It is also great with your favorite crackers. You can add broken-up spaghetti noodles for a little more heft." Brad closed his note with this sage advice: "Eat well—Live well."

2 pounds ground sirloin

One 15½-ounce can red beans, drained and well rinsed (I like red beans much better than kidney beans in chili; they have a lighter flavor and the taste blends better)

1 large onion (I enjoy Vidalias in season), finely chopped

Two 10¾-ounce cans Campbell's condensed tomato soup

McCormick's Hot Mexican-Style chili powder to taste

½ teaspoon salt

2 tablespoons Chi-Chi's hot salsa

Campbell's tomato juice for thinning, if necessary

1. In a large skillet over medium-high heat, cook the ground beef until no longer pink, breaking up any clumps. Add the remaining ingredients, except the tomato juice, stir well, bring to a simmer, reduce the heat to low, and cook for 30 minutes, stirring occasionally.

2. If necessary, thin the chili with tomato juice.

MAKES 3 TO 4 SERVINGS (LESS IF IT IS COLD OUTSIDE)

JAMES GANG RACING
CHECKERED FLAG CHILI

My friend Paul James is the communications manager at Harley-Davidson. Here is the secret recipe that he uses to fuel his racing team. "I've been working for Harley-Davidson and Buell for the past four years, but I've been a motorcycle enthusiast all my life. When I was old enough to hang on, my dad took me on a series of summer motorcycle adventures from coast to coast. We followed the Oregon Trail out West and roamed the South visiting Civil War battlefields. I saw much of the U.S. on the back of my dad's motorcycle. Later, I got a dirt bike and learned to ride myself. My first car was a motorcycle. And I've never been without one since. I commute to work every day aboard my 1998 Buell S1-W. I also compete on the weekends aboard my Buell Lightning Series-spec roadracer in the regional Championship Cup series and the national Formula USA series."

3 pounds ground round

2 tablespoons chopped garlic

2 cups diced onions

2 pounds bacon, diced

¼ teaspoon salt

½ teaspoon black pepper

5 quarts tomatoes, peeled and diced

Two 16-ounce cans unseasoned tomato sauce

2 tablespoons barbecue sauce

2 cups diced celery

2 Hungarian hot peppers, diced

2 jalapeño peppers, diced

2 large green bell peppers, seeded and diced

Two 16-ounce cans hot chile beans

One 16-ounce can sliced black olives, drained

Chili powder to taste

Shredded cheddar cheese and sour cream for serving

1. In a large skillet over medium-high heat, cook the beef, garlic, and onions until the meat is no longer pink. Drain off the fat and set aside.

2. In another large skillet over medium-high heat, fry the bacon until crisp. Drain, then mix with the ground round. Add the salt and pepper and cook over low heat for 5 minutes, stirring often.

3. In a large pot, bring the tomatoes to a boil, add the tomato sauce, barbecue sauce, and celery, and cook for 5 minutes. Add all the peppers and bring to a boil. Turn the heat down to medium-low, add the ground beef and bacon, and simmer for 45 minutes, stirring every 10 minutes. Add the beans and olives, simmer for 10 minutes, then add the chili powder to taste. (Add 1 tablespoon and allow to simmer 5 minutes before adding more.)

4. Serve with shredded cheddar cheese and sour cream.

MAKES ABOUT 7 QUARTS

OUT OF TIME RACING'S CHUCK WAGON BEANS

This recipe comes from the Out of Time Racing team, which is owned by the Zalewski family. They are currently racing in two All Harley Drag Racing Association (AHDRA) classes, Top Fuel and Pro Fuel. These folks call New Jersey home but you can catch them racing all over America. Check out AHDRA races if you get a chance—the thundering action is sure to quicken your heartbeat, just like this recipe will fire up your appetite. It is no little wonder why these guys run at speeds nearing 200 mph after having a bowl full of their secret racing grub.

1 pound sliced bacon, cut up, fried, and drained on paper towels

3 pounds ground beef, browned and drained

3 medium-size onions, chopped and sautéed in the bacon grease until tender

One 14-ounce can beef broth

1½ cloves garlic, chopped

1½ cups ketchup

3 tablespoons yellow mustard

1½ teaspoons salt

½ teaspoon black pepper

Three 16-ounce cans Bush's baked beans

Combine all the ingredients in a large baking dish and bake for 1½ hours in a preheated 375°F oven.

FEEDS A WHOLE RACE TEAM AND MORE

NEUG'S BLACK BEAN AND SAUSAGE CHILI

Neugene Seaborn of Grandville, Michigan, and his Four Fires N-Da Hole Chili Team sent me their contest-winning chili recipe. "This recipe was derived from a couple of my other chili recipes, and made especially for the Grand Rapids LOH Chili Cook-Off. It has the right ingredients to be selected first place winner in this year's LOH Chili Cook-Off. The secret is in the sausage! Riding my Hog and cooking are passions for a lifetime. Sharing them with friends and helping raise money for our American veterans are as satisfying as dinner and dessert. Ride Free!"

3 pounds ground beef

2 tablespoons olive oil

1½ medium-size onions, diced

2 tablespoons garlic powder

3 tablespoons ground chipotle chili pepper

One 15½-ounce can black beans, drained

Two 28-ounce cans diced tomatoes

Two 12-ounce cans tomato sauce

One 6-ounce can tomato paste

18 ounces andouille sausage

One 8-ounce jar medium-hot chipotle salsa

1. In a large pot or skillet, brown the ground beef over medium-high heat. Drain the fat from the beef and set beef aside.

2. Heat the olive oil in a medium-size stock pot over medium-high heat. Add the onions and cook, stirring, until nicely browned and caramelized, 10 to 12 minutes. Do not burn! Add the spices and mix thoroughly. Add the cooked beef, beans, tomatoes, and tomato sauce

and paste and cook over medium heat for about 1 hour, stirring occasionally to keep from sticking to the bottom of the pot.

3. Cut the andouille sausage in half lengthwise, then cut into ¼-inch-thick slices. Cook them in a medium-size skillet over medium heat for about 10 minutes. Do not drain! Add the sausage and salsa to the chili mixture and cook an additional 30 to 45 minutes.

MAKES 12 QUARTS

CHILE PEPPER RANCH BEANS

My friend Joel Gregory, who publishes *Chile Pepper* magazine, sent this medium fiery recipe to me. The recipe is the culinary creation of *Chile Pepper* editor David K. "Gib" Gibson, who told me it is "a version of pinto beans from the ranch country of western and northern Texas." I hope you enjoy this recipe as much as I enjoy their magazine, which featured me on the cover of the November/December 2001 issue as Santa Claus with the Burpee Biker Billy Jalapeño show bike, a 1999 Twin Cam 88 Road King Classic.

1 pound dried pinto beans, rinsed and picked over

1 pound salt pork or bacon, cut into small cubes

2 medium-size onions, chopped

2 large jalapeños, finely chopped

4 large cloves garlic, minced

¼ cup Texas-style chili powder

1 teaspoon finely ground black pepper

Salt

1. Put the beans into a 6-quart stockpot and add enough cold water to cover. Soak the beans overnight.

2. Drain the beans thoroughly in a colander; rinse and drain again. Return the beans to the stockpot. Add the remaining ingredients, except salt, and enough cold water to cover everything. Stir well. Bring to a boil over high heat. Reduce the heat to low and let the beans simmer, uncovered, for about 6 hours, stirring only occasionally.

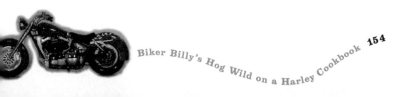

3. Thirty minutes before the cooking time is finished, add salt to taste. Serve hot.

MAKES 10 TO 12 SERVINGS

SASHA'S CHICKEN CROSSROADS CHILI

S asha Mullins from New York, New York, submitted this recipe, which came to her courtesy of her Uncle John Winkelman. Sasha is a Harley Lady, author, singer, songwriter, and a friend of mine. You might see her at motorcycle rallies and events or storming the pavement of the Big Apple on her 1999 Harley-Davidson. Could this recipe be why the chicken crossed the road or could this be what happened to the chicken on the other side? Only the chicken knows for sure and it isn't spilling the beans.

2½ to 3 pounds bone-in chicken breasts (about 3 whole breasts; don't remove the skin)

6 cups chicken broth

2 tablespoons extra virgin olive oil

2 medium-size onions, chopped (about 2 cups)

8 cloves garlic, crushed

Four 3-inch-long hot peppers, any kind or a combination, chopped

1 tablespoon ground cumin

1 tablespoon dried oregano

½ teaspoon ground cinnamon

1 pound dried small white, navy, or Great Northern beans, picked over, soaked overnight in water to cover, and drained

Salt

Your favorite bottled hot sauce to taste

4 cups shredded Monterey Jack or sharp cheddar cheese

¼ cup fresh cilantro leaves (optional), chopped

Sour cream

Tomato salsa

Lime wedges

1. In a 5- to 6-quart pot, combine the chicken with the broth. Bring to a simmer over medium-low heat and poach the chicken, uncovered, until just cooked, 18 to 20 minutes. Remove from the heat and let the chicken cool in the broth for about 15 minutes. Remove the chicken from the broth. Pour the broth into a large mixing bowl and skim off the fat. Reserve the broth. When the chicken is cool enough to handle, remove and discard the skin and bones. Shred or cube the chicken.

2. Rinse and dry the same pot, then warm the oil over medium heat and cook the onions, stirring, until just browned. Add the garlic and cook, stirring, for another 30 seconds. Add the hot peppers, cumin, oregano, cinnamon, beans, and the reserved broth, stir well, partially cover the pot, and reduce the heat so the beans cook at a brisk simmer until really tender, an hour to an hour and a half.

3. Stir in the chicken and let simmer 2 to 3 minutes. Taste and season to your liking with salt and hot sauce. Just before serving, stir in 1 cup of the shredded cheese and sprinkle with the cilantro, if using. Serve hot, garnished with sour cream, the remaining cheese, tomato salsa, and lime.

MAKES 8 SERVINGS

SPANKY'S CHUCKSTER-STYLE CHICKEN CHILI

Mike Sanford of Tampa, Florida, a.k.a. Spanky, offered this recipe for your enjoyment and his tale of a man and his Harley dream. In Mike's own words, "I started riding in 1974 and dreamed of touring the USA on a big bike and seeing the wonderful sights of our country. A 26-year career in the US Air Force took me all over the world and forced me to put my tour on hold, but the dream never died. In November 1999, I returned from my final overseas assignment and took delivery of a new Road Glide FLTRI to begin my Harley adventure. I spent my last year in the US Air Force assigned in southern Georgia, where I hooked up with other military riders and spent every possible weekend riding to locations throughout the

Southeast. During that first year of Harley ownership, I rode to Bike Week 2000, the Alabama State H.O.G. rally, the Bainbridge Georgia Bike Fest, Biketoberfest 2000, and Key West, Florida.

"On 1 Jan 2001, I retired from the Air Force and moved back home to Tampa to finish my preparations and fulfill my dream of touring the USA. After enjoying Bike Week 2001, I loaded my bike on 9 April and departed Tampa, bound for the West Coast. Along the way, I stopped to see old Air Force friends and visit the sights in northern Florida, New Orleans, San Antonio, Abilene, Carlsbad Caverns, New Mexico, Tucson, Phoenix, Las Vegas, and finally Los Angeles and the Pacific Ocean. After spending a few days with family, I turned around and made my way back to the East Coast. Along the way I camped at the Grand Canyon and stopped in Albuquerque, Denver, St. Louis, Dayton, Gettysburg, Washington, D.C., Hampton, Virginia, and Boston. While staying with friends in Boston, I took a day trip in the rain to attend the final day of the Mass Gathering National H.O.G. Rally in Worcester, Massachusetts, on 2 June.

"I finished my 2001 Tour of America in 74 days, putting a total of 10,600 miles on the bike. Since returning home in June 2001, I have ridden back to Gettysburg for the Pennsylvania State H.O.G. Rally, up to Montreal, Canada, and toured the White Mountains of Vermont and New Hampshire to watch the fall colors change. In 2002, I have experienced the wonders of Bike Week 2002 and Rolling Thunder XV in Washington, D.C., and the Laconia and Sturgis 2002 rallies.

"I guess you can say I crammed a lot of the Harley Experience into a very short period of time, and I hope to ride till I'm too damn old to walk! Ride safe and ride often." All I can say is, WOW, that is some dream come true, Mike. See folks, if your dreams are H-D dreams, they come true with style. About his recipe Mike said, "This recipe is dedicated to a good friend, Chuck Rivera, hence the title Chuckster-Style Chicken Chili. The recipe sounds kinda weird, and I've never seen it in a cookbook, but trust me, once you've tried it, you'll be hooked! Due to its main ingredients (white northern beans and chicken), it doesn't look like traditional chili, but don't let its appearance put you off. I've taken it to many a biker party and I don't take any home at the end of the night! Lots of folks think it also tastes great as a dip and scoop it up with plain corn tortilla chips. It's the perfect recipe for home, parties, or a campground meal at Sturgis . . . inexpensive, simple, full of flavor, and always a hit!

"I always make this in a Crock-Pot since it slow cooks the chili and I think it improves the taste. In addition, you can let it cook all day while you're out on a ride and you'll come home to the wonderful smell of a home cooked meal. And there's no danger of finding burnt chili stuck to the bottom of your pot! If you don't have a Crock-Pot, slow cooking on your stove will work nicely but you'll have to stir often to prevent burning. I've cooked it with both fresh and canned chicken meat and strongly recommend use of fresh chicken, even though the canned meat version didn't taste too bad. I know there are other white/light colored beans out there and you're welcome to experiment, but I can't guarantee the same tasty results I've obtained with white northern beans. I use onion and garlic powder, in addition to fresh onion and garlic, because I like full flavor and want the texture provided by the chopped onion. I've also cooked this by simply dumping all the raw ingredients into the Crock-Pot and letting it all cook at the same time. It always comes out tasting great!"

Believe him, he is both a Harley man and a retired Air Force man.

One 15½-ounce can Great Northern beans

Two 4½-ounce cans chopped green chiles

1 teaspoon ground cumin

1 teaspoon onion powder

1 teaspoon garlic powder

1 teaspoon salt

1 small onion, diced

3 cloves garlic, crushed and chopped

**3 skinless, boneless chicken breasts, chopped into small pieces
(or substitute canned chicken meat of same approximate weight)**

1. Heat the beans and chopped chiles in a slow cooker. Add the cumin, onion powder, garlic powder, and salt.

2. In a medium-size pan, heat a little bit of oil, add the onion and garlic, and cook, stirring, for a few minutes. Add the chopped chicken pieces and cook thoroughly. Add this to the slow cooker, stir to combine, and slow cook for at least 8 hours, simmering until all ingredients are thoroughly blended. It looks like lumpy refried beans when it's done! Season to taste and serve.

MAKES 8 TO 10 SERVINGS

N O T E If you're cooking this on the stove, let it simmer for at least 4 hours.

Mike Sanford and his 1999 Road Glide FLTRI

DUDLEY PERKINS'S HARLEY-DAVIDSON'S FRISCO CHILI

Here is a chili recipe from Kelly Mills, who is the corporate chef at Dudley Perkins Co. Harley-Davidson in San Francisco, California. Kelly told me, "Dudley Perkins Co. is the oldest Harley-Davidson dealership in the world. In 1914 Dudley Perkins, a legend in his own time as a racer, established this Harley-Davidson Motorcycle dealership. Ownership transferred directly to his son, Dudley Perkins, Jr. Then ownership transferred directly to his son, Thomas Perkins, who currently oversees daily operations with his son and daughter, Christopher and Nicole, both waiting patiently in the wings for their time. We offer motorcycle sales, parts and accessories, and service. Our commitment to customer satisfaction is legendary. Our customers expect only the best, we offer only the best." In that spirit, they offer you their family chili recipe. The passion for Harley-Davidson is truly a family affair.

¼ cup olive oil

2 pounds ground turkey

¼ cup chopped garlic

Salt

Black pepper

2 cups diced (¾-inch) yellow onions

2 cups seeded and diced (¾-inch) green bell peppers

2 cups seeded and diced (¾-inch) red bell peppers

3 tablespoons pasilla chile powder

1 tablespoon dried oregano

1 tablespoon ground cumin

1 tablespoon granulated garlic

1 cup masa flour

Two 15½-ounce cans black beans, drained

Two 10-ounce cans chopped tomatoes

4 ears white corn, blackened and kernels removed from cob

Sugar

Worcestershire sauce

Leaves from 1 bunch fresh cilantro, chopped

1 can chipotle peppers packed in adobo sauce, pureed

1. Heat the oil in a 4-quart heavy stockpot over medium-high heat, add the turkey and chopped garlic and brown, stirring, until the turkey is cooked through. Season with salt and pepper. Add the onions and bell peppers, then stir in the pasilla powder, oregano, cumin, and granulated garlic and cook for 5 minutes. Add the masa and stir until thickened, about 5 minutes. Add the black beans, tomatoes, and corn and taste for seasoning, adding salt, black pepper, sugar, and Worcestershire sauce to taste. Reduce the heat to medium-low and simmer until the vegetables are tender.

2. When ready to serve, stir in the cilantro and add the chipotle puree with caution.

MAKES 8 SERVINGS

MARTHA NORRIS STRATMAN'S BEASTIFUL BUFFALO CHILI

Martha Norris Stratman from Wentzville, Missouri, sent me her wild and woolly chili recipe with this note: "I was quite a young lass when my father started taking my brothers and me to motorcycle races—flat track, that is—and the best of them all, the Springfield Mile. Although there were some national championships won on other bikes, there is nothing through the years like the sound of a 750 on the hunt for glory. During this same time my brothers and I started to compete in chili cook-offs, placing several times for the chili and always winning for showmanship. A world-renowned chili cook, Joe Defrates, once told us, 'If there was more beer in the chili and less in the cooks, you'd have some world championship chili.' Oh, well, the lessons of youth. After a whole lot of fun, I decided on the solo cook-off circuit. I won two chicken wing cook-offs for my seriously spicy and flavorful Jamaican Flappers, which surprised the heck out of my family. I was very fortunate growing up to be exposed to almost every food I'd ever want to try and a few I'd rather forget (fried brain sandwiches—YUCK!). We always had hot peppers and hot sauce in the house and used to have the proverbial sibling rivalry of who could eat the hottest stuff. My brother always set me up for the fall. Today, we all still ride and eat really hot stuff. I love the search for the new and different fires you get to encounter on your way through the winding roads of life.

"I first saw my husband many years ago. He was this wild-looking dude with the ugliest bike I'd ever seen—it's covered with a buffalo head and hide. I thought he might be too. From time to time, I'd see him at a motorcycle event, marveling at the draw of his buffalo bike and amazed by his following. Years later, I was introduced to him again—a clean-cut looking gentleman. Little did I know he was the Buffalo Man. When I had him over for that first dinner and told him to help himself to one of the hot sauce bottles, he was awestruck at my collection. It has been a great journey from that moment on. Our mutual love of motorcycle races, hot food, and, yes, the mighty bison brought us together and have kept the fires burning.

"Being an old chili cook (Team Bowl Evil), I thought I could formulate a recipe that would encompass a few of our passions—great

chili, healthy buffalo meat, and some heat! You can modify the intensity of this recipe to suit your palate. Here is Beastiful Buffalo Chili, dedicated to my loving husband, RK Stratman."

Serve it with some additional diced onions, shredded sharp cheddar cheese, and sour cream on the side.

1 tablespoon light olive oil

1 medium-size onion, diced

2 bottles dark beer (I prefer Guinness Stout)

1 heaping tablespoon chopped garlic

2 jalapeños, diced (seeded, if you're a wimp)

1 serrano pepper, diced (seed them if you've got to)

1 habanero pepper (optional—for the real heat eater!), diced (again, seeded if you can't take the heat)

1 pound ground buffalo burger

3/4 cup chili powder

1 tablespoon dried oregano

1 tablespoon ground cumin (yeah, I know how to pronounce it)

1 1/2 teaspoons paprika

1/2 teaspoon salt

1 teaspoon ground red pepper

One 8-ounce can unseasoned tomato sauce

One 16-ounce can peeled whole tomatoes, squished into pieces (don't add the seeds if you can help it)

Two 15 1/2-ounce cans black beans, drained

1/4 cup masa flour

1/4 cup water

1. Heat the oil in a large, heavy stockpot over medium heat. Add the onion and cook, stirring, until it is translucent. Open the first beer and have a few quaffs while you are stirring the onion. Add the garlic and peppers and stir around for a couple more minutes. Don't lean directly over the pot while the peppers are cooking, unless, of course, you have a sinus problem you'd like cleared up. Crumble the buffalo into the pot, making sure there are no big hunks o' meat. You want to stir the buffalo to make sure it cooks evenly but doesn't brown. Cook it slowly and keep the lumps out. If it looks like there is not

enough oil in the pan, add a little of your beer, which adds depth to the chili and keeps you from finishing the first bottle too soon.

2. When the meat is cooked, add the seasonings, tomato sauce, and tomatoes. Stir it together good, turn the heat down to a low simmer, and cover. Check the chili religiously every 10 to 15 minutes, because it is a wondrous experience to be brewing such a fine concoction and also you want your guests to think you are going through a great deal of work! And, of course, you will need to get to that second beer somewhere in the midst of the simmering. Let the chili meld for at least half an hour but it will be much better if you give it an hour.

3. Add the black beans and simmer another half hour. If it looks too thick, add a little of your beer or some water. About 15 minutes before serving, combine the masa flour with the water and mix into the chili. Let cook over medium heat for 15 minutes.

MAKES 6 TO 20 SERVINGS, DEPENDING

"Buffalo Man" RK Stratman and
Martha on his costumed 1980 FLT

RUSS AND CINDY STOUGH'S SPICY VENISON AND BEANS

Russ and Cindy Stough from Clare, Michigan, sent me this venison recipe and said, "We returned from a truly marvelous trip back east on our 95th Anniversary Road King Classic and one of the many highlights of that journey was watching my husband, Russ, cooking spicy breakfast burritos on stage with you at Roeder's H-D in Monroeville, Ohio, at their 30th Anniversary party. I promised to send you a recipe and this is one of our favorites. The area in central Michigan that we live in is abundant with deer, so rather than run over them, we hunt 'em and eat 'em! This spicy venison is great in pita bread, tortillas, or over rice. If it ain't hot enough for ya, add some of your peppers! You seem to add the heat to everything! Thanks for the wonderful memory, I have a great picture of you holding your big knife to my husband's throat! Keep on ridin' and cookin' with fire!" It was self-defense, I swear—Russ was gonna eat all the breakfast burritos. Enjoy Russ and Cindy's venison and beans—better to eat the deer than get killed by them when they run across the road.

 5 strips bacon

 1 large onion, coarsely chopped

 1½ pounds lean venison, trimmed of fat and cut into ½-inch cubes

 Two 15½-ounce cans kidney beans

 ½ cup water

 1 tablespoon Tabasco sauce

 1 jalapeño, or more to your taste, seeded and chopped

 ½ teaspoon chili powder

 1 tablespoon crushed garlic

 1 tablespoon Worcestershire sauce

 Salt and black pepper to taste

1. Cut the bacon into ½-inch pieces and fry in a large skillet until almost crispy. Add the onion and venison and cook, stirring, until the meat is no longer pink.

2. Add the remaining ingredients, stir, and simmer, uncovered, for 20 to 30 minutes. It will thicken up. Serve on rolls, rice, or tortillas. Spice it up if you like!

MAKES 6 TO 8 SERVINGS

DALE MATTINGLY'S BEAN GUMBO

This recipe is from Chef Dale, who was my assistant during the Louisiana Bike Expo in New Orleans at the Superdome in 2002. Dale told me he came up with this recipe "to get a different taste from the plain red beans and rice that we have been eating in New Orleans forever." Try Chef Dale's Bean Gumbo and create your own special New Orleans taste treat.

2 pounds dried red kidney beans, rinsed and picked over

1 pound dried baby lima beans, rinsed and picked over

1 pound dried Great Northern beans, rinsed and picked over

2 pounds smoked sausage, sliced

2 pounds pickled pork or ham, cut into cubes

6 medium-size yellow onions, chopped

2 bunches scallions, ends trimmed and chopped

2 large green bell peppers, seeded and chopped

2 cloves garlic, chopped

Cajun seasoning

Lemon pepper

Garlic powder

Onion powder

White pepper

Tabasco sauce

Place the beans in a large stock pot, cover with water, and place over high heat. Add the sausage and pickled pork. Add all the veggies. Season to taste with the seasonings. Bring the water to a boil, then reduce the heat to medium heat and cook until the beans are soft and creamy, 2 to 3 hours. Serve over hot rice and enjoy.

MAKES 12 HUNGRY CAJUN-SIZE SERVINGS

TOLL ROADS:
MAIN DISHES

T oll roads—the big highways—are a sure bet if you want to cover a lot of miles in one day. These roads often have the fewest entrances and exits and therefore less merging traffic. They also usually have good signage and service areas located at convenient intervals—all good things for a motorcycle rider. I am, however, not that big a fan of toll roads; after living in New Jersey for many years, I got tired of paying tolls on roads that had been built and paid for many times over. This is especially true of bridges, like those going into New York City. I do understand that the bridge tolls are a method of deterring vehicular traffic from entering an overcrowded city but since motorcycles are one of the best solutions to traffic congestion, I firmly believe they should be allowed to pass toll free to encourage more people to ride to work. In defense of toll roads, I will say that traffic does wear out a road over time and some toll roads are very well maintained because of the availability of repair funds. But motorcycles don't wear out a road like a car or big truck will, so to my way of thinking, again, motorcycles should pass free or at a very reduced toll to encourage more road users to ride a bike and reduce road wear.

There is one time of year that I truly love toll roads and that is winter. For many years, I rode with a winter riding group called the Polar Bears. This New Jersey–based, American Motorcyclist Association (AMA)–sanctioned club rode all winter long from October to March. While it is a club and each week featured a new ride, it was organized in a unique way. Every Sunday there was a ride that ended at a different location, ranging from Delaware to New York to Pennsylvania and, of course, all around New Jersey. What was unique was that there was no set start site for each ride. The idea was that each rider started from home and rode out to the meeting place and shared food and talk, then headed home again. Points were awarded based on attendance and the mileage from your home to the end site of the week. If you rode enough weeks and or/far enough, you earned enough points to complete the "tour" and became a Polar Bear.

Now back to the reason I really liked toll roads in the winter. Winter in New Jersey can be cold and the roads can be very dangerous for riding a motorcycle. This is especially true if you want or need to cover a large distance during the short daylight hours. Well, the toll roads in New Jersey were often the cleanest, driest roads available, even shortly after a winter storm. So, my buddies and I often rode them every weekend during the winter. The only downside was removing my warm gloves to dig out the tolls, brrrrr. Now thinking about those frozen rides makes me think of food because we were always headed to meet at a restaurant. Anyone who rides in the colder months knows that besides wearing the proper riding gear, there is one other important preparation for winter riding. That is to eat a good meal, since without fuel, your body can't make the warmth it needs to keep you safe and alert on the bike.

This chapter is filled with hearty main dishes to build a meal around, all perfect to warm you for a winter's ride. They are, of course, equally welcome all year long, so cook some of them and dig in. After you are finished eating, grab some cash and ride them big toll roads.

CRANKSHAFT CURRY

This is a spicy, aromatic one-dish meal. I enjoy curried dishes a lot and I hope you like this one. It's not a traditional curry, as the rice is cooked with the curry. Sometimes you want something flavorful without a lot of fuss or clean up, leaving more time to shoot the breeze with your buddies or polish that big Harley in preparation for Sunday's run. So windup this Crankshaft and polish the bike's case while you digest.

There are two ingredients in this dish that you may be unfamiliar with: Texmati rice and garam marsala. First, Texmati rice: this is a cross between long-grain American rice and Indian basmati rice. It delivers a fantastic flavor and an aroma that is reminiscent of buttered popcorn. A product of American agriculture, hence the Tex in Texmati, this rice is easy and fast cooking like American long-grain rice, while imparting some of the flavor of Indian basmati rice, which takes much longer to cook. You can substitute long-grain or basmati rice but follow the package directions regarding cooking times, as there can be a big difference from one type or brand of rice to another.

Garam marsala is a commercially prepared Indian spice blend that is used in many recipes for curries. It often contains ground coriander, cinnamon, nutmeg, mace, star anise, cumin, turmeric, pepper, cardamom, and ground ginger, though individual blends may vary. You can find it in specialty and health food stores and the spice section of some larger supermarkets.

2 tablespoons canola oil

1 medium-size onion, cut into matchsticks

1 medium-size red potato, cut into ½-inch cubes

1 teaspoon ground cumin

½ teaspoon turmeric

½ teaspoon garlic powder

1 teaspoon garam masala

¼ teaspoon cayenne pepper

1 teaspoon dried cilantro

1 teaspoon salt

1 teaspoon white pepper

1 cup Texmati rice

1 cup frozen peas, thawed and drained

2 cups water

1. In a large skillet, heat the canola oil over medium heat, add the onion and potato, and cook, stirring, until the onion is tender, 10 to 12 minutes.

2. Add the cumin, turmeric, garlic powder, garam masala, cayenne, cilantro, salt, and white pepper, stir well, and cook, stirring, for 1 minute. Add the rice and cook, stirring, for 1 minute. Add the peas and water, bring to a boil, and reduce the heat to low. Cook, covered, until the rice is tender, 20 to 25 minutes. Serve immediately.

MAKES 6 TO 8 SERVINGS

EGGPLANT EXHAUST PIPES

Like the bark of straight pipes on a Harley howling in the distance will make your head lift up and tilt toward that sweet sound, so will the aroma of this recipe get your attention. These rolls of breaded and fried eggplants are stuffed with a tasty seasoned cheese blend. Cook 'em up and serve them at the next gathering of your H.O.G. buddies, then sit back and listen to them howl with culinary delight, like a Twin Cam 88 roaring down a mountain road.

FOR THE EGGPLANT

1 tablespoon dried basil

1 teaspoon dried oregano

1 teaspoon sweet paprika

1 tablespoon onion powder

1 tablespoon garlic powder

1 teaspoon black pepper

½ teaspoon red pepper flakes

1 cup boiling water

1 cup extra virgin olive oil

1 medium-size eggplant, cut lengthwise into ¼-inch-thick slices

FOR THE FILLING

1½ cups ricotta cheese

½ cup freshly grated Parmesan cheese

½ cup shredded mozzarella cheese

½ teaspoon dried basil

½ teaspoon dried oregano

½ teaspoon salt

½ teaspoon black pepper

After-Burner Pasta Sauce (page 119)

Shredded mozzarella cheese

1. Build a fire.

2. In a small heat proof bowl, combine the basil, oregano, paprika, onion powder, garlic powder, black pepper, red pepper flakes, and boiling water, stir well, and allow to cool to room temperature. Add the

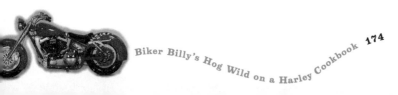

olive oil and stir well. Brush the mixture on both sides of the eggplant slices, then grill them until tender and browned, 3 to 5 minutes per side, brushing them with the flavored oil each time you turn them. Remove from the grill and allow to cool to room temperature.

3. In a medium-size mixing bowl, combine the filling ingredients, stirring well to blend in the spices.

4. Preheat the oven to 350°F.

5. Cover the bottom of a large baking dish with a layer of pasta sauce. Take a slice of grilled eggplant, place a spoonful of filling at one end, roll the eggplant around it, and place in the baking dish. Spoon some sauce over each rolled eggplant, then sprinkle mozzarella cheese on top of each. Repeat until all the eggplant slices are rolled. Bake until the mozzarella is golden brown and the sauce is bubbly, 15 to 20 minutes.

MAKES 4 TO 6 SERVINGS

JULIE ROSE KAPP'S THE WORLD'S BEST EGGPLANT

My friend Julie Rose Kapp from Hickory, North Carolina, shared this recipe with me and told about her family's love for Harleys and the American spirit of adventure both here and abroad. "My brother has always ridden Harley-Davidsons. There were many weekends that he and I would take long road trips on his bike. We both have a great spirit of adventure and we would just get on his bike and ride to anywhere. I've always loved motorcycles, and especially Harleys. They truly represent the free spirit that is America! This recipe was developed for my older brother who has always ridden Harleys. He came to visit me in Japan, while I was there teaching English as a second language. He fell in love with the Asian version of eggplant, which is long and thin and very easy to adapt into recipes as a meat substitute. Even though the eggplant is fried in my recipe, it can also be sliced into wedges and grilled over charcoal. That's as good as or better than the fried version!" From halfway around the world, a recipe fit for any Harley rider. Julie uses black sesame seeds, which she gets in Asian market; they have a stronger sesame flavor than regular sesame seeds, so keep that in mind if you must substitute.

FOR THE SAUCE

1 medium-size white onion, diced

2 Thai or serrano peppers, halved

⅓ cup Thai soy sauce or tamari

2 tablespoons tomato paste (or ketchup in a pinch)

2 tablespoons firmly packed brown sugar

2 tablespoons mirin or dry sherry

2 tablespoons black sesame seeds

¼ cup minced garlic

2 teaspoons peeled and grated fresh ginger (Julie uses the jarred stuff)

½ cup rice wine or white wine vinegar

2 tablespoons fresh lime juice

2 quarts peanut oil

2 medium-size eggplants, peeled and cut into 2-inch chunks

1 large egg, beaten

½ cup all-purpose flour

Steamed rice

½ cup chopped fresh cilantro leaves for garnish

1. Combine the sauce ingredients in a bowl and allow to sit at room temperature 1 to 3 hours.

2. In a large, heavy, deep-sided skillet, heat the peanut oil just to smoking and turn down the heat to medium-high.

3. Place the eggplants in a large mixing bowl, pour the egg over it, and toss until coated. Add the flour and toss until coated. Working in batches, taking care not to crowd the pan, carefully put the eggplant in the hot oil and fry 3 to 5 minutes, turning once to brown evenly. With a slotted spoon, remove from the oil and drain on paper towels. Turn the heat off under the oil.

Biker Billy's Hog Wild on a Harley Cookbook

4. In a wok or large skillet, bring the sauce to a simmer and add the cooked eggplant. Toss and cook until the sauce is thickened, about 3 minutes. Serve over steamed rice garnished with the cilantro.

MAKES 6 SERVINGS

BLACK BEAN LOAF

Black beans are the black leather of the food world; they pack flavor and style in a small dark package. In this recipe I have blended them with some of my favorite Tex-Mex flavors. Packed in with eggs, rice, and cheese, this is a high-protein loaf that will fuel your body for a long ride. Serve it like a meat loaf or slice and serve in a bun like a burger—the choice is yours. The pleasure is in the eating, just like the joy of a road trip is in the adventure of getting there. Saddle up and enjoy this tasty dish, then hit the road.

¼ cup extra virgin olive oil

1 medium-size onion, cut into matchsticks

2 tablespoons chopped garlic

One 15½-ounce can black beans

1 tablespoon dark molasses

1 tablespoon liquid smoke

1 tablespoon dried parsley

2 teaspoons dried cilantro

1 teaspoon ground cumin

½ teaspoon ground coriander

1 teaspoon salt

1 teaspoon black pepper

1 cup dark beer

3 cups cooked Texmati rice

2 jumbo eggs, beaten

2 cups shredded cheddar cheese

1. Preheat the oven to 350°F. Grease a 1½-quart loaf pan.

2. Heat the olive oil in large skillet over high heat, add the onion, and cook, stirring, until brown, 3 to 5 minutes. Reduce the heat to medium, add the garlic, and cook stirring, until the garlic begins to color, about 1 minute. Add black beans, molasses, liquid smoke, parsley, cilantro, cumin, coriander, salt, black pepper, and dark beer and simmer until the liquid is almost gone, 12 to 15 minutes. Remove from the heat and allow to cool to room temperature.

3. Combine the rice, eggs, and cheddar cheese with the cooled bean mixture, stirring well to combine. Transfer to the loaf pan, lightly packing it down. Bake until the top is browned, 20 to 25 minutes. Let it rest for about 5 minutes, then slice like meat loaf.

MAKES 1 LOAF

BURNING BEAN CURD LOAF

Dreaming of the "Blue Plate Special" at that greasy spoon you always stop for dinner at on your favorite evening ride, but you know you need to cut back on your fat and cholesterol intake? Well, here is a meat-free loaf that will keep your taste buds revved-up. While it is not free of fat or cholesterol, it contains less of both than a meat version and it tastes darn good. Try it, then ride by that restaurant and have a cup of Joe so you can still see your favorite waitress.

This loaf is made with chickpea flour, which is ground-up dried chickpeas (garbanzo beans). Its pale yellow flour adds a special flavor and the nutritional value of a legume. You will find chickpea flour in health food and specialty food stores or the organic food section of upscale supermarkets. If you can't find it, try substituting whole wheat flour.

¼ cup extra virgin olive oil

1 medium-size onion, cut into matchsticks

2 canned chipotle peppers packed in adobo sauce, minced

2 carrots, shredded

One 16-ounce can chickpeas, drained

2 tablespoons chopped garlic

1 tablespoon dried parsley

1½ teaspoons onion powder

1½ teaspoons garlic powder

1½ teaspoons ground cumin

1 teaspoon ground coriander

1 teaspoon turmeric

1 teaspoon salt

1 teaspoon black pepper

1 pound extra firm tofu, drained and shredded

2 jumbo eggs, beaten

¼ cup chickpea flour

1. Heat the olive oil in a large skillet over medium heat. Add the onion, chipotles, and carrots, stir well to coat with the oil, and cook, stirring, until the onion is tender, 3 to 5 minutes. Add the chickpeas and garlic, stir well, and cook, stirring, until the onion begins to brown, 3 to 5 minutes. Remove from the heat. Add the parsley, onion powder, garlic powder, cumin, coriander, turmeric, salt, and black pepper, stir well, and allow to cool to room temperature.

2. Preheat the oven to 350°F. Grease a 1½-quart loaf pan.

3. In a large mixing bowl, combine the sautéed mixture with the bean curd and toss well to mix. Add the eggs and mix well. Add the chickpea flour and mix well. Transfer the mixture to the loaf pan, packing it down firmly.

4. Bake until the top is golden brown, 50 to 60 minutes. Let it rest for about 5 minutes, then slice it like meat loaf. Serve hot.

MAKES 1 LOAF

TEMPEH MARSALA

Tempeh is an interesting protein source made from fermented soybeans and grains. It has what can be called a nutty or sometimes smoky flavor. It is a staple food in Indonesia. In this recipe I have prepared it with my own special Marsala sauce for a memorable main course. You will find tempeh in health food and specialty food stores or the organic food or produce section of upscale supermarkets.

1 cup Marsala wine

½ teaspoon salt

½ teaspoon white pepper

¼ cup extra virgin olive oil

One 8-ounce package tempeh, cut into 4 "steaks"

1 medium-size onion, diced

2 cups sliced mushrooms

2 tablespoons chopped garlic

1. Combine the Marsala, salt, and white pepper in a small bowl, whisk together, and set aside.

2. Heat the olive oil in a large skillet over medium heat. Place the tempeh steaks in the skillet, add the onion and mushrooms, and pan-fry until the tempeh is brown, 3 to 5 minutes. Turn the tempeh over, add the garlic, and fry until the other side is brown, another 3 to 5 minutes. Add the wine mixture, reduce the heat to low, and simmer for 1 to 2 minutes. Serve immediately.

MAKES 4 SERVINGS

WHERE'S THE BEEF STIR-FRY

"**W**here's the beef?" is a line from a commercial long ago. Well, you might ask, where's the beef in this recipe? You won't miss it a bit since seitan has a great meaty texture and a rich flavor. Seitan is a protein source made from wheat gluten. Wheat gluten is a complex protein that is abundant in hard wheats like durum. The meaty texture is so incredible that some vegetarians just won't eat it. It makes a great tool in your efforts to reduce fat and cholesterol intake so you can live longer to ride that Harley longer. You will find seitan in health food and specialty food stores or the organic food and produce sections of upscale supermarkets, often next to the tofu.

⅓ cup light soy sauce

1 tablespoon cornstarch

¼ teaspoon cayenne pepper

¼ cup extra virgin olive oil

One 8-ounce package seitan, drained and cut into bite-size pieces

1 medium-size onion, cut into matchsticks

8 baby carrots, cut into matchsticks

1 red bell pepper, seeded and cut into matchsticks

3 scallions, ends trimmed and cut into ½-inch-thick slices

2 stalks broccoli, cut into bite-size florets

2 tablespoons chopped garlic

1 tablespoon peeled and minced fresh ginger

1. In a small bowl, combine the soy sauce, cornstarch, and cayenne, stir well, and set aside.

2. Heat the olive oil in a large wok over high heat. Add the seitan and stir-fry until it begins to brown, 3 to 5 minutes. Add the onion and carrots and stir-fry for 2 minutes. Add the red bell pepper, scallions, broccoli, garlic, and ginger and stir-fry until the broccoli turns dark green but is still crispy, 3 to 5 minutes. Add the soy sauce mixture, toss well to coat, stir-fry for 1 minute, and serve immediately.

MAKES 4 SERVINGS

HD@RT GALLERY'S EZ BLUE CHEESE FISH FILLETS

The HD@rt Gallery in Fort Davis, Texas, is a great place to shop for Harley-Davidson–inspired artwork. Many of my artist/biker friends have their work on display there; if you can't make it to Fort Davis, Texas, you can find them on the Web at www.HD@art.com. Rick O'Donnell, who owns and operates the gallery, sent in this easy cheesy recipe.

6 good-size fish fillets (about 2 pounds), preferably catfish, but just about any white-fleshed fish will work fine

1 teaspoon black or white pepper

1 teaspoon salt (optional; Rick doesn't use salt)

1 tub crumbled blue cheese (that's the stinky cheese)

Preheat the oven to 350°F. Wash and pat dry the fillets. Place the fillets in a single layer in a large baking pan and coat with the pepper and salt, if desired. Sprinkle the blue cheese evenly over the fillets. Place in the oven and bake until the fish flakes when tested with a fork, 16 to 20 minutes.

MAKES 6 SERVINGS

LISA PETERS'S BAKED SALMON

This is a simple salmon recipe from my friend Lisa Peters, who is from Concord, New Hampshire. Lisa works many motorcycle events providing healing massages. She tells me, "I've yet to meet someone that couldn't use a great massage! Plus, I get to be outside enjoying the beautiful rumble of all those throaty Harley-Davidsons. I, as of the writing of this blurb, don't have a bike of my own . . . BUT . . . I'm saving for a sweet 82 FXR rubber-mounted shovel head! Hey, may as well start with the good stuff. So, if you see me out on the circuit, stop and get a massage . . . how else am I gonna be able to buy my Harley? Just look for the Massage Lady with the fox tail!!!"

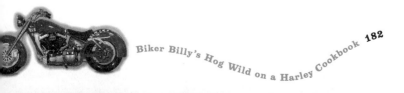

2 to 3 pounds salmon fillets, any remaining pinbones pulled out

Olive oil

Honey

Butter, cut into thin slices

Dried basil

Dried oregano

Salt

Black pepper

1 medium-size onion, thinly sliced

Wine

1. Preheat the oven to 350°F.

2. Lay the salmon fillets in a single layer in an aluminum foil–lined baking pan and drizzle evenly with some olive oil and honey. Lay some thin slices of butter the length of the fillet, then sprinkle with basil, oregano, salt, and black pepper. Lay the onion slices on top. Pour some wine or water in the bottom of the pan, cover with aluminum foil, and bake until the salmon flakes when you test it with a fork, 35 to 40 minutes.

MAKES 4 TO 6 SERVINGS

ART GOMPPER'S GRILLED GINGER SALMON WITH MANGO SALSA

In 1998 I joined my good friend Art Gompper from Milwaukee, Wisconsin, on the ride from Spokane, Washington, to Milwaukee, Wisconsin, for Harley's 95th anniversary ride. Art works for Harley-Davidson and was producing the 95th anniversary film. We had a great time celebrating, riding across this great country, and sharing some good food and good times. Art knows his food and his Harleys and he rides like the wind too, so try his recipe for a ride on the culinary wild side.

"I started riding dirt bikes at fourteen. My first Harley-Davidson was a 250cc Sprint, which I rode throughout high school and I've been riding ever since. My current ride is a 2002 FXDX Super Glide Sport. It's my sixth Dyna and I really like it a lot. I'm a big fan of fish and eat sea creatures whenever possible. This salmon recipe always tastes really fresh and the color is outstanding. It can be prepared to travel, cuz all you have to do is wrap it up in foil to cook on a grill or open fire. It's a great camping recipe if you can keep it cool while traveling. The smell of this dish, especially after a long ride, is like a welcome reward." Listen to Art. Take a long ride on your Harley, then come home and reward yourself with Art's Grilled Ginger Salmon with Mango Salsa.

2 ripe mangoes

1 red onion

3 to 5 of your favorite tomatoes

2 cloves garlic, peeled

2 teaspoons chopped fresh cilantro leaves

3 medium-size jalapeños

½ teaspoon salt

1 teaspoon sugar

Juice of ½ lime

1 nice habanero pepper (optional)

1 large salmon fillet, any pinbones removed

1 jar pickled ginger (sushi style)

Cooked white rice

1. Peel and cut the mangoes and onion into chunks. Cut the tomatoes into manageable chunks. Combine the mangoes, onion, tomatoes, garlic, cilantro, jalapeños, salt, sugar, lime juice, and habanero, if you are using it, in a food processor and have at it until the chunks are to your liking. Refrigerate while the salmon cooks.

2. Build a fire.

3. Place the salmon fillet on a big sheet of aluminum foil (enough foil to cover the fish after you pretty it up). Line the edge of the salmon with strips of the pickled ginger all the way around. Brush or scoop the mango salsa over the top and cover completely with the foil. Place

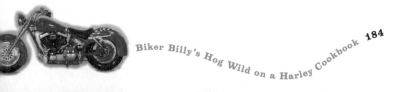

on the grill and cook for 20 minutes. Fold the foil back and continue to cook, uncovered, until the fish flakes when tested with a fork. Serve with rice and more mango salsa.

MAKES 4 SERVINGS

CHRIS ERICSEN'S RED CHILI PEPPER SALMON

Chris Ericsen from Portland, Oregon, wrote with a novel idea, saying, "I'm in school to be a chef and I love bikes, so why not put the two together?" Hey, wait a minute, I started to do that a long time ago—it's a GREAT IDEA! Chris went on to say, "I got into hot foods from my dad's biker friends and have grown up trying to make hot food. We go to the drags and cook good food and race fast bikes. Hot pipes and hot pans." Eat Hot and Ride Safe, Chris. Alright!

FOR THE POACHING LIQUID

1½ bottles dry white wine

4½ cups water

3 carrots, thinly sliced

1½ medium-size onions, thinly sliced

2 stalks celery, thinly sliced

2 cloves garlic, smashed

7 to 10 fresh parsley sprigs

6 to 10 fresh thyme sprigs

2 fresh rosemary sprigs

2 bay leaves

Juice of 2 oranges

Salt to taste

Eight 7-ounce salmon fillets

½ pound brown sugar

1 cup Vietnamese chili garlic sauce

3 tablespoons red pepper flakes

1 teaspoon cayenne pepper

Eight 7-ounce salmon fillets

1. In a large saucepan, bring the poaching liquid ingredients to a boil and continue to boil until reduced by half. Strain through a fine mesh strainer, discard the solids, and pour into a large skillet or poacher. Bring to a very gentle simmer.

2. Combine the brown sugar, chili garlic sauce, red pepper, and cayenne pepper in a medium-size bowl, then rub into each salmon fillet. Wrap each fillet tightly in cheesecloth and completely submerge in the simmering liquid. Try to keep at an even temperature. The salmon is done when the fillets feel springy to the touch.

3. Remove the salmon from the poaching liquid, unwrap the cheesecloth, and serve.

MAKES 8 SERVINGS

JOHN HUDGINS'S
SHARKIN JERK WAHOO

John Hudgins of Whittier, California, sent in this recipe and told me he and his wife, Billie, "stumbled on to the idea during a tour of the Northwest in '99 on my 95 Bad Boy 'Old Blue.'" When they returned home, he "developed this recipe after Billie had Jamaican jerk chicken at the Hamilton River House in Grant's Pass, Oregon, during our 'vroom '99.' I combined the consensus ingredients I liked the sound of from several recipes I found on the net with the only store-bought sauce I could find that contained Scotch bonnet peppers." Try this recipe that was inspired by an experience touring America on a Harley; while you enjoy it, make plans for your own tour.

½ cup **World Harbors Blue Mountain Jamaican-Style Jerk Sauce or equivalent (should contain citrus juice and habanero, a.k.a. Scotch bonnet)**

½ teaspoon **ground cinnamon**

Rounded ½ teaspoon **dried thyme**

¼ teaspoon **freshly ground black pepper**

Rounded ¼ teaspoon **ground nutmeg**

1 **scallion, ends trimmed and chopped**

¾ teaspoon **dried oregano (not crushed) plus ½ teaspoon dried oregano, crushed**

1 teaspoon **habanero sauce (John uses Mazzetta brand)**

One 2- to 3-pound **wahoo fillet**

1. In a medium-size mixing bowl, mix everything but the wahoo together. You can use thyme that hasn't been ground and extra oregano for that dropped-on-the-sawdust-covered-floor effect I find so appealing, but you probably should still add some ground thyme to ensure that essential flavor. The amount of habanero added can vary to taste, but extreme caution is advised.

2. Cut your 'hoo into 1-inch-thick (or thinner if you prefer more jerk per ounce) steaks, trying to keep them parallel so the sauce doesn't run off. Lay the steaks in a glass, plastic, or ceramic dish. One with a rippled bottom comes in handy but isn't required. Spoon your sauce over fish. Flip the steaks over, coating the edges with sauce as you do

so. Coat the other side, cover with plastic wrap, and let sit overnight in the refrigerator.

3. When ready to eat, build a medium fire. Remove the wahoo from the marinade and grill 5 to 7 minutes a side. Do not overcook. On the subject of overcooking fish, I have found that if you take it off the fire while it is still a little sticky in the middle, it continues to cook to the proper doneness after it is removed. Remember, you can always cook more, but I have never been able to reverse an overcooked dish.

MAKES 6 TO 8 SERVINGS

Billie and John Hudgins with his 1995 Harley-Davidson Bad Boy, a.k.a. the "Shark Glide"

RICK AND LYNNE SINGER'S CRAWFISH LYNNE

This recipe is from Rick and Lynne Singer of Black Forest, Colorado. Rick told me, "Lynne and I have two hobbies, our 1996 Softail Custom and cooking. We spend our summers touring the mountains of Colorado and New Mexico, along with a pilgrimage to Sturgis. We take time out of our riding to cater wedding receptions for our biker friends and their kids. During our travels, we look for small eateries to sample the local cuisine, looking for ideas and tastes to add to our 'cookbook.' Having moved from the Florida Gulf Coast (Pensacola) to Colorado, we missed Mardi Gras with its spicy food, beer, and beads. This year we hosted our inaugural 'Crew of H.O.G. Mardi Gras Bash.' Since the weather in February in Colorado is not the best for riding, it gave us an excuse to gather our H.O.G. buddies for an evening of fun and planning of summer rides. Lynne and I concocted this recipe to introduce our friends to the pleasures of crawfish. Those who did not arrive early only got to hear others rave about it." Do you need a better reason to get to a H.O.G. party on time? Just remember to Ride Safe on your way there and back home again.

¼ cup (½ stick) butter

1 cup chopped yellow onions

¼ cup seeded and chopped green bell pepper

¼ cup seeded and chopped red bell pepper plus 1 finely chopped tablespoon for garnish

½ cup chopped celery

2 tablespoons minced shallots

1 tablespoon minced garlic

1½ tablespoons Rick and Lynne Singer's Spice Mix (page 191)

1 pound peeled crawfish tails

1 cup heavy cream

2 tablespoons all-purpose flour

2 tablespoons chopped fresh parsley leaves

¼ cup freshly grated Parmesan cheese

Cooked white rice or pasta of your choice

2 tablespoons chopped fresh chives

1. In a large skillet, heat the butter over medium heat until melted, then add the onion, bell peppers, celery, shallots, garlic, and spice mix and cook, stirring, until the vegetables are golden and wilted, about 8 minutes.

2. Add the crawfish tails and, stirring a few times, cook for about 4 minutes. Add the cream till the desired consistency is reached. Dissolve the flour in a small amount of cream and add to the pan. Stir until the mixture thickens, about 2 minutes.

3. Remove from the heat and stir in the parsley and Parmesan. Serve over rice or pasta garnished with the chives and red peppers.

MAKES 4 SERVINGS

Rick and Lynne Singer

Rick and Lynne Singer's Spice Mixture

1½ teaspoons salt

1 teaspoon paprika

½ teaspoon white pepper

¼ teaspoon onion powder

¼ teaspoon garlic powder

¼ teaspoon dry mustard

¼ teaspoon cayenne pepper

¼ teaspoon black pepper

⅛ teaspoon dried thyme

⅛ teaspoon dried basil

Mix the ingredients in a bowl and set aside.

MAKES 1½ TABLESPOONS

SUSAN BUCK'S UN-FRIED CHICKEN

My friend Susan Buck sent in this recipe. Susan is a Harley rider and journalist from New York City; you may recognize her name from Thunder Press, where she was the editor of the East Coast edition for many years. Here is what Susan shared with me: "I took over as the family cook in my early teens. I liked cooking more than anyone else in the family seemed to, and the results were usually better than anything the parental units concocted. My first lessons were from *Better Homes & Gardens*, *McCall's*, and newspaper clippings, and an awful lot of trial and error. I learned there were recipes that could be altered, and others that must be followed to the letter. Billy, bless you, writes recipes that can be altered, but serve as an excellent guide for the basics. In sympathy to all, this one can as well.

"I love chicken because it tastes good prepared so many ways. It's also cheap, plentiful, and most folks like it. Even during a ten-year stretch of vegetarianism, the smell of fried chicken always made my mouth water. In 2001, at the recommendation of a wonderful nutritionist, I came back to carnivorism. Chicken is a rich source of protein, nearly a third by weight—a 3.5-ounce serving has about an ounce. A three-pound chicken has nearly the same amount of bone as a 4-pound chicken; you get more meat, especially breast meat, with the heavier ones. Chicken's fat content can be controlled easily too. Remove the skin and any visible yellow lumps with a sharp knife, as well as any stray innards. While frying is generally the preferred method of cooking fast food, chicken is not really fast food; it must be cooked thoroughly for flavor as well as safety.

"Frying is not necessary for the flavor or texture. With very little oil and a hot oven, the same fragrance and taste can be achieved without the messy stove and without eating empty fat calories. Spend those on dessert! The secret to delicious, juicy poultry with a light, spicy, crispy crust is cook it hot and fast. Ovens vary, so to avoid over-cooked, dry tough meat, you must watch carefully for the last few minutes."

One 3½-pound broiler-fryer chicken, whole or parts

Cooking spray, like Pam, or a light oil in a spray bottle

FOR THE COATING

1 cup all-purpose or whole wheat flour

½ teaspoon baking powder

2 teaspoons poultry seasoning

1 teaspoon ground nutmeg

2 teaspoons garlic powder

2 teaspoons paprika

2 teaspoons chili powder

2 teaspoons seasoned salt (Susan likes Soul Seasoning, but any will work)

2 teaspoons Vegit, Mrs. Dash, or other no-salt seasoning mix

½ teaspoon black pepper

1 jumbo or 2 large eggs

½ teaspoon seasoned salt (optional)

1. Clean the chicken well; remove the skin, if desired, and all excess fat beneath the skin. Cut into small pieces: legs off the thighs, wings off the breasts, smallest part of the wing cut away. Cut the breast

quarter in half at the point where the cartilage meets the breastbone, about halfway down from the wishbone to the end of the cartilage.

2. Preheat the oven to 450°F. Coat a baking sheet generously with cooking spray.

3. Combine the coating ingredients in a large mixing bowl or paper bag. In a medium-size mixing bowl, beat the egg with the seasoned salt, if using.

4. Dip the chicken in the beaten egg, then in the flour mix, to coat thoroughly. Place on the greased baking sheet, the largest pieces to the corners, the smallest in the middle.

Sprinkle the chicken with a little extra flour, then spray with oil again for a few seconds.

5. Bake for 30 minutes. Test by slicing into the top of a leg or thigh; if the juices are clear, it's done. If the juices are too pink, cook a little longer, rechecking every 3 minutes to avoid overcooking. Let stand about 5 minutes before serving.

MAKES 3 TO 4 SERVINGS

NOTE Susan makes larger batches of the coating mix and stores it in a reusable, covered bowl. Doubling this recipe yields enough coating for about 2 chickens. It also works nicely on pork chops; bake ⅓-inch-thick pork chops 10 to 12 minutes, 1-inch-thick chops, 15 to 17 minutes.

Susan Buck on her 1994 Harley-Davidson FXR

SUSAN'S CHICKEN WITH GRAVY

Susan Buck also sends along this little recipe to accompany her Un-Fried Chicken (page 191). She told me that "by accident, I discovered that seasoned flour makes a great gravy." Here is her "accidental" gravy. Try the chicken with or without the gravy or just make the gravy for your mashed potatoes or biscuits.

One 3½-pound broiler-fryer chicken, cut into serving pieces

FOR THE GRAVY SEASONING:

1 cup all-purpose or whole wheat flour

½ teaspoon baking powder

2 teaspoons poultry seasoning

1 teaspoon ground nutmeg

2 teaspoons garlic powder

2 teaspoons paprika

2 teaspoons chili powder

2 teaspoons seasoned salt (Susan likes Soul Seasoning, but says any kind will work)

2 teaspoons Vegit, Mrs. Dash, or other no-salt seasoning

½ teaspoon black pepper

1. Lightly brown the chicken parts in a skillet.

2. Add enough water to cover chicken halfway.

3. Combine the gravy seasoning ingredients and sprinkle generously over the chicken. Turn the pieces over, sprinkle with a bit more of the flour. Simmer, covered, over medium heat for 10 to 15 minutes. Turn the parts over and simmer until done, another 5 to 10 minutes. Test by checking a thigh near the joint; the juice should run clear. You will get a golden gravy with virtually no stirring and no lumps. Just add mashed potatoes.

MAKES 3 TO 4 SERVINGS

JERRY BROWN'S GREASED CHICKEN RIMS

Jerry Brown from Kokomo, Indiana, shared this recipe. "I like the older Harleys. My Harley is an 82 FXRS and is combined with another love of mine, Mickey Mouse. Yeah, I love Walt Disney World—strange for a biker to admit that but it is painted right on my tank. I have never been mechanically inclined, yet I love working on this bike. Our local neighborhoood biker shop, Moody Cycles (www. moodycycle.com), has led me all the way through the customization of my bike. I did all the work, but they talked me through the hard stuff. My wife and I annually attend the ABATE of Indiana Boogie. We tent camp with other couples and watch all the madness go by while I take care of the cooking for the thirteen people in our group. Finding something to cook at a tent camping motorcycle event is hard to do. So I came up with a prep-ahead, cooler-save entree that goes over great at every gathering of hungry bikers. Harley-Davidsons, pretty biker babes, Biker Brotherhood, and good eats—what else is there?" You heard it straight from Jerry, what more is there?

4 Biker Billy jalapeños (preferably from your own garden)

4 boneless, skinless chicken breasts

Salt

Black peppercorns, cracked

1 pound peppered bacon

½ cup (1 stick) butter

1. Slice the jalapeños into ⅛-inch-thick slices under cold water.

2. On a cutting board, pound out the chicken breasts to ⅛-inch thickness with a tenderizing mallet. Salt and pepper the rough side of the chicken. Place the sliced jalapeños at the closest end of the chicken in a single horizontal line from side to side. Start rolling up the chicken breast from the jalapeño end as if rolling up a beach towel. Once rolled, completely wrap with a single layer of bacon strips. Wrap with aluminum foil just like a Tootsie Roll. Freeze in a plastic freezer bag until travel time.

3. Place the foil-wrapped chicken on a hot grill. Turn often, cooking about 20 minutes. Slice the foil with a sharp knife and remove. Keep cooking on the grill until the bacon is crispy golden brown.

4. When serving, slice off small pinwheels and arrange on a plate around a campfire baked potato or ear of sweet corn.

VARIATIONS The jalapeños can be replaced with or added to asparagus, pepper cheese, tomatoes, or anything your heart desires.

MAKES 4 SERVINGS

N O T E When removing the foil, some grease will come out, so watch for flame-ups. The chicken will stay together in the roll without using any fasteners because of the steam cooking in the foil while wrapped.

Louie Smith and his 1998 Police Bike FLHTP

LOUIE SMITH'S BIKER HOBO DELITE

Louie Smith of Dover, Florida, sent in this traveling man's recipe, saying, "I love Harley to the fullest. I've worked for *Full Throttle* in Tampa for about six years now. I do a bike night in Poke County on State Route 60 at the Twilight Zone every Tuesday. This recipe is

easy to fix and you can make it just about anywhere on the road or at home. It's an old recipe that that the hobos used to fix on the road."

1 boneless, skinless chicken breast

2 medium-size red or white potatoes

2 carrots

1 stalk celery

1 small onion

½ red bell pepper

½ green bell pepper

1 red cayenne pepper

¼ teaspoon Original Mrs. Dash seasoning

Pinch of salt

Pinch of black pepper

3 tablespoons Italian salad dressing

2 tablespoons BBQ sauce

¼ teaspoon chicken bouillon

1. Lay the chicken breast on a big piece of aluminum foil. Cut the potatoes, carrot, celery, onion, and bell peppers, and cayenne into ¼-inch pieces. Add everything to the chicken and close the foil up tight.

2. Place in a preheated 425°F oven or on a grill or campfire for about an hour.

3. Put on a plate or eat right out of the foil. It's a great dish.

MAKES 1 SERVING

KITTIE RUSSELL'S HEARTY HARLEY CHICKEN TERIYAKI

Kittie Russell from Corpus Christi, Texas, shared her recipe, saying, "My love for food started when I was born, but my taste for good food came later, as did my love for Harley-Davidson. I think my love for Harley-Davidson must have started the first time I saw Catfish on one. He was fourteen and I was twelve. Boy, did they look good!! I climbed on the back with him and we drove down a wet street.

My blouse got covered with dirty water but it was the most thrilling thing I had ever done in my twelve years. Now, at sixty-two, he still looks good on his 1987 classic Harley-Davidson.

"This is a hearty meal for Harley riders. It saves time cooking, giving you more time to spend with your bike, yet it's great tasting and easy to fix. You can also take it on cookouts and heat it on the grill."

2 whole chickens, cut into serving pieces

Salt and pepper

1 cup honey

1 cup teriyaki sauce

1. Wash the chicken, pat dry, and season with salt and pepper. Place in a single layer in a large baking pan.

2. In a medium-size mixing bowl, mix together the honey and teriyaki sauce. Pour evenly over the chicken. Let stand in the refrigerator overnight covered with aluminum foil.

3. Preheat the oven to 350°F and bake, covered, about 1½ hours. Uncover and bake about 20 minutes longer. Serve over rice, mashed potatoes, pasta, or whatever you like.

MAKES 8 TO 10 SERVINGS

Kittie Russell's soul mate, Walter Lee "Catfish" Siros, with his 1986 FXSTC Softail Custom

JOHN GILES'S
SWEET-AND-SOUR CHICKEN

I met John Giles, the lead guitarist and vocalist for the legendary Leon Russell Group, at Battlefield Harley-Davidson in Gettysburg, Pennsylvania, when I shared the bill with them at the second birthday shindig. Hailing from Antioch, Tennessee, John says that this recipe, "like my Road King, is sweet and spicy!"

1/4 cup olive oil

1 large onion, thinly sliced

2 cloves garlic, crushed

1/2 green bell pepper, seeded and thinly sliced

1/2 red bell pepper, seeded and thinly sliced

1 small head broccoli, cut into small florets

2 boneless, skinless chicken breasts, cut into serving pieces

Salt

Pepper

6 tablespoons malt vinegar

6 tablespoons ketchup

6 tablespoons honey

6 tablespoons soy sauce

1/2 cup water

1 tablespoon cornstarch

3 cups steamed rice

1. Preheat the oven to 350°F. Heat the oil in a large skillet or wok over medium-high heat. Add the onion, garlic, bell peppers, and broccoli and cook, stirring, for about 5 minutes. Add the chicken, season with salt and pepper to taste, and cook, stirring until the chicken is lightly browned. Transfer to a covered baking dish, place in the oven, and bake for 20 minutes.

2. Meanwhile, in the skillet, bring the vinegar to a boil and cook until reduced by half, about 1 minute. Stir in the ketchup, honey, soy sauce, and water and simmer for 3 minutes over medium heat. Add the cornstarch and stir until the mixture thickens, then add the chicken and veggies. Serve over steamed rice.

VARIATION Add a few hot peppers when sautéing the veggies to fire it up a little!

MAKES 4 SERVINGS

John Giles on his 1998 Road King Classic (FLHRCI)

Pete Collins on his 1997 Fat Boy

PETE COLLINS'S PATIO DADDYO'S FAT AND SCREAMIN' CHICKEN

Pete Collins of Hicksville, New York, sent in this recipe, saying, "I am a graduate of Johnson and Wales culinary school, a certified Kansas City Barbecue Society judge, and owner of The Patio Daddyo.com. I have been riding Harleys all my life and recently did 11.68 on my 1997 Fat Boy. We always use to go to Hooters on our Harleys and have buffalo chicken wings. Now my friends like to come out to my place and let me cook something a little bit more extravagant and tasty, so I usually smoke ribs and cook this chicken on my Hot Rod Grill. This dish goes well placed over a salad, then topped with blue cheese dressing." Riding to eat and eating to ride—who would have imagined that?

½ cup hot sauce (preferably Frank's Hot Sauce)

½ cup (1 stick) butter

6 slices deli ham

2 boneless, skinless chicken breasts

4 slices Munster cheese

1. In a small saucepan, combine the butter and hot sauce over medium heat, stirring until the butter melts.

2. Dredge the ham in the sauce and set aside. Dredge the chicken thoroughly in the sauce, place on a hot grill, and grill until almost cooked through, about 3 minutes per side. Place the 3 slices of the marinated ham over each breast, then close the grill lid and let cook for 2 minutes. Lift the lid, place 2 slices of the Munster cheese on each breast on top of the ham, close the lid, and let the cheese melt thoroughly.

MAKES 2 SERVINGS

VICKY ALCOCK'S CHICKEN FROM HELL

Vicky Alcock of Pink Hill, North Carolina, really put it right in a few words: "I love damn good food, and a damn good ride." In regard to the recipe: "It don't take much time, which gives me more time to do things, like putt around with the ol' man." Righteously put, Vicky.

1 chicken

Salt and pepper

1 bottle Texas Pete or any brand of hot sauce like that

1. Preheat the oven to 350°F.

2. Place the chicken in a baking pan and season with salt and pepper. Put a little water in the bottom of the pan and pour the Texas Pete all over the chicken and in the water.

3. Bake until the chicken is no longer pink at the joints and is as brown as you want.

MAKES 4 SERVINGS

CRAIG THORPE'S TRICKED OUT TURKEY MADRAS

I have spent many a night riding my Harley through New Jersey working up a killer appetite—something about all that fresh air and riding past 24-hour diners gets your appetite going. Seems that this phenomenon happens to other Harley riders too. Craig Thorpe from Lindenwold, New Jersey, shared the result of his midnight ride in the Garden State with this recipe. As Craig puts it, "I like to prepare this dish after a nice long ride on my Heritage Softail through the pine barrens of New Jersey or on a cold winter night when I'm longing for the wind in my face. Just like that buzz you get from riding, so this dish will also delight you and leave you yearning for more." That's the way to tell it, Craig, riding and cooking. Try Craig's recipe and get a taste for riding in the pine barrens of New Jersey—just watch out for the Jersey Devil.

One 14-ounce can chicken broth

1 large green apple

1 large onion, cut into a few large pieces

½ cup (1 stick) butter or margarine

3 tablespoons hot curry powder

1 tablespoon all-purpose flour

1 pound cooked turkey, diced

4 ounces dry-roasted unsalted peanuts

Steamed rice

Mango chutney

2 to 3 scallions, ends trimmed and chopped

1. Heat the chicken broth in a small saucepan and keep warm until needed.

2. Peel and core the apple, then chop into very small pieces in a food processor along with the onion. Melt ¼ cup (½ stick) of the butter in a wok over medium heat, add the apple-onion mixture, and cook, stirring often, until lightly caramelized. Reduce the heat to low, add the remaining ¼ cup (½ stick) butter, the curry powder, and flour, and cook, stirring constantly, until you have a thick paste. Slowly add the warm chicken broth to the wok while constantly stirring until you have a medium thick sauce. At this point, add the turkey and peanuts and continue to cook over low heat for 2 minutes.

3. Serve over steamed rice and garnish with mango chutney and the chopped green onions.

DRAGON FIRE STEAK

After a long hot summer ride, do you have one of those "I could eat a horse"–sized appetites? Well, if you do, these fiery steaks will set you up just right. Get them marinating before you start your ride and they will be ready for the grill when you return. While your steaks are cooking, listen to the music of the hot metal sounds from your cooling Harley mixing with the sizzling of the steaks on the grill; combine that with the smoky grilling aromas and you might think your meal is being cooked on the flames of a dragon. One bite and you'll know the dragon's fire is the combination of hot banana and habanero peppers.

> **2 tablespoons extra virgin olive oil**
>
> **1 medium-size onion, cut into matchsticks**
>
> **2 tablespoons chopped garlic**
>
> **1 habanero pepper, seeded**
>
> **¼ cup seeded and sliced banana peppers**
>
> **½ cup teriyaki sauce**
>
> **½ cup light soy sauce**
>
> **1 tablespoon dark molasses**
>
> **1 tablespoon honey**
>
> **1 teaspoon liquid smoke**
>
> **½ teaspoon ground ginger**
>
> **1 teaspoon black pepper**
>
> **Two 8- to 10-ounce New York strip steaks**

1. Heat the olive oil in a medium-size skillet over medium heat, add the onion and garlic, and cook, stirring, until the onion is tender, 3 to 5 minutes. Add the habanero and banana peppers and cook, stirring, until the onion begins to brown, 3 to 5 minutes. Add the teriyaki sauce, soy sauce, molasses, honey, liquid smoke, ginger, and black pepper, stir well, and simmer for 2 minutes. Remove from the heat and allow to cool to room temperature. Remove and discard the habanero pepper.

2. Place the steaks in a shallow bowl and cover with the marinade. Cover the bowl with plastic wrap and refrigerate for at least 4 hours or overnight, turning the steaks over several times to ensure thorough marinating.

3. When ready to cook, build a fire.

4. Remove the steaks from the marinade, pour the marinade into a small saucepan, and warm over low heat. Grill the steaks to taste, brushing often with the marinade.

5. Serve the steaks with some of the onions and banana peppers as a garnish.

MAKES 2 SERVINGS

LISA'S SLOPPY JOE
BISCUIT CUPS

Here is another tasty recipe from my Harley-riding buddy Lisa Peters of Concord, New Hampshire.

> 1 pound lean ground beef
>
> ¼ cup finely chopped celery
>
> ¼ cup finely chopped onion
>
> ¼ cup seeded and finely chopped green bell pepper
>
> ½ cup barbecue sauce of your choice
>
> ¼ teaspoon salt
>
> One 20-ounce can refrigerated buttermilk biscuits
>
> 5 slices (1 ounce each) cheddar cheese, quartered

1. Preheat the oven to 400°F.

2. In a large nonstick skillet over medium heat, brown the beef, celery, onion, and bell pepper long enough for the beef to lose its pink. Break up the beef as you cook it. Pour off the grease drippings. Stir in barbecue sauce and salt. Simmer, uncovered, for a couple minutes more. Remove from the heat.

3. Place one biscuit into each of 10 ungreased standard-size muffin cups. Press the dough firmly into the bottom and up side of each cup. Spoon about ¼ cup beef mixture into each biscuit cup. Bake until the edges of the biscuits are golden brown, 10 to 15 minutes.

4. Place 2 pieces of cheese on top of each biscuit cup and bake a bit more, until the cheese melts. Remove from the oven and let stand for 1 minute. Loosen the edges of each biscuit cup before removing from the tin.

MAKES 10 BISCUIT CUPS

Josh Placa's Grandpa's Oil Pan Stew

My buddy Joshua Placa sent in this recipe from his grandpa. Somehow I suspect they both spent too much time riding bare-headed in the Arizona sun, then drank a few too many cups of Grandma's Wild Eggnog (page 14). So enjoy the laugh, but don't even think of cooking it if you ever want to ride again.

What you'll need:

1. Leftover corn
2. Leftover carrots
3. Leftover roast beast (any past-fresh meat)
4. Black pepper
5. Older potatoes
6. Leftover tomato sauce
7. Aged peas
8. Garlic
9. Oil pan

1. Rummage through your fridge until you find all the ingredients. In a pinch, frozen vegetables will do, but the meat must have been sitting around since last Sunday's supper.

2. Go to the junkyard for an early model Ford or Chevy oil pan, preferably off your favorite old car. Or, if you just happen to have pulled your motor for spring maintenance, removing the oil pan is only a matter of a dozen bolts or so. Use a truck pan for parties. Be careful not to let any of the gaskets fall into the pan. This could ruin the stew's flavor.

3. Into the oil pan, carefully put all the leftovers. Doesn't much matter what proportion. Add tomato sauce to a nice, pasty thickness. Sprinkle in 4 heaping tablespoons pepper and 3 tablespoons garlic, maybe a little salt. No need to add oil. Stir.

4. Bake at 350°F for 1 hour.

SERVES 4

SUSAN'S BASIC MEATBALLS

Here is another fine recipe from my friend and fellow Harley rider Susan Buck. Listen to what Susan has to say: "This takes about an hour, start to finish, and while not terribly difficult, it is quite labor intensive—measuring, chopping, mixing. It comes from my grandmother, a 'handful of this, three shakes of that' kind of cook who was pretty good once in a while. Sometimes, the dish was anyone's guess. She proved some skills are transmitted genetically, as only my brother can make her signature apple pie. I always made better chicken than either of them.

"Estelle was the one family member who didn't throw a fit when I started riding a motorcycle to visit her each week. She lived in Brooklyn, about 17 miles and a 40 to 70 minute drive, depending on traffic. 'There's an angel over your shoulder,' she'd say. I wondered if she was trying to convince herself or me that she wasn't worrying. I did have an accident about a year after I started riding, but luckily sustained little visible damage. At eighty-two, she didn't walk much faster than I did with several bruised ligaments. But that didn't stop the cooking lessons."

¼ to ⅓ cup water, as needed

½ cup seasoned dry bread crumbs (or crumbs made from 1 slice bread, ½ bagel or pita, or ½ cup plain oats plus 1 tablespoon extra soy sauce)

1 large egg

2 tablespoons soy sauce

2 teaspoons dried oregano

½ teaspoon black pepper

Scant ½ teaspoon cayenne pepper

4 cloves garlic, minced

½ small onion, minced (about ¼ cup)

⅓ cup grated Romano cheese (optional)

1 to 1¼ pounds lean ground beef

2 tablespoons olive oil

3 to 3½ cups pasta sauce, homemade or store-bought (arrabbiata is a nice choice)

1. Add the water to the bread crumbs, just enough to moisten them, then beat in the egg and soy sauce. Add the oregano, black pepper, cayenne, garlic, onion, and cheese. The mixture should be loose and muddy; if it is too crumbly, add a little more water or soy sauce by tablespoons.

2. Add the beef, a little at a time, mixing thoroughly. Take a level, standard ice-cream scoopful, roll it out between your hands a few times, and place on a clean plate. You'll get 12 to 15 meatballs.

3. Heat the olive oil in a 9-inch skillet over medium-high heat. Brown the meatballs, covered, turning 3 to 4 times to crust all sides, 7 to 8 minutes. When done, drain on a plate lined with paper towels.

4. Scrape the skillet clean, but do not wash—leave a film of oil. Pour about 1 cup of the pasta sauce into the skillet and heat over low heat. Add the meatballs gently, then more sauce, leaving the meatballs about an inch above the sauce. Simmer, covered, for about 20 minutes. (By now, you should be heating the water for pasta.)

5. Turn the meatballs two or three times while cooking. Add 2 to 8 tablespoons of water if the sauce gets too thick to prevent scorching or sticking. The sauce will reduce as it simmers again, incorporating the flavor of the meat. Serve hot over the pasta of your choice.

MAKES 4 TO 5 SERVINGS, WITH PASTA, SALAD, AND PERHAPS SPINACH SAUTÉED WITH GARLIC, LEMON, AND OIL. AND A HEARTY RED WINE . . .

N O T E If you really love garlic, mince and brown 4 cloves and 1 small onion and add that to the meatball mixture, along with 2 cloves raw minced garlic. You can throw on more pepper, too, if you like spicier meatballs.

RON JANICKI'S BIKER'S BRAISED BEEF

My buddy Ron Janicki has life pretty well figured out—eat great food, ride a Harley, and work in the motorcycle industry. Here is another one of his yummy recipes and a few words about working in this fun business. "After 30 years with the Eastman Kodak Co., I have found another great American success story—Vanson Leathers. Vanson is America's largest producer of motorcycle apparel: racing suits, jackets, pants, chaps, bags, gloves, and accessories. We manufacture everything in our Fall River, Massachusetts, facility. We are the definition of an American company."

> **Vegetable oil**
>
> **3 to 4 pounds boneless chuck roast, trimmed of fat and cut into bite-size pieces**
>
> **1 large onion, chopped**
>
> **One 10- to 12-ounce can unseasoned tomato sauce**
>
> **Water (equal to amount of tomato sauce)**
>
> **2 tablespoons Worcestershire sauce**
>
> **Salt**

Coat the bottom of a Dutch oven with vegetable oil and place over medium heat. Add the beef and onion and cook, stirring, until the meat is brown. Add the tomato sauce, water, and Worcestershire sauce, cover, reduce the heat to low, and simmer for 2 to 2½ hours. Season with salt and serve.

MAKES 10 TO 12 SERVINGS

SUKOSHI FAHEY'S GOULASH FOR THE ROAD

I have a lot of great friends who work in the motorcycle industry; one of them is Sukoshi Fahey from Mukileto, Washington. Says Sukoshi, "I love to eat and I love to ride motorcycles. Sometimes it's hard to know which I love more. I've been around motorcycles since I was seventeen and have been in the industry for over 20 years. My world is made up of round and black—as in motorcycle tires. I work for Avon tires and as far as I'm concerned, there's nothing better for a Harley.

"When it comes to cooking, if it's easy to make and doesn't require a ton of ingredients and lasts a while, then that's the recipe for me. So sit back, cruise a while, and enjoy the scenery." It's easy to see why we are friends—we both share the same loves.

½ cup white rice

2 onions, diced (use 4 onions to ward off germs and vampires)

1 pound hamburger

¼ to ⅓ cup molasses

Bunch of ketchup

1 large can brown beans

1. Cook the rice according to the package directions.

2. Cook the onions and hamburger in a medium-size skillet over medium-high heat until the meat is browned, then drain the fat. Add the molasses and ketchup (just squeeze in until the meat changes to an orange color). Add the cooked rice and beans and stir well. If you're like Biker Billy, just add lots of spices to suit your taste and enjoy.

MAKES 6 TO 8 SERVINGS

YVONNE ROBERTS'S POORBOYS

Here is a real interesting recipe from America's heartland and Harley rider Yvonne Roberts of Taylorville, Illinois. Yvonne, in her own words, has "been riding most of my life, bitch & solo. Got three in the garage. I belong to Midstate ABATE of Illinois. I do our newsletter, our web page, backup PR, and activities committee. There's nothing better than the vibration under ya . . . okay, men qualify too, can't just have one or the other . . . hmmm, yes ya can." Somehow I think she would choose her Harley. She had this to say about food, life, and her ride of choice: "This recipe is how I like my men and my Harley . . . spicy! So simple to create, and makes ya think there's some Italian in the house." Sound like Yvonne know what she wants, so run, don't walk, to the kitchen and whip up a batch of Yvonne Roberts's poorboys and enjoy the ride.

1 tablespoon garlic powder

1 tablespoon salt

1 tablespoon black pepper

1 tablespoon dry mustard

3 tablespoons Worcestershire sauce

One 3-pound chuck roast or venison roast

1 chicken bouillon cube

10 to 12 hard rolls

Peperoncini peppers

1. Combine the garlic powder, salt, black pepper, mustard, and Worcestershire sauce in a small bowl into a paste and rub all over the roast.

2. Put the roast in a slow cooker set on on low and cook all day or overnight. Transfer the roast to a plate and let rest for 5 to 10 minutes, then shred with a fork.

3. Add the chicken bouillon cube to the juice in the slow cooker, stir to dissolve, and add the shredded meat back to cooker to combine. Serve on hard rolls, along with peperoncini peppers.

MAKES 10 TO 12 SERVINGS

ROSE ELSWORTH'S
CUBE STEAK

Rose Elsworth from Lenoir City, Tennessee, told me, "I like to cook and make different kinds of concoctions by adding stuff a recipe doesn't even call for, just making the best of what I've got. As for riding a Harley, I've ridden a few different bikes in my time and the best ride is the Harley. You remember the old saying, you never forget your first pig, well, you get the picture.

"If you're not a fan of cube steak, you will be after you eat this. As for a connection to Harley-Davidson, I guess the only thing to say is I like 'em both."

All-purpose flour

4 good-size cube steaks

Oil to brown the steaks in

½ green bell pepper, seeded and sliced

½ red bell pepper, seeded and sliced

1 small onion, preferably Vidalia, sliced

About 6 medium-size potatoes, peeled and sliced

One 15-ounce can green beans

Salt and pepper

1. Flour the cube steaks, shaking off any excess, and, in a large skillet over medium-high heat, brown them on both sides.

2. In another large skillet or in an electric skillet, combine the remaining ingredients. When the steaks are browned, place them on top, cover, and cook over medium-low heat until the steaks and vegetables are tender, about 40 minutes, adding water as necessary to keep everything from sticking.

MAKES 4 SERVINGS

COOT'S SAUERKRAUT AND KIELBASA

Betsy (Cooter) King is a financial manager for a law firm in Washington, D.C. "Ever since my husband took me for my first ride on a Harley, I've been in love—with both my husband and the Harley. There is a bond that Harley riders have and I feel it every time we attend a Harley biker event. We are active members in our H.O.G. chapter and each year attend as many Harley (or bike) events that we can. Riding our Harley has become a lifestyle for us, one that we enjoy tremendously. You meet the nicest darn people in the world riding Harleys and I'm thrilled to be among them. So, let's ride! And when the riding is done, let's eat!" There you have it, folks, what more do you need to hear to get out on your Harley and join in on the fun.

Says Betsy, "The secret to this recipe is, the longer it cooks, the sweeter it gets. This recipe can be done in a Crock-Pot also (on high). Put it in the Crock-Pot and take a ride—it will be ready when you get back!"

> One 27-ounce can or 23-ounce bag sauerkraut
>
> 1 large onion, diced
>
> 1/4 teaspoon white pepper
>
> 3/4 cup sugar
>
> 2 cans or bottles beer (any brand)
>
> 3 cups water
>
> One or two 16-ounce rings kielbasa

1. Place the sauerkraut, including its juice, in a large pot. Top with the onion and sprinkle with the white pepper and sugar, then pour in the beer and add enough water to completely cover the sauerkraut and onions with liquid. Bring to a boil.

2. Reduce the heat to a simmer, place the kielbasa on top of the simmering sauerkraut, and continue to simmer for 4 to 6 hours.

MAKES 6 TO 8 SERVINGS

HD@RT GALLERY JALAPEÑO CHOPS

Rick O'Donnell, owner of The HD@rt Gallery in Fort Davis, Texas, sent along this great pork chop recipe. It is as fiery as the west Texas sun. Try Rick's Harley-inspired culinary artwork and feel the fire.

> **6 cloves garlic, crushed**
>
> **3 good-sized jalapeños, sliced, or one 4-ounce can diced jalapeños, drained**
>
> **1 cup firmly packed brown sugar**
>
> **2 tablespoons salt**
>
> **1 tablespoon cayenne pepper**
>
> **1 can beer**
>
> **4 good-size pork chops**

1. In a medium-size mixing bowl combine the garlic, jalapeños, brown sugar, salt, cayenne, and beer, stirring until the sugar and salt dissolve.

2. Wash the pork chops, then place them in a single layer in a baking pan and cover with the marinade mixture. Refrigerate, covered with plastic wrap, for 2 to 4 hours, turning the pork chops occasionally.

3. Preheat either your grill or your oven to 400°F.

4. Grill the pork chops until firm, 12 to 15 minutes, turning two to three times during grilling. If you cook these in the oven, roast until firm, 10 to 12 minutes.

MAKES 4 SERVINGS

CHRIS FILE'S RAGIN' CAJUN PORK ROAST WITH RED CABBAGE SLAW

Chris File of Forest Hills, New York, tells me, "I teach cooking school and tell my students, 'learn how to cook and you can work anywhere, just jump on your bike and see the world, cooking and learning.'" Great advice, Chris. He also told me about his experience as a chef who rides a Harley Road King Classic whose license plate reads 4CHEF. "As a Cordon Bleu Paris-trained chef, I spend my days cooking fancy meals that take a team of professionals to cook, serve, and clean. On MY DAYS, I like to ride my Hog, not spend all day cooking it; I want my old lady having fun, not helping me in the kitchen. Unfortunately, all my bros want to see what the Chef can do. So, here it is . . . easy as pie. Do it the night before and there are like two dishes to clean. It looks and, more importantly, tastes like you worked all day." I couldn't agree more, so follow Chris's advice and recipe, enjoy the food, and enjoy the ride.

FOR CHRIS FILE'S RAGIN' RED CABBAGE SLAW

2 cups mayonnaise

1 tablespoon Dijon mustard

¼ cup chili powder

1 tablespoon cayenne pepper

1 tablespoon ground cumin

Juice of 2 limes

1 bunch scallions, ends trimmed and chopped

Leaves from 1 bunch fresh cilantro, chopped

4 jalapeños, seeded and chopped

1 large red onion, chopped

2 red bell peppers, seeded and chopped

1 head red cabbage, cored and shredded

FOR CHRIS FILE'S RAGIN' PORK LOIN ROAST

One 4-pound pork loin

8 ounces tasso ham, thinly sliced

8 ounces jalapeño pepper jack cheese, thinly sliced

½ cup dry bread crumbs

5 tablespoons chili powder

1 tablespoon cayenne pepper

1 tablespoon ground cumin

Salt

Black pepper

Butcher's twine

Oil for roast

1. To make the cabbage slaw, in a large mixing bowl, mix together all the slaw ingredients, except the cabbage, until well combined. (This by itself is a great sauce for almost anything from fried fish to iceberg lettuce.) Add the shredded cabbage and toss until well coated with the sauce. Cover with plastic wrap and refrigerate for at least 3 hours. It will be best the day after, but do not hold for more than 3 days.

2. To make the roast, make a cut the length of the loin going about halfway in. Open this flap and make a cut perpendicular to it up the other side. The loin should now unfold like a trifold wallet. Lay in the tasso ham. Next layer the cheese. Now sprinkle over the bread crumbs, which will absorb any excess moisture and ensure a moist roast. (If you wish, you can spice up the bread crumbs with the chili powder, cayenne, and cumin. If not, use the spice mixture as a dry rub on the outside of the roast.) Season to taste with salt and black pepper. Now fold the flaps of the meat back over the ham and cheese and, using butcher's twine, tie the roast up.

3. Preheat the oven to 400°F.

4. Coat the bottom of a Dutch oven with vegetable oil over medium-high heat, then brown the loin on all sides. Cover the pan and roast until an instant-read meat thermometer inserted in the thickest part reads 150°F, about 45 minutes.

5. Remove from the oven, remove the string, let rest for 10 minutes, slice, and serve with slaw on the side. Also good the next day cold on hero rolls with the slaw as a topping.

SERVES 4 BIG GUYS

BILL CRAFTON'S CAN'T-MISS RIBS THAT COOK WHILE YOU RIDE

Bill Crafton of Slatington, Pennsylvania, has an interesting story to tell about life and Harley-Davidsons. "After years as a journalist, both in the streets and in management, I finally realized the stress just wasn't worth it and bagged the whole deal. I was fortunate enough to be able to take a couple of years at that point to see the country on my Harley and let my brain and soul heal. The first thing I'd do in a new town was ask the locals what their favorite restaurant was, then ask the restaurant what their most-requested dish was. And I often ordered dessert first. I figure the *Titanic* was full of people waiting on the dessert cart. One waitress said she was going to tell my mother on me. Anyway, I learned to judge an area by its scenery, its people, and its food. Every area has its specialties, things you just can't get anywhere else, so I started seeking out recipes to try to duplicate when I got home. The most flavorful recipes seemed to be in the New Orleans area, so I stayed there longer than some other places, and really enjoy cooking Creole dishes for friends and family. My grown kids often call for recipes they remember having at the dinner table when they were younger.

"I now travel full-time from bike show to bike show as an event vendor, so I need simple recipes I can fix quickly at the site, like this can't-miss rib recipe. You'll never fix them any other way. They are the juiciest, most tender, most flavorful baby back ribs that cook themselves while you're out riding for the day. Come home tired and hungry? No problem! It's all ready." Look for Bill on the rally circuit—just follow the aroma of these ribs. Now that is a man with a plan.

2 slabs baby back ribs

1 large yellow onion

1 large bottle of your favorite barbecue sauce (Bill prefers KC Masterpiece, Original Recipe)

1. Cut the slab of baby back ribs into sections of about 4 ribs each. Slice the onion and separate the slices into rings.

2. In a large slow cooker, put in a layer of ribs. Cover that with a layer of onion rings. Cover that with a layer of barbecue sauce. Repeat that layering until the slow cooker is full, making sure the last layer is a thick coating of sauce. Put the lid on, and cook on high for an hour, then turn it to low, and cook for 8 hours. *Voilà!* The meat will be so tender that it will separate from the bone, and the meat so tasty and juicy, you'll never fix ribs any other way. I like using the leftover sauce in the bottom as a gravy for mashed potatoes or fries served with the ribs.

MAKES 4 SERVINGS

Bill Crafton on his 1999 Harley-Davidson Ultra Classic

LARRY LANGLINAIS'S HONEY-GLAZED RIBS

Larry Langlinais from New Iberia, Louisiana, sent me his rib recipe. "Well, I love to ride my Harley and I love to eat. As the saying goes, you can call me anything you want, but don't call me late for supper. I attended the Bonnie and Clyde Festival in Gibsland, Louisiana—there were plenty of barbecue pits and bikes, maybe even more pits than bikes. Anyway, I sampled quite a lot of different barbecue, asking about the ingredients. I came up with the idea for this winning combination, then we went off to the supermarket. Boy, you should have seen us all, in the pouring rain, carrying charcoal, beer, and meat, etc. back to the campsite on the scoots."

> 1 jar honey
>
> 1 bottle A-1 steak sauce
>
> 1 bottle Lea & Perrins Worcestershire sauce
>
> As many country-style ribs as you can get on the pit

1. In a large mixing bowl, combine the honey and steak sauce, then add the Worcestershire sauce to your own liking.

2. Barbecue the ribs to your favorite length of time; 20 minutes before finishing, start basting with the honey mixture. Man, this will make you want to slap your grandma, they're so good. Enjoy with a cold beer or your whiskey of choice.

MAKES A PITFUL OF RIBS

DAN KLEMENCIC'S
BROWN SUGAR VENISON

My good friend Dan Klemencic from Milwaukee, Wisconsin, works at the Motor Company. He has the cool job of creating the beautiful Harley-Davidson Genuine Parts and Accessory Catalogs. When Dan sent in his recipe, he told me, "I love to be outdoors as much as possible, no matter the season. The doors on my house, the windows on my truck, and the face shield on my helmet stay open as much as possible. I hate air conditioning. You could call me an outdoorsman, but not in the classic sense. I do love to hunt and fish, but I also love to golf and ride my Harley. What is it about riding a motorcycle that makes one so hungry? Fresh air? Heightened senses? Whatever it is, long rides and hearty meals go hand in hand. Not only is Wisconsin a great place to ride a motorcycle, it also is a hunting and fishing paradise. With that in mind, here is my favorite wild game recipe."

1 venison loin or backstrap

¼ cup (½ stick) butter or margarine

¼ cup packed brown sugar

¼ cup soy sauce

1. Fire up your grill.

2. Trim all the fat and and/or silverskin from the venison. Cut the venison into lengths about 4 inches long, 6 to 8 ounces each.

3. In a small saucepan, melt the butter over medium heat. Add the brown sugar and soy sauce and cook, stirring constantly, until the brown sugar melts and the sauce begins to bubble.

4. Place the venison on the grill. Grill on one side until just seared. Turn the venison over and brush with the brown sugar mixture. Continue to grill, brushing frequently with the brown sugar mixture. Turn the meat a few times, grilling on both sides, until cooked to your desired degree of doneness.

MAKES 2 TO 3 SERVINGS PER POUND OF VENISON

SERVICE ROADS:
SIDE DISHES

Service roads are the pathways to the things you often need while touring on your Harley-Davidson. Things such as restaurants, gas stations, motels, and the like are waiting for you on service roads all across America. The big roads would not be the same without the benefit of service roads.

I remember one time when I was crossing Canada, it was late at night and I was very low on gas. Up ahead I saw what I was searching for, an open gas station. I exited the highway and headed down the service road. It had been raining on me for hours and I was anxious to get my tank filled and find a room for the night before everything closed. Next to the gas station and along the side of the service road was what appeared to be a large parking lot. Well, in my rush to get to the gas station I decided to take a diagonal across the parking lot.

As I entered the lot at about 35 mph, I discovered that what had looked like wet asphalt was, in fact, mud with a nice layer of water on top. Well, my dresser turned into an 800-pound dirt bike in a flash. As I did a good imitation of a flat track racer entering turn one, the mud made a grand sucking sound and stopped the bike. With my bike stuck axle-deep sitting upright in the Manitoba mud, I dismounted and walked with a squish per footstep through the mud to the gas station. After much work by two guys from the station and myself, the bike was freed from the mud. A good half hour of work with a hose, my bike and I were clean enough to buy gas. I found mud in nooks and cranny of the bike for many months. After that experience I came to have a great appreciation for service roads.

This chapter has the culinary equivalent of service roads—side dishes. Remember that if you want to enjoy your dessert without delay, eat your side dishes first; they are there for a reason, to balance out your nutrition. So take it from me, the fast way to dessert is to stay on the Service Roads and eat your Side Dishes.

MAMA COVUCCI'S BROCCOLI CASSEROLE ITALIANO

Frank Covucci from Pickerington, Ohio, is an old friend of mine from the Jersey days. We both have moved on to new places, for me Asheville, North Carolina, for Frank it is Ohio. Even though Frank lives in a mostly flat state, he tells me, "I am living my dream job as Director of Travel and Tours for the American Motorcyclist Association. What this means is that I get paid to lead groups of riders on organized motorcycle tours. AMA Tours offers fabulous trips all around the world, and I get to ride many different types of motorcycles, including Harley-Davidsons. One of my best memories is of riding a new Harley Electra Glide across the canyon country of Utah and Arizona, while enjoying a tape of spiritual Navajo music through the bike's excellent stereo. If you want to join AMA Tours on an upcoming trip, call me at 800-AMA-JOIN. See you on the road!" Yes, Frank knows how to work and live—lucky man. He went on to say, "To handle those long days on the road, the pounding of the pavement, the blast of the wind, the nightly debauchery, Harley riders need a well-balanced meal. And the best dishes combine protein, vitamins, and green vegetables, such as the all-conquering broccoli. Broccoli, at least according to the association of broccoli growers, is claimed to cure just about every disease, including enhancing one's sexual stamina. Mama Covucci's Broccoli Casserole Italiano combines broccoli with most of the other major food groups to provide a delicious dish that is a meal in itself. *Molto buono!*" Did I tell you that Frank is way tall and in killer shape? Must be all the broccoli.

Oil for sautéing the onion

1 onion, chopped

1 pound ground beef

1 cup dry bread crumbs

1 jar unseasoned tomato sauce

8 ounces mozzarella cheese

8 ounces sharp cheddar cheese

Three 10-ounce packages frozen broccoli, thawed

1. Preheat the oven to 350°F.

2. Sauté the onion in oil. Add the ground beef and brown it over medium-high heat. Drain the grease, then add the bread crumbs and pour in a little of the tomato sauce. Stir it all together and let it simmer for a few minutes while you shred all the cheese.

3. Get a deep casserole dish and start the assembly process. The casserole should be layered as follows: broccoli, meat, cheeses, sauce. Make two layers. Finally, bake for 1 hour and serve hot.

MAKES 8 TO 10 SERVINGS

STEVE PIEHL'S HAM AND BROCCOLI CASSEROLE

My friend Steve Piehl from Milwaukee, Wisconsin, sent in this comforting dish and told me, "I've worked at Harley-Davidson for over 20 years, but I was a motorcyclist even before that. I'll never forget my first ride on a Harley, a 1980 Sportster. What an experience!!! Now I spend most of my riding time on my 2001 Road King and my work time talking to the media about my favorite subject, Harley-Davidson.

"I grew up in a family of seven kids, so most of my favorite foods are casseroles and dinner soups. This is one of my favorites and one that we've even adapted for our kids, who don't like broccoli (just put all of the broccoli on the 'adult side'). To me, sitting down at the table to a meal of this dish says, 'I'm home.' Just like the feeling I get when I roll into the driveway after a great trip on my Road King."

> One 6-ounce package long-grain and wild rice (like Uncle Ben's)
> One 10-ounce package frozen chopped broccoli
> 2 cups cubed ham
> 1 cup shredded Wisconsin sharp cheddar cheese
> One 14 ¾-ounce can condensed cream of celery soup
> ½ to ¾ cup mayonnaise, to your taste
> 2 teaspoons Dijon mustard
> ¼ cup freshly grated Parmesan cheese
> 2 tablespoons butter or margarine
> ½ cup dry bread crumbs

1. Preheat the oven to 350°F.

2. Spread the rice over the bottom of a buttered 9 x 13-inch casserole. Top with the broccoli, then the ham, then the cheddar cheese. Blend the soup with the mayonnaise and mustard and pour over the casserole. Sprinkle with the Parmesan cheese. In a small saucepan, melt the butter and mix with the bread crumbs. Top the casserole with the crumbs.

3. Bake until heated through and bubbly, 30 to 45 minutes. Can be made the day before and reheated.

MAKES 4 TO 6 SERVINGS

Steve Piehl on his 2001 blue and silver fuel-injected Road King

CRUSHED CAULIFLOWER

My friend Kelly McEnany from Asheville, North Carolina, told me about a dish that used cauliflower like mashed potatoes. The idea sounded so good that I rode home and made it in my own fiery way. The flavor of the cauliflower makes spuds look like duds. I have served this to people who dislike cauliflower and they loved it. It's a great way to get the little bikers in your house eat their veggies.

1 medium-size head cauliflower, cut into bite-size florets and steamed until tender

3 tablespoons butter, softened

¼ teaspoon white pepper

¼ teaspoon salt

¼ teaspoon cayenne pepper

½ teaspoon garlic powder

2 tablespoons half-and-half

1. In a food processor, combine the cauliflower, butter, white pepper, salt, cayenne, and garlic powder and pulse several times to break up the cauliflower florets.

2. With the machine running, slowly add the half-and-half through the feed tube and process until the cauliflower is smooth. (If the cauliflower is very moist, you may not need all the half-and-half.)

MAKES 4 TO 6 SERVINGS

CHICANE CURRIED CAULIFLOWER

Your head will be snapping left and right looking for the source of the great aromas from this dish, just like the front wheel of a Buell being pushed through a chicane on a racetrack. And when you finally find your way to the steaming pot and try a forkful, you will feel like you just entered the winner's circle. Whip some of this up and race your way to the culinary winner's circle.

¼ cup canola oil

1 teaspoon ground cumin

½ teaspoon ground coriander

2 tablespoons peeled and minced fresh ginger

2 tablespoons chopped garlic

1 teaspoon turmeric

1 teaspoon dried cilantro

1 teaspoon cayenne pepper

1 teaspoon salt

½ teaspoon white pepper

1 medium-size head cauliflower, cut into bite-size florets

1 cup water

1. Heat the canola oil in a large skillet over medium-high heat. Add the cumin, coriander, ginger, garlic, turmeric, cilantro, cayenne, salt, and white pepper and cook, stirring, until the spices become fragrant, about 3 minutes.

2. Add the cauliflower, stir well to coat, and cook, stirring, for 3 minutes. Add the water, stir well, and reduce the heat to medium. Cook, covered, until the liquid is gone, 20 to 25 minutes. Serve immediately.

MAKES 4 TO 6 SERVINGS

BIG BOB'S BODACIOUS
BAKED BEANS

Here is a sure-fire recipe from Bob Rawhouser, a motorcycle roller test rider at Harley-Davidson for 10 years. Bob rides a 2002 Road King.

> **2 pounds dried Great Northern beans, picked over, rinsed, and soaked in water to cover overnight**
>
> **2 onions, chopped**
>
> **2 tablespoons prepared mustard**
>
> **2 cups ketchup**
>
> **2 cups firmly packed brown sugar**
>
> **1 tablespoon honey**
>
> **1 pound bacon, cut into small pieces**

Preheat the oven to 350°F. Drain the beans and place in a baking pan. Add the onions, mustard, ketchup, brown sugar, and honey and mix thoroughly. Layer the bacon on top of the mixture. Bake, uncovered, until browned on top, about 35 minutes.

MAKES 8 TO 12 SERVINGS

ANGELA TLACK'S
SPICY BAKED BEANS
IN BELGIAN ALE

Angela Tlack from Morris Plains, New Jersey, sent in this yummy recipe and this message: "Okay, okay, I have to come clean. My husband races dirt bikes in Enduros. But he still gives the big thumbs up to the Harleys. As long as you're on any kind of motorcycle, that's OK with him. He's a moto-head and I'm a culinary student. I've learned to love bikes through him and he's learned to love food through me. Any chance we can, we bring out the Dual Sport and take weekend rides through the countryside of NJ, NY, and PA. We love to stop at local mom-and-pop roadside places and grab a bite to

eat. That's where you find the best food. What else could be better—both of us indulging in our passions!" Sounds like they enjoy sharing their passions—I bet there is a Harley in their future. Not everyone is lucky enough to have a big Harley in his or her garage, but that luck seems to start with an appreciation of America's Motor Company's machines.

Angela has this to say about her recipe: "As an aspiring culinary student with a husband who has a passion for bikes, I try to combine our two loves as much as possible. My baked beans are totally delicious, if I do say so myself. Many a biker has raved that they're the best ever! They have an unexpected kick, but one that isn't too overpowering. Spice freaks, spice posers, and vegetarians all love 'em! These are great to bring to biker parties—easy to make, easy to transport, and easy going down. Everybody loves baked beans! They give you the added fuel needed for that next ride!" Her beans do sound yummy, but if you want to feed them to a vegetarian, please omit the bacon and sauté the onions in 2 tablespoons olive oil.

7 strips bacon, chopped

1 medium-size Spanish onion, chopped

¾ cup barbecue sauce (a good quality bottled brand or Angela Tlack's Damn Good BBQ Sauce, page 285)

⅓ cup ketchup

¾ cup Belgian-style ale (such as Chimay or Duvel)

¼ cup molasses

3 tablespoons spicy golden mustard

3 tablespoons firmly packed brown sugar

2 tablespoons Worcestershire sauce

1 canned chipotle pepper packed in adobo sauce, finely chopped, or ¼ to ¾ teaspoon ground chipotle (add more or less, according to desired spiciness)

Six 15½-ounce cans Great Northern beans, drained

2 tablespoon chopped fresh cilantro leaves

1. Preheat the oven to 350°F.

2. Cook the bacon in a heavy pan over medium heat until crispy. Drain on paper towels and remove all but 2 tablespoons of the fat from the pan.

3. Cook the onion in the drippings over medium heat, stirring, until translucent. Transfer to a large mixing bowl. Add the bacon, barbecue sauce, and ketchup, then mix in the Belgian ale. Blend in the molasses, mustard, brown sugar, Worcestershire sauce, and chipotle pepper with a whisk. Add the beans and stir well. Pour into a glass 9 x 13-inch glass baking dish and bake, uncovered, until the sauce is thickened and bubbly, about 1 hour.

4. Sprinkle with the chopped cilantro and serve while hot.

MAKES 8 TO 10 SERVINGS

BIG FRED'S ASS-SQUEALIN' BEANS

Talk about a recipe that will live up to its name! Fred Newcomer from Tacoma, Washington, sent in this musical delight and relayed this: "Ass-Squealin' Beans will be the hit of your party! You can't believe how great they are until you try them. Some folks like to use them as a dip for tortilla chips; others just eat them with a spoon. A big bowl of Ass-Squealin' Beans and an ice cold Pabst Blue Ribbon is a culinary combination that can't be beat!" There you have it, straight from the source.

3 very large onions

1 pound sliced bacon

Four 16-ounce cans pinto beans with jalapeños

¾ cup firmly packed brown sugar

1 cup hickory barbecue sauce

1. Chop the onions. You'll have a huge mound of them, but they'll cook down.

2. In a large skillet, fry the bacon until crisp, then let drain on paper towels. Keep the hot grease in the pan and add the onions. Cook, stirring, for about 5 minutes.

3. In a big slow cooker, stir together the onions, beans, brown sugar, and barbecue sauce. Add the bacon after breaking the strips into 1-inch pieces. Put the cooker on high until boiling. Cover, turn the setting to low, and let cook for 3 hours, stirring occasionally.

MAKES 15 SERVINGS

Fred Newcomer on his 1996 Road King, loaded with chrome and a Vance and Hines exhaust

Phoenix Joseph and her 2001 Heritage Softail Classic, named "Amethyst"

PHOENIX JOSEPH'S HAWAIIAN BAKED BEANS

A Lady of Harley rider from North Carolina, Phoenix Joseph sent in this recipe and said, "I have been riding for eleven years and have had my Harley for eight years. I am half Italian, so I grew up around good cooks and good food! Nothing beats a good recipe or a good winding road for the soul!! This is a recipe that my mother used to make. I have no idea where she found it, so to me it has always been a family recipe. It is great for picnics and is delicious hot or cold. I love this recipe and I love to ride!" It is one love we all share—riding and food.

¼ cup cooking oil

1 medium-size onion, chopped

1 medium-size green bell pepper, seeded and chopped

One 10-ounce can pineapple chunks, drained and sliced

Three 15-ounce cans pork and beans

Salt and pepper to taste

1. In a large skillet, heat the oil over medium heat. Add the onion and bell pepper and cook, stirring, until almost tender. Add the sliced pineapple and cook, stirring a few times, until the pineapple is slightly brown. Turn off the heat, add the pork and beans, and season with salt and pepper. Mix well.

2. Turn into a 2-quart casserole dish, cover, and bake for 45 minutes in a preheated 350°F oven. Caution: The beans are extremely hot when done. Let them cool a bit before serving.

MAKES 6 TO 8 SERVINGS

MEAN GREEN BEANS

This is a great way to cook up some of those green beans you have been growing in your garden. Or it makes a great excuse to take your Harley for a tour of all the farm stands within a day's ride of your home—like you really need an excuse to ride.

1/4 teaspoon sugar

1/2 teaspoon salt

1/2 teaspoon black pepper

1/2 teaspoon ground ginger

1 tablespoon light soy sauce

1 tablespoon light teriyaki sauce

1/4 cup water

2 tablespoons extra virgin olive oil

1 jalapeño, seeded and thinly sliced

1 medium-size onion, cut into matchsticks

2 cloves garlic, elephant if you can find it, thinly sliced

1 cup fresh green beans cut into 2-inch pieces

1. In a small heatproof bowl, combine the sugar, salt, black pepper, ginger, soy sauce, teriyaki sauce, and water and stir well. Heat in a microwave oven on half power for 30 seconds or in a small saucepan over medium heat, stir well, and set aside.

2. Heat the olive oil in a medium-size skillet over high heat. Add the jalapeño and cook, stirring, for 2 minutes. Add the onion and garlic and cook, stirring, for 2 minutes. Add the green beans and cook, stirring, until the onion begins to brown, about 2 minutes. Add the sauce, stir well, cover, remove from the heat, and allow to steam for 2 minutes.

3. Stir well to get any of the tasty browned bits off the bottom of the pan and serve immediately.

MAKES 2 SERVINGS

STROKER TOMATOES AND REDLINE ZUCCHINI

This innocent looking side dish packs some serious firepower, like a stock-looking bike with a stroker motor may look tame, until you hit the starter button that is, and the beast comes alive. One forkful and you will know that you have your hands on something wild. Use that fork with care and if you get all fired up, consider a ride around the county to cool yourself off.

This recipe uses the pepper that the W. Atlee Burpee Company, America's oldest and best seed company, named after me, truly a great honor. As wonderful as that was, the pepper is even better, large, very hot, and flavorful. You will need to grow them yourself to enjoy them, which is the best way, after all. For seeds, go to my Web site, www.bikerbilly.com or to Burpee's Web site, www.burpee.com. While you're waiting for your Hot Pepper Biker Billy Hybrid to grow, just use more of the wimpy store-bought jalapeños.

3 tablespoons extra virgin olive oil

1 medium-size onion, cut into matchsticks

1 Biker Billy hybrid or other jalapeño, seeded and thinly sliced

2 cloves garlic, elephant if you can find it, thinly sliced

4 cups zucchini quartered lengthwise and cut into ¼-inch-thick slices

2 cups coarsely chopped fresh tomatoes with their juices

2 tablespoons dried basil

1 teaspoon dried oregano

1 teaspoon ground savory

1 teaspoon dried chervil

1½ teaspoons salt

1 teaspoon black pepper

1. Heat the olive oil in a large saucepan over high heat. Add the jalapeño, onion, and garlic and cook, stirring, until the onion begins to brown, 5 to 7 minutes. Reduce the heat to medium, add the zucchini, stir well to coat with oil, and cook, stirring, until the zucchini is tender, 5 to 7 minutes.

2. Add the remaining ingredients, stir well, cover, and simmer for 10 minutes. Remove the cover and simmer until the tomatoes are reduced to a thick sauce, 20 to 25 minutes. Serve hot.

MAKES 4 TO 6 SERVINGS

SMASHED BUCKET BUTTERNUT SQUASH

Kaboom, you just dropped that new high dollar custom-painted helmet on the ground. That makes you so mad; well, at least your head wasn't in it. While you attempt to cool off and consider how much it will cost to repair the paint, try cooking some of this squash—you can let all your anger out while smashing the squash. Then after you eat some, you might need a ride without that fancy dancy bucket to cool off from the cayenne fire. Just remember to Ride Safe so you can return to Eat Hot again.

1 medium-size butternut squash, seeded, peeled, and cut into
½-inch dice

1 medium-size apple, peeled, cored, cut into ½-inch dice

½ cup raisins

½ cup firmly packed light brown sugar

¼ teaspoon cayenne pepper

½ teaspoon salt

½ teaspoon white pepper

1 tablespoon butter, softened

1 cup water

⅓ cup half-and-half

1. Preheat the oven to 400°F. Grease a 1½-quart loaf pan.

2. Combine the squash, apple, and raisins in the prepared loaf pan, tossing well to mix.

3. In a small mixing bowl, combine the brown sugar, cayenne, salt, white pepper, butter, and water and whisk together well. Pour the sugar mixture into the loaf pan and stir well. Bake until the squash is tender, 40 to 45 minutes, stirring several times during baking to keep it moist.

4. Remove from oven, transfer to a food processor, and process for 1 minute, scraping down the sides of the bowl as needed. Add the half-and-half and process until smooth, 1 to 2 minutes. Serve immediately.

MAKES 4 TO 6 SERVINGS

PAM KRUTSCH'S ONION

Pam Krutsch of Rosemont, Illinois, sent in this recipe. "This recipe is simple to make, so make yourself two." A lady of few words, so make yourself some of her onions and see if you agree.

1 large onion

Butter or margarine

2 strips bacon

Salt and pepper

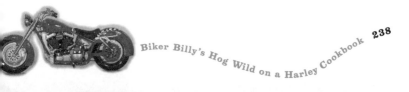

1. Peel the skin off the onion. Core out the center, but not all the way through, to make a well in the onion. Load up the well with butter or margarine. Wrap the bacon strips around the onion to cross over the well. Season with salt and pepper.

2. Wrap in aluminum foil and twist the top of the foil to close tight. Toss on the fire and cook until soft.

MAKES 1 SERVING

WILD ONE STUFFED MUSHROOMS

This is a side dish fit for the "Wild One." With enough flavor to win a barroom brawl, these mushrooms are also great as an appetizer. But there is no need to fight over the last serving—just cook up a double batch. Alright!

4 portobello mushrooms

2 tablespoons extra virgin olive oil, plus extra for greasing the dish and brushing the mushrooms

1 small onion, minced

2 canned chipotle peppers packed in adobo sauce, minced

2 tablespoons chopped garlic

½ cup vegetable broth

1 cup cooked wild rice

1 teaspoon dried chervil

1 teaspoon dried chives

½ teaspoon ground savory

½ teaspoon dried basil

½ teaspoon dried thyme

1 teaspoon dried parsley

½ teaspoon salt

½ teaspoon white pepper

¼ cup shredded Asiago cheese

¼ cup freshly grated Parmesan cheese

1. Preheat the oven to 400°F. Grease a 9-inch square or 9 x 13-inch baking dish with olive oil.

2. Remove the stems from the portobello mushrooms, mince the stems, and set aside. Place the mushroom caps upside down on the baking dish and brush with olive oil. Bake until the mushroom caps become dark and juicy, about 15 minutes.

3. Heat the 2 tablespoons olive oil in a small skillet over medium heat. Add the onion and chipotles and cook, stirring, until the onion is golden brown, 5 to 7 minutes. Add the chopped mushroom stems and garlic and cook, stirring, until the mushrooms begin to darken, 2 to 3 minutes. Add the broth, rice, chervil, chives, savory, basil, thyme, parsley, salt, and white pepper and simmer until the liquid is almost gone, 5 to 7 minutes. Add the cheeses and stir well.

4. Divide the rice mixture among the portobello caps, mounding it nicely. Bake until the tops are lightly browned, 20 to 25 minutes. Serve warm.

MAKES 4 SERVINGS

LISA PETERS'S
TUNA-STUFFED POTATOES

Here is a tasty stuffed baked potato recipe from my Harley-riding friend Lisa Peters. Lisa calls Concord, New Hampshire, home, a place where they get some pretty cold winters. These baked potatoes will warm you up nicely after a cold winter's ride. While Lisa did not add any hot peppers, don't let that stop you from adding some fire to increase the warming factor.

4 large baking potatoes

6 to 8 ounces cheddar cheese, shredded

One 7-ounce can water-packed albacore tuna, drained and flaked

½ cup shredded carrots

⅓ cup finely chopped scallions or onion

1. Preheat the oven to 425°F.

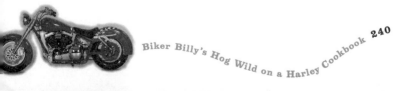

2. Scrub the potatoes, dry, and prick with a fork. Bake until soft, about 1 hour. Take the potatoes out of the oven and reduce the oven temperature to 350°F.

3. Using care while handling the hot potatoes, cut a slice from the top of each one. Carefully scoop out the insides of the potatoes without breaking the skin. Set the skins aside.

4. In a medium-size mixing bowl, beat potatoes till smooth, then stir in the cheese, tuna, carrots, and scallions. Spoon the potato mixture back into the potato skins. Place the stuffed potatoes on a baking sheet and bake until heated through to the center, 25 to 30 minutes. Serve hot.

MAKES 4 STUFFED POTATOES

RIGHTEOUS RED POTATOES

These oven-roasted red potatoes will do you right. They have a warm, satisfying flavor and a moderate dose of fire. As a side dish for barbecued steak, chicken, or your favorite main dish, they can't be beat. If you have any leftovers, they are great cold in salads like Suicide Shift Salad (page 77).

> ¼ cup extra virgin olive oil
>
> 2 tablespoons chopped garlic
>
> ¼ teaspoon cayenne pepper
>
> 1 teaspoon sweet paprika
>
> 1 teaspoon dried rosemary
>
> ½ teaspoon salt
>
> ½ teaspoon black pepper
>
> 6 medium-size red potatoes, quartered

1. Preheat the oven to 350°F.

2. In a small microwave-safe bowl, combine the olive oil, garlic, cayenne, paprika, rosemary, salt, and black pepper, stir well to mix, and microwave at half power for 1 minute or heat in a small saucepan over medium heat.

3. Place the potatoes in a large mixing bowl, add the flavored oil, and stir well to completely coat the potatoes. Transfer the potatoes to a baking sheet and arrange in a single layer. Pour the oil remaining in the bowl over the potatoes. Bake, turning a few times, until golden brown, 60 to 75 minutes. Serve hot.

MAKES 4 TO 6 SERVINGS

KATHY AUSTIN'S TATER TOT CHEESE CASSEROLE

Kathy Austin from Houston, Texas, told me, "I finally got my first Harley at the ripe old age of forty-three. I figured I had waited long enough. Soon after that, I got married and my husband, Joseph, got his own Harley. Now we ride as much as we can! This is a great quick recipe that kids and adults both love! This is NOT a diet recipe—lots of fat but VERY good. It's so quick that you can whip it up, bake, eat, and still have enough daylight left outside to ride the open road!" Dinner and a ride sound like a sweet idea.

> 2 teaspoons butter
>
> 2 large eggs
>
> 2 cups milk
>
> Salt and pepper to taste
>
> 1 teaspoon onion powder
>
> 1 teaspoon garlic powder
>
> 2 cups shredded cheddar cheese
>
> 2 cups shredded Monterey Jack cheese (you can use pepper Jack cheese if you're brave enough!)
>
> 1 cup chopped ham or cooked sausage or hamburger
>
> One 2-pound bag frozen tater tots (you can use cubed hash browns in a pinch), thawed

1. Preheat the oven to 350°F. Grease a large baking dish (9 x 13-inch at least) with the butter.

2. In a large mixing bowl, mix together the eggs and milk, whisking well. Season with salt, pepper, and the onion and garlic powders. Add 1 cup of the cheddar and 1 cup of the Monterey Jack. Mix well, then add the ham and tater tots. Mix it all up well.

3. Pour the mixture into the prepared dish and sprinkle the top evenly with each of the remaining cheeses. (Yes, it's *a lot* of cheese, but worth it!) Place in the oven and bake until the top is browned, 40 to 45 minutes.

MAKES 4 TO 6 SERVINGS

Kathy Austin

LISA'S SWEET POTATO CAKES

Besides riding Harleys and working as a massage therapist at both rallies and her office, Lisa is a professional chef. This is another of her tasty recipes. They will make a great side dish for you next dinner or lunch gathering. Maybe you should cook up two batches so your H.O.G. buddies can take some home.

> **4 large sweet potatoes, peeled**
>
> **3 large eggs**
>
> **1 cup all-purpose flour**
>
> **1½ teaspoons salt**
>
> **⅛ teaspoon freshly ground black pepper**
>
> **2 tablespoons cooking oil of your choice**

1. Place the sweet potatoes in a large saucepan of water, bring to a boil, and let boil until tender. Drain, then mash. Add the eggs, flour, salt, and black pepper and mix until well blended.

2. Heat the oil on a large griddle. Drop the batter from a large spoon onto the hot griddle and brown on both sides. As you turn the pancakes, flatten them slightly with a metal spatula. Add more oil to the griddle as needed to finish the cakes. Serve hot with butter or honey or both.

MAKES ABOUT FIFTEEN 3-INCH PANCAKES

CABIN FEVER CASSEROLE

In the depths of winter, motorcyclists in the northern states suffer from a disease called Cabin Fever. That dreaded disorder arises when the Harleys are snowed in in the garage and the groundhog says six more weeks of winter. While you may want to cook up some groundhog stew, don't blame the little fur ball—instead, cook up some of this comforting casserole, then relax on the sofa with some road maps and travel guides and plan your big spring tour.

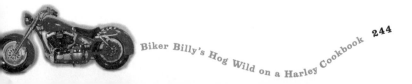

1 medium-size onion, minced

1 red bell pepper, seeded and minced

One 16-ounce package frozen corn, thawed and drained

One 8-ounce package frozen snow peas, thawed and drained

1 teaspoon onion powder

1 teaspoon garlic powder

1 teaspoon celery seeds

½ teaspoon ground savory

1 tablespoon dried parsley

½ teaspoon cayenne pepper

1 teaspoon dried chervil

1 teaspoon salt

½ teaspoon white pepper

½ cup shredded mild cheddar cheese

½ cup shredded mozzarella cheese

1 cup sour cream

¼ cup half-and-half

1 cup crumbled Ritz crackers

¼ cup (½ stick) butter, melted

1. Preheat the oven to 350°F. Grease a 1½-quart loaf pan.

2. In a large mixing bowl, combine the onion, bell pepper, corn, and snow peas and toss well to mix. Add the onion powder, garlic powder, celery seeds, savory, parsley, cayenne, chervil, salt, and white pepper and toss well to mix. Add the cheeses, sour cream, and half-and-half and stir well to mix.

3. Transfer the mixture to the prepared loaf pan. Cover evenly with the crumbled Ritz crackers and drizzle with the melted butter. Bake until the top is golden brown, 50 to 60 minutes. Serve immediately.

MAKES 6 TO 8 SERVINGS

SCREAMING YELLOW RICE

Like a Harley-Davidson VR 1000 race bike screaming down the front straightaway at the Daytona International Speedway, this rice takes your breath away. With a color that makes ordinary yellow rice look pale, this rice delivers a V-twin blast of flavor. At home with the most potent Mexican dishes, it will become a family favorite. Serve this after your next ride and your riding buddies will scream for more. So what are you waiting for? Rev up that stove and get cooking.

2 cups water

½ teaspoon salt

½ teaspoon white pepper

1 teaspoon turmeric

1 tablespoon dried cilantro

¼ teaspoon cayenne pepper

1 teaspoon saffron threads

1 tablespoon lightly salted butter

1 cup long-grain rice

Bring the water to a boil in a medium-size saucepan, then add the salt, white pepper, turmeric, cilantro, cayenne, saffron, and butter. Stir until the butter is melted, then add the rice and stir well. Cover, reduce the heat to low, and cook until the rice is tender and the liquid is absorbed, 20 to 25 minutes. Fluff the rice with a fork and serve immediately.

MAKES 6 TO 8 SERVINGS

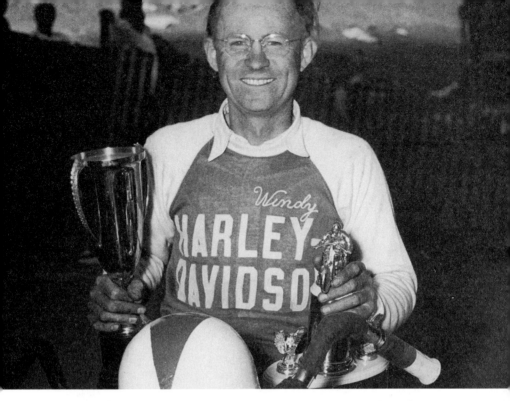

PAVEMENT ENDS:
DESSERTS

G o riding in some parts of the country and you will come across a sign that reads "Pavement Ends." Depending on your type of bike and skill level, this either means turn around quick or enter into a new adventure.

I have ventured past the pavement on my Harley-Davidson Road King Police Bike a few times over the years. Sometimes I have found a very manageable road of hard-packed earth or gravel that led to a place of great scenic beauty I might never have seen if I had turned around. But more than a few times I have found myself riding on a treacherous surface at a very slow speed for miles with no reasonable place to turn around, wondering where in the world I was going to end up.

One time in particular I was riding in the Blue Ridge Mountains. I had left the Blue Ridge Parkway for gas and was on my way back to the parkway when I spied a cool-looking little road heading off into the shade of a great canopy of trees. Since it was a sultry August afternoon, the shade looked mighty inviting, so I turned up the road. Well, in short order that little paved road started to wind up the mountainside and, without the benefit of a "Pavement Ends" sign, the pavement turned into hard pack. I rode on, since it was a nice surface and a gentle grade. The road rounded a bend and the grade increased sharply; the surface was now covered with small loose stones. I stopped and looked up the hill. It did not take me long to decide I should turn around and head back to the relative safety of tarmac. One problem became very clear; I was already on a piece of road too steep and a surface too loose to turn the bike around on. I had one and only one choice, to ride up the hill to the next turn, where I could see what looked like a level area. I started up the hill and the rear tire began to slip a little and throw stones around inside the rear fender. After a few white-knuckled minutes, I reached the very small level area and saw the road got even steeper ahead of me. Well, I did manage to almost turn the bike around in that little barely level area. When I was almost pointed straight back down the road, the bike started to slide downhill. Did I mention there were huge rain gullies along the sides of the road? Guess where I stopped sliding? That's right, in the rain gully, both wheels off the ground and my bike resting unharmed on the crash bars. After I removed my leathers and appraised the situation, I decided I needed to hike back down the road and seek some help. I could have used my cell phone but I was in an area too remote to get a signal (figures, doesn't it). Thankfully, halfway down the hill I met the mailman. He gave me a lift up the hill to the bike. With his help and the help of a gentleman who came along, we piled enough rocks under the wheels to allow me, with their help and the engine, to get the bike back on the road. After thanking them and putting my leathers on, I rode/slid my way back to the main road. Talk about an adventure. Needless to say, I now think twice before I risk riding uphill past the pavement's end on a dresser.

But you don't have to think twice about trying the recipes at the pavement's end—your only risk is enjoying them so much that you gain some pounds. I can recommend a road that will burn off that weight in no time flat.

DENA SHEETS'S BITE ME MOLASSES COOKIES

Here is another recipe from Harley rider Dena Sheets from Lead, South Dakota. "I developed this one about 25 years ago. These are for the sweet lovers—you're going to get your daily dose of sugar." These are as sweet as taking delivery of your new Harley—okay, almost as sweet.

- ¾ cup vegetable shortening
- 1 cup packed brown sugar
- 1 large egg
- One 12-ounce jar molasses
- 3½ to 4 cups all-purpose flour (enough to make a pretty stiff dough)
- 2 teaspoons baking soda
- ¼ teaspoon salt
- ½ teaspoon ground cloves
- 2 teaspoons ground cinnamon
- 1 teaspoon ground ginger
- Sugar to roll balls in

1. Preheat the oven to 350°F.

2. In a large mixing bowl, combine the shortening, brown sugar, egg, molasses, flour, baking soda, salt, cloves, cinnamon, and ginger until well mixed.

3. Roll the dough into 1-inch balls, then roll them in sugar to coat evenly. Place on an ungreased baking sheet and bake until slightly cracked on top, about 10 minutes. Let cool, then serve.

MAKES 2 DOZEN COOKIES

TOLL ROAD COOKIES

Y ou travel the road, you pay the toll. I guess that idea stemmed from a desire to have road users pay directly for the cost of the road's construction. Seems to me that some of the roads that were built in this manner must have been paid for more than several times over. Funny thing how once they get into your pocket, they never leave. Well, these cookies are just like that—once you eat one, you never want to stop. This recipe in my version of the classic concept of tollhouse cookies; like anything mechanical or edible left around this biker, it will be customized to suit my taste—did you expect anything less?

½ cup (1 stick) butter, softened

1 cup packed light brown sugar

1½ teaspoons vanilla extract

1 teaspoon cayenne pepper

½ teaspoon salt

1½ teaspoons baking powder

1 jumbo egg, beaten

1½ cups all-purpose flour

1 cup semisweet chocolate chips

½ cup walnuts, chopped

Oil or butter-flavored cooking spray

1. **HAND DOUGH METHOD:** Place the butter in a large mixing bowl and cut up with a dough cutter or two knives. Add the brown sugar and mix together until creamy. Add the vanilla, cayenne, salt, and baking powder and cut together well. Add the egg and cut together until smooth. Add the flour ¼ cup at a time, cutting together with each addition until a dough has formed. Add the chocolate chips and walnuts and knead until the chips and nuts are evenly distributed throughout the dough.

FOOD PROCESSOR DOUGH METHOD: Place the butter in a food processor and pulse several times. While the blades are running, slowly add the brown sugar through the feed tube and process until creamy. It may be necessary to stop the machine and scrape down the side of the bowl a few times. Add the vanilla, cayenne, salt, baking powder, and egg and process until well blended, about 1 minute. Add the flour ¼ cup at a time, processing for about 1 minute with each addition. Continue to process until the dough forms a ball that revolves around the processor bowl. It may be necessary to stop processing periodically to scrape down the sides of the bowl. Add the chocolate chips and walnuts and pulse until the chips and nuts are evenly distributed throughout the dough. I have found that the chopping blades will cut the chips up if you pulse them too much. If the chips don't integrate into the dough with a few pulses, remove the dough from the food processor and finish by hand in a mixing bowl.

2. Preheat the oven to 400°F. Grease a cookie sheet.

3. Form the dough into 1-inch balls, flatten between your palms, and place on the cookie sheet, leaving ½ inch between them. Bake 8 to 10 minutes for chewy cookies or 10 to 12 minutes for crispy cookies.

4. Transfer the cookies to a plate and allow to cool.

MAKES ABOUT TWENTY-FOUR 2-INCH COOKIES

LISA PETERS'S PEANUT BUTTER COOKIES

Although I love chocolate and am addicted to it, I do believe that peanut butter cookies are my favorite. This cookie recipe from Lisa Peters of Concord, New Hampshire, has a wonderful aroma while baking and a great peanut butter taste. Great for that H.O.G bake sale or for a pre-ride meeting treat, enjoy them as they are or, if you like something a little fierier, add some cayenne pepper like I do.

½ cup (1 stick) butter

⅔ cup honey

1 large egg

1 cup peanut butter (Lisa uses the no-sugar natural stuff)

½ teaspoon salt

½ teaspoon baking soda

½ teaspoon vanilla extract

Cayenne pepper to taste (optional)

1 to 1½ cups sifted all-purpose flour, as needed

1. Preheat the oven to 375°F. Grease a cookie sheet.

2. In a large mixing bowl, beat the butter till soft and smooth, then add the honey and cream it in. Add the egg, peanut butter, salt, baking soda, vanilla, and cayenne, if using, and beat in well. Add 1 cup of the flour and mix well. Add as much additional flour as needed to achieve a firm dough; the final amount depends on how oily the peanut butter is.

3. Drop by spoonfuls onto the prepared cookie sheet. Press flat with a fork in a tic tac toe pattern. Bake until golden, 10 to 20 minutes.

MAKES 30 TO 36 COOKIES

PEANUT BUTTER PANHEAD COOKIES

As I have said, I do love peanut butter cookies. I named these cookies for my favorite vintage Harley-Davidson motor, the Panhead. I love Panheads and hope someday to acquire one of them. Until then, I will just look at the inspirational picture of one on my office wall and enjoy riding my Evo Road King and Buell. But I can have these killer cookies anytime I want and so can you. The cayenne pepper gives these cookies the equivalent of an electric leg and will kick-start your taste buds.

½ cup (1 stick) butter, softened

1½ cups packed light brown sugar

1 cup chunky peanut butter

1 tablespoon vanilla extract

1 teaspoon cayenne pepper

¾ teaspoon salt

¾ teaspoon baking soda

1 jumbo egg

1¾ cups all-purpose flour

¼ cup half-and-half

1. **HAND DOUGH METHOD:** Place the butter in a large mixing bowl and cut up with a dough cutter or two knives. Add the brown sugar and mix together until creamy. Add the peanut butter, vanilla, cayenne, salt, and baking soda and cut together well. Add the egg and cut together until smooth. Add the flour ¼ cup at a time, cutting together with each addition until a dough has formed.

FOOD PROCESSOR DOUGH METHOD: Place the butter in a food processor and pulse several times. While the machine running, slowly add the brown sugar through the feed tube and process until creamy. It may be necessary to scrape down the side of the bowl a few times. Add the peanut butter, vanilla, cayenne, salt, baking soda, and egg and process until well blended, about 1 minute. Add the flour ¼ cup at a time, processing for about 1 minute with each addition. Continue to process until the dough forms a ball that revolves around the processor bowl. It may be necessary to stop processing periodically to scrape down the side of the bowl.

2. Preheat the oven to 400°F. Grease a cookie sheet.

3. Form the dough into 1-inch balls, flatten between your palms, and place on the prepared cookie sheet, leaving 1 inch between them. Use a fork to press a tic tac toe pattern into each cookie. Bake for 8 to 10 minutes for chewy cookies or 10 to 12 minutes for crispy cookies.

4. Transfer the cookies to a plate and allow to cool.

MAKES ABOUT TWENTY-FOUR 2-INCH COOKIES

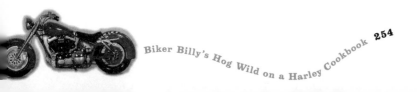

Marty Rosenblum on his 1994 FXSTS Springer Softail

GRANDMA RESSMAN'S POLISH SUGAR COOKIES

My great friend Dr. Martin Jack Rosenblum is the historian for the Harley-Davidson Motor Company. Marty shared this family jewel of a recipe with me and relayed some of this recipe's meaning to him. "When I was in my teens, my Grandmother Ressman let me hide my motorcycles in her chicken coop. My parents at first did not approve of my passion for riding. Grandma Sarah Ressman kept my secret. I would often work on my bikes in her coop, which was out behind her garden and garage, and then come into her house for these cookies. Later on, when I had a rockabilly band, we would practice in her garage, which also hid our equipment truck. We would all eat Grandma Ressman's Polish Sugar Cookies before our gigs, as we loaded the 1940s panel truck. I think of her every time my daughter, Sarah, makes this recipe. Now when I eat these cookies, I think of that venerable Harley-Davidson Sportster from the late fifties in the chicken coop, all the wild music, and my dear Grandma Ressman serving cookies she learned how to make in Poland. Make a batch yourself for your saddlebags. Even the crumbs taste good." I am sure Grandma Ressman would be pleased if you enjoyed these cookies.

½ cup (1 stick) butter, softened

½ cup sugar

1 large egg, beaten

¼ cup milk

1 capful vanilla extract

2 cups all-purpose flour

1 teaspoon baking powder

½ teaspoon baking soda

1. In a large mixing bowl, cream the butter, then add the sugar and combine well.

2. In a small mixing bowl, combine the beaten egg, milk, and vanilla.

3. In a medium-size mixing bowl, sift the dry ingredients together. Alternately, add the flour and milk mixtures to the butter-and-sugar mixture, beating gently but thoroughly

4. Spoon out cookies to your preferred size on greased cookie sheets and bake in a preheated 400°F oven for 15 minutes.

MAKES 24 TO 30 COOKIES

WILD FIRE H.O.G. CHAPTER SUGAR COOKIES

This recipe comes from Pearl Christopherson, who is a member of the Wild Fire H.O.G. Chapter in Peshtigo, Wisconsin. Pearl tells us, "Here's a fun cookie recipe that is easy to make and has ingredients one usually has in the house. My family and friends like it because the cookies are large, soft, and thicker than usual. I use my Harley-Davidson cookie cutter and frost them with a buttercream frosting. I then pack them up, place them in my H-D saddlebags, and deliver them to my grandchildren, friends, and potluck at H.O.G. meetings. This grandmother doesn't sit in a chair and knit, but does bake, ride, and share cookies. Cookies and Harleys together bring smiles. Hope you enjoy them." Way to go, Pearl! You will find Pearl's H-D Buttercream Frosting on page 258.

3 large eggs

1⅔ cups sugar

1 cup butter-flavored Crisco vegetable shortening

1 teaspoon salt

2 teaspoons baking powder

2 teaspoons baking soda

2 teaspoons vanilla extract

1 cup sour milk (see Note)

5 cups sifted all-purpose flour

1. In a large mixing bowl, combine the eggs, sugar, and Crisco and beat together well. Add the salt, baking powder, baking soda, vanilla, and sour milk and mix well. Add the flour 1 cup at a time, mixing well after each addition.

2. Gather the dough up into a ball, cover with plastic wrap, and chill.

3. When ready to bake, preheat the oven to 350°F.

4. On a lightly floured work surface, roll the dough out to thickness of about ¼ inch and use a cookie cutter to cut your cookies. Reroll the scraps and cut out more cookies until you don't have enough left to do it anymore. Bake in the oven until set and lightly golden at the edges, about 8 minutes. Let cool completely and frost, if desired.

MAKES ABOUT 5 DOZEN COOKIES

N O T E You can sour fresh milk with 1 tablespoon vinegar or lemon juice.

Pearl Christopherson on her 2000 Dyna Low Rider with 33,000 miles

PEARL'S H-D BUTTERCREAM FROSTING

This great frosting recipe comes from Pearl Christopherson, who is a member of the Wild Fire H.O.G. Chapter in Peshtigo, Wisconsin. You can use it on Pearl's Wild Fire H.O.G. Chapter Sugar Cookies (page 256) or on any cookie for a more festive presentation. Pearl says, "Leftovers freeze well or go great on graham crackers. I use orange food coloring to frost H-D cookies and outline them in brown." Ahh, the art of cookies, just like custom Harley, is an expression of one's own individual creativity.

> 1 cup butter-flavored Crisco vegetable shortening
>
> 3 cups confectioners' sugar
>
> 1 teaspoon salt
>
> 1½ teaspoons vanilla extract
>
> 1 large egg white
>
> 1 cup whole milk

In a large mixing bowl, beat all the ingredients together till creamy.

MAKES ABOUT 5 CUPS FROSTING

PAULA'S CHOCOLATE TAHINI SHORTBREAD

My good friend Paula Bishop from Asheville, North Carolina, shared this fantastic recipe. Paula makes the most incredible chocolate desserts, from truffles to pies to unbelievably yummy cakes. Did I tell you I am a chocolate addict? This recipe combines three of my personal favorites and when Paula told me about it, I knew it had to be in this cookbook. If you are ever in Asheville and find Paula's chocolates, buy them and prepare for a true chocolate delight. Until then, try this recipe and dream—sweet dreams, that is. Alright, Paula!

¾ cup (1½ sticks) butter (if you use unsalted, add a pinch salt)

¾ cup bittersweet bar chocolate broken into pieces

½ cups tahini (sesame paste)

1 cup packed light brown sugar

½ cup ground or finely chopped pecans or walnuts, plus halves for garnish

2 cups all-purpose flour

1. Preheat the oven to 375°F.

2. In the top of a double boiler set over simmering water, melt the butter and chocolate together. Add the tahini and mix well. Add the brown sugar and mix, then add the nuts and mix. Sprinkle in the flour and mix; the dough should be pretty stiff at this point.

3. Transfer and press the dough down into a shallow 10 x 14-inch baking pan (or into a couple of pie pans) so that the dough is about ¼ inch thick. You can add a few pecan/walnut halves on top for decoration at this point, by pressing them into the dough. Bake the shortbread for about 15 minutes, checking frequently, every couple of minutes, until the edges start to brown. Be careful not to overbake it.

4. While it's still warm, cut each shortbread into pieces—don't wait until it is cool or it will crumble.

MAKES ABOUT FORTY-TWO 1½ X 2-INCH COOKIES

OUT OF TIME PEANUT BUTTER BROWNIES

What do you eat when you win a motorcycle drag race? Well, if you race for the "Z man," you get an Out of Time Brownie. Andy "Z man" Zalewski from New Jersey, who owns and operates the Out of Time Racing Team, sent in this yummy dessert. Remember to grab one before you serve them 'cause they will disappear as fast as a Top Fuel Harley leaves the green light at the AHDRA races.

4 ounces unsweetened chocolate

⅔ cup vegetable shortening

2 cups sugar

4 large eggs

1 teaspoon vanilla extract

1¼ cups all-purpose flour

1 teaspoon baking powder

1 teaspoon salt

1 cup chopped nuts

One 8-ounce jar Jif peanut butter

1. Preheat the oven to 350°F. Grease a 9 x 13-inch baking pan.

2. Melt the chocolate and shortening together in large saucepan over low heat. Remove from the heat.

3. Mix in the sugar, eggs, and vanilla, then stir in the flour, baking powder, salt, and nuts. Transfer to the prepared pan and spread evenly. Bake until it starts to pull away from the sides of the pan, about 30 minutes. Be careful not to overbake.

4. Let cool slightly, then spread the peanut butter over the top, cut into bars, and serve with a tall glass of cold milk.

MAKES ABOUT 12 BROWNIES

MAMA MEDERSKI'S HOGGIN' THE BROWNIES

Miriam Mederski from the Motorcycle Hall of Fame Museum shared this yummy recipe. "I was making these brownies long before my son Mark took up motorcycling. Although not everybody likes nuts in their brownies, around here they are as standard as chrome on a Harley. I suppose lattice crust peach pie is my specialty, but these brownies offered for dessert usually worked to get my young men out of the garage and to the dinner table."

2 ounces unsweetened chocolate

2 cups (4 sticks) butter

1 cup sugar

½ cup chopped English walnuts

1 scant cup all-purpose flour

2 large eggs, well beaten

1. Preheat the oven to 325°F. Grease and flour a 9-inch square glass or ceramic baking dish.

2. In a large, heavy saucepan over low heat, melt and combine the chocolate and butter. Mix in the remaining ingredients one at a time. Pour the batter into the prepared baking dish and bake until the center is set and the edges are just starting to pull away from the edges of the pan, about 40 minutes.

MAKES 9 TO 12 SERVINGS

RANDY DUNN'S GRANDMA'S RAISED DONUTS

Here is a family recipe from my good friend Randy Dunn, who calls Milwaukee, Wisconsin, home when he is not on the road. Randy is the marketing manager for the Harley-Davidson Demonstration Ride and Traveling Museum Programs. Says Randy, "The traveling museum pulls enough motorcycles and memorabilia from the archives department to fill a 53-foot semi trailer with two slide-out sides. This gives the public the opportunity to view the branches of the Harley-Davidson motorcycle family tree. The theme and displays of the Traveling Museum change periodically so that the public can view 'new' pieces of the Motor Company's history every few years. The Traveling Museum visits major motorcycle rallies and over 200 dealerships a year.

"The Demonstration Ride program, which keeps me traveling the country eight months out of the year, is produced to present the current models and new innovations Harley-Davidson Motor Company develops each year. The 'Demo Rides,' as they are most often called, give customers the opportunity to see and ride current model year Harley-Davidson and Buell motorcycles.

"With all this traveling, I rarely get to cook or enjoy a real home-cooked meal. Though there are many great restaurants out there, there is nothing like a meal individually prepared for the enjoyment of a few friends. More importantly, there is nothing like a 'treat' prepared with only the love a grandmother can bake her food.

"I was raised in the central western part of Illinois in the small community of Macomb. My grandmother Clara Brewer was raised on the farm and stayed there until my grandfather died, then she moved next door to the house I grew up in. Grandma knew how to cook all the great foods from the farm and that alone could fill a cookbook, even though now most doctors say it is bad for you. I have a hard time believing that, since my grandmother lived an active life until she passed away at 102 years old.

"As a youth growing up, my favorite treat was Grandma's raised donuts. We kids would beg her to make them for us and she would come over to the house and create her masterpiece. Half of the fun of getting donuts was the intricate game of cat and mouse, with Grandma being the cat, standing guard over the morsels, and we three kids the mice, ready to snatch a bite whenever possible. Since these donuts take time to raise, it was our scheme to acquire, for early consumption, as many of the 'raw' donuts as possible. The uncooked donuts had a sweetness to them that made them almost as delectable as the finished product. As the donuts sat out on the counter to rise, we would perform distracting maneuvers and 'hit and run' tactics to procure as much appetite-spoiling delights as possible.

"Grandma would always say, 'If you don't stop eating the dough, there won't be enough left for donuts.' There always seemed to be enough for both. Here is what you will need for ingredients and how to prepare them."

2 packets active dry yeast

¼ cup lukewarm water

¾ cup lukewarm milk

¼ cup granulated sugar

1 teaspoon salt

1 teaspoon vanilla extract

1 large egg

¼ cup vegetable shortening

3½ to 3¾ cups all-purpose flour, as needed

Granulated sugar or 2 cups confectioners' sugar for coating

1. Soften the yeast in the water. In a large mixing bowl, combine the milk, sugar, salt, and vanilla together. Add the yeast mixture, stir in the egg, shortening, and half of the flour, and mix well. Slowly add the remaining flour to the mixture until it obtains a typical dough consistency. Any remaining flour is used to spread on your kneading board to keep the dough from sticking to the surface.

2. Knead the dough on a lightly floured board a few times. Place in a clean bowl, cover with a clean kitchen cloth, and let rise in a warm place until the dough is light. My grandmother used to place the covered bowl of dough in the back porch window to let the sun warm it up. This would cause it to double in size in about 2 hours. As a second option, Grandma would place the bowl over the pilot light area of the stove and let it warm the bowl. Actual time depends on the warmth of the surrounding air. This is a process where you have to keep checking the mixture to see when it doubles in size. Punch the dough down and let it rise again until doubled in size.

3. On a lightly floured board, roll out the dough ½ inch, as it will puff up to about 1 inch when fried and cut with a donut cutter. Reroll the scraps and cut out more donuts until you can't cut out anymore. Place the donuts and donut holes on a baking sheet and let rise until very light. Leave uncovered to form a hard crust.

4. In a deep-fryer or large, deep pot, heat 2 inches of oil until a donut hole dropped in the hot oil browns. Deep-fry the donuts in batches, being careful not to crowd them, until golden brown on both sides. Remove from the oil using a slotted spoon or tons. Let the excess oil drip off the donut when removing it from the pot, then roll them in granulated sugar or a glaze made with the confectioners' sugar mixed with enough water to achieve the consistency of a soft paste. When the warm donut comes into contact with the glaze, it will soften the glaze, which will melt and stick to the donut. If the glaze is too hard,

it will tear the donut and if too soft, it will run off the donut and not give a good coating. Place the coated donuts on wax paper or in a plastic container until cool and ready to serve. Eat them while they're fresh.

MAKES 3 DOZEN AVERAGE-SIZE DONUTS PLUS HOLES
(SEE NOTE)

NOTE Randy says, "The recipe will make 3 dozen average-sized donuts plus holes. Since you cut the donuts from the dough after it rises, you cannot take the holes and roll them back out for more donuts. As kids, we preferred to pilfer the holes when raw, as we could grab them and get them in our mouths in one shot and no one was the wiser, except for the Cheshire Cat grins on our guilty faces. The holes are also great little morsels after cooked and rolled in a powdered sugar and maple flavoring glaze. Sure brings back a lot of fond childhood memories of playing 'cat and mouse' with Mom and Grandma when they fixed them. It was a perpetual game until the last donuts were cooked and coated. Even then, we were always sneaking around, getting a donut from the Tupperware between meals and in the evenings, until every last one was consumed."

STEPHEN SCHATZGER'S SMOOTH RIDE RICE PUDDING

Sasha Mullins, my Harley-riding friend from NYC, sent in this family recipe. She says, "Here's a recipe from my cousin Stephen. I'll tell you this is *the best* rice pudding I have ever had. And it's such a delicate presentation, presented by a burly biker. I have a darling photo of Stephen with his family surrounding him on the bike. For burly road hogs, double the recipe. For your biker kids, top with whipped cream. For your biker lady, top with whipped cream and a cherry!" Stephen Schatzger and family call West Islip, New York, home.

6 cups milk

½ cup raw white rice

½ teaspoon salt (optional)

2 large eggs

1 teaspoon vanilla extract

¾ cup sugar

Raisins to your liking

Ground cinnamon

Ground nutmeg

1. Combine the milk, rice, and salt in heavy-bottomed 2-quart saucepan over medium-low heat and simmer, uncovered, for 1 hour, stirring occasionally.

2. In another 2-quart saucepan, combine the eggs, vanilla, and sugar over medium heat until hot, but do not let it boil, as this will easily burn. Add to the rice mixture and cook and stir for 1 minute.

3. Pour the pudding into a serving dish and add raisins to your taste. Sprinkle with cinnamon and nutmeg. Let cool, then chill well before serving. Dig in!

MAKES ABOUT 8 SERVINGS

From left to right: Jessica, Liz, Stephen, Stephanie, and Kimberly Schatzger gathered around Stephen's 2002 Harley-Davidson Road King

VIRDA AND MAE'S WHEELIE-POPPING PEACH COBBLER

Here is a yummy dessert from one of my old-time Harley friends. I first met Virda, a Harley-Davidson district manager, at A.D. Farrows's Harley-Davidson's 85th anniversary celebration. "I've been with Harley for almost nine years. I love to cook and to ride. I met my husband at a motorcycle rally. We had a very classy bona fide motorcycle wedding. The entire wedding party rode up in leathers on flower-draped bikes. I rode in on a Road King, decked out in white leathers, white lace chaps with a train, and a veil on my helmet. My husband wore white leathers too. The pastor, being a rider, included Harley in the vows: 'Promise to love, honor, and cherish on a Harley, off a Harley.' The ceremony ended with a procession of 40 to 50 motorcycles. Now we have two beautiful babies—an '01 S.E. Road Glide and '94 Fat Boy. We love to go on overnight trips. After coming home from the road, there's nothing better than having a home-cooked meal complete with a homemade dessert."

> 3 to 4 cups peeled, pitted, and sliced peaches, frozen (thawed) or fresh
>
> ¼ cup water
>
> 1¾ cups sugar
>
> 3 teaspoons ground cinnamon
>
> ¼ teaspoon ground nutmeg
>
> 2 teaspoons vanilla extract
>
> 3 tablespoons butter
>
> 1 cup self-rising flour
>
> ⅔ cup milk
>
> 1 teaspoon baking powder

1. Place the peaches and water in a large saucepan. Add ¾ cup of the sugar, 2 teaspoons of the cinnamon, ⅛ teaspoon of the nutmeg, and 1 teaspoon of the vanilla. Simmer for 15 to 20 minutes over low heat.

2. Preheat the oven to 350°F. Melt the butter in a flameproof 7 x 11-inch glass baking dish (or one big enough to hold the peaches) while the oven is preheating.

3. In a medium-size mixing bowl, combine the flour, milk, baking powder, remaining 1 cup sugar, 1 teaspoon cinnamon, $\frac{1}{8}$ teaspoon nutmeg, and 1 teaspoon vanilla. Pour the batter into the baking dish and add the peaches. Bake until browned on top, 30 to 40 minutes.

MAKES 6 TO 8 SERVINGS OR FEEDS 2 HUSBANDS

DEB BALLARD'S STRAWBERRY SURPRIZE

"I've been riding with my husband for a quite some time but this past May I got my own bike and since then have somehow racked up 4,000 miles in a little over two months," says Deb Ballard of Frankfort, Kentucky. "We're leaving for Sturgis next week and I just can't wait for this experience. I LOVE the feel of that wind & vibrations & the singing of my pipes—mmmmmmm, it doesn't get much better than this. This is an awesome dessert, my hubby's fav treat, besides yours truly."

2 small packages instant vanilla pudding

3½ cups cold milk

1½ cups graham cracker crumbs

½ cup sugar

⅓ cup butter, melted

Two 8-ounce packages cream cheese, softened

2 tablespoons milk

3½ cups Cool Whip

2 pints fresh strawberries, hulled and sliced

1. Prepare the pudding according to the package direction using the cold milk. Put in the refrigerator to chill.

2. When the pudding is chilled, combine the graham cracker crumbs, ¼ cup of the sugar, and the melted butter in a medium-size mixing bowl and press into the bottom of a 9 x 13-inch baking pan.

3. In a large mixing bowl with an electric mixer, beat the cream cheese with the remaining ¼ cup sugar and the milk until smooth.

Fold in half of the Cool Whip. Spread evenly over the graham cracker crust. Arrange the strawberries evenly on top. Spread the chilled pudding over the strawberries. Spread the remaining Cool Whip over the top. (You can also mix the remaining Cool Whip with the vanilla pudding and spread over the strawberries, making one layer instead of two.) Chill until ready to serve.

MAKES ABOUT 24 SERVINGS

Deb Ballard and her 1999 Dyna Low Rider

LISA'S CARROT CAKE

This simple carrot cake is from Lisa Peters of Concord, New Hampshire. Bake it before your ride and enjoy it on your return, a sweet treat for the ride's end. Make it an even richer treat by spreading a little cream cheese on top of a slice of this cake. If you take the approach of let me have my dessert first, then start your day with a piece of this for breakfast.

1¼ cups canola oil

1½ cups honey

4 large eggs

3 cups all-purpose, whole wheat, or spelt flour

2 teaspoons baking soda

1 tablespoon ground cinnamon

1 teaspoon ground ginger (optional)

1 teaspoon ground cloves (optional)

5 cups grated carrots

1 teaspoon salt

1. Preheat the oven to 350°F.

2. Blend the oil and honey together in a large mixing bowl. Add the eggs one at a time, beating well after each addition. Add the flour, baking soda, cinnamon, ginger and cloves, if using, carrots, and salt and mix well.

3. Pour the batter into a 9 x 12-inch baking pan. Bake until a toothpick inserted in the center comes out clean, about 30 minutes.

MAKES 9 TO 12 SERVINGS

JOHN HENKEL'S PRISON BREAK CAKE

John Henkel of Sandusky, Ohio, is a Harley rider and artist. He sent in this recipe and said, "This cake is soo good, it could cause a prison break!!! We love to have this the day after a long night of partying and riding!! It could probably be called our hangover cake.

Anyway, with a tall glass of ice cold milk, it will make your tongue slap your brains out!!!"

FOR THE CAKE

3 cups all-purpose flour

2 cups granulated sugar

3 large eggs

1 cup vegetable oil

One 8-ounce can crushed pineapple, drained

2 cups peeled and chopped bananas

1 teaspoon baking soda

1 teaspoon salt

1 teaspoon ground cinnamon

½ teaspoon vanilla extract

1 cup pecans, chopped

FOR THE FROSTING

One 8-ounce package cream cheese, softened

½ cup (1 stick) butter, softened

One 1-pound box confectioners' sugar

1 teaspoon vanilla extract

1. Preheat the oven to 350°F. Grease and flour a 9 x 13-inch baking pan, knocking out any excess.

2. In a large mixing bowl, mix together the cake ingredients until combined, but do not beat. Pour into the prepared pan and bake until a toothpick inserted into the center comes out clean, 35 to 40 minutes. Let cool on a wire rack.

3. In a large mixing bowl, beat together the frosting ingredients to your desired frosting consistency.

4. Once the cake has cooled completely, frost the top of the cake and serve in squares.

MAKES 12 SERVINGS

GILES FAMILY CHEESECAKE

John Giles of Nashville, Tennessee, shared his family recipe and told me, "I'm lead guitarist and vocalist for the legendary Leon Russell and tour with Leon, doing 100 to 120 shows a year. I'm also a proud owner of a '98 FLHRCI. This cheesecake is as smooth as a Road King on a country road."

1¾ cups graham cracker crumbs

⅓ cup butter, melted

1¼ cups sugar

Three 8-ounce packages cream cheese, softened

2 teaspoons vanilla extract

3 large eggs

1 cup sour cream

1. In a medium-size mixing bowl, combine the crumbs, melted butter, and ¼ cup of the sugar. Press the crumbs into the bottom and 1½ inches up the sides of an 8- or 9-inch springform pan; set aside.

2. In a large mixing bowl with electric mixer on high speed, beat the cream cheese, remaining 1 cup sugar, and the vanilla until creamy. Beat in the eggs, one at a time. Blend in the sour cream. Transfer to the prepared pan and smooth out the top.

3. Bake in a preheated 350°F oven until the center is set, 60 to 70 minutes. Turn off the oven, leaving the door slightly ajar, and leave the cheesecake in the oven for 1 hour.

4. Remove from the oven; let cool completely. Chill for 4 hours or overnight before slicing.

MAKES 8 SERVINGS

John Giles on tour

KOSCO H-D'S TOLLHOUSE COOKIE PIE

Here is a sinfully delicious dessert from my friends at Kosco Harley-Davidson and Buell in Kinnelon, New Jersey. Lou Kosco, Jr., sent in this family recipe. If you are in the area, stop by and say hi to Lou or any one of the three generations of the Kosco family who can be found at the dealership. While you're there, as Lou, Jr., puts it, enjoy "a hot cup of coffee, and good conversation with fellow bikers." That, after all, is the Harley way—good friends, hospitality, and one hell of a good motorcycle.

> **2 large eggs**
> **½ cup all-purpose flour**
> **½ cup granulated sugar**
> **½ cup packed light brown sugar**
> **¾ cup (1½ sticks) butter**
> **1 cup semisweet chocolate chips**
> **One 9-inch pie shell**

1. Preheat the oven to 325°F.

2. In a large mixing bowl, beat the eggs until foamy. Beat in the flour, and both sugars. Stir in the chips.

3. Spoon the filling into the pie shell. Bake until golden brown, 55 to 60 minutes. Let cool on a wire rack and serve warm with whipped cream or ice cream.

MAKES ONE 9-INCH PIE; 6 TO 12 SERVINGS

TO DIE PUMPKIN PIE

Talk about desserts to die for, this high-performance biker-style pie will lay you out with a smile. The aromas from this pie will fill your kitchen with hungry bikers. Just warn all those sweet tooths that this pie packs a surprise. Its warming but not scorching fire is thanks to the cayenne. Besides packing firepower, the pepper also brings the other flavors to life. This pie is truly worthy of playing the

last act of a memorable holiday feast. Some vanilla ice cream or whipped cream will soothe the tender tongues at your dinner table.

4 large eggs

3 cups light cream

¾ cup packed light brown sugar

¾ cup granulated sugar

½ teaspoon ground ginger

½ teaspoon ground nutmeg

½ teaspoon ground cloves

1 teaspoon cayenne pepper

1 teaspoon ground cinnamon

3 cups fresh pumpkin, prebaked (see Note)

1 packaged piecrust mix, prepared for a double-crust 9-inch pie

1. In a large mixing bowl, beat the eggs using an electric blender on low speed. Add the cream and mix until well blended. Add both sugars, the ginger, nutmeg, cloves, cayenne, and cinnamon and blend until smooth, about 2 minutes. Add the pumpkin and blend until smooth, about 3 minutes. (You can blend this by hand but it takes a lot more effort.)

2. Preheat the oven to 425°F. Roll out and place the crusts in two 9-inch pie pans and pinch-flute the edges into a nice-looking ridge. Divide the filling between the two pie crusts. Bake at 425°F for 15 minutes, the reduce the oven temperature to 350°F and bake until a fork inserted in the center of the pie comes out clean, about another 45 minutes. Serve warm or chilled, as you prefer.

MAKES TWO 9-INCH PIES; 8 TO 12 SERVINGS TOTAL

N O T E To prepare the pumpkin, cut a 2- to 3-pound pumpkin in half, scrape out and discard the seeds and membranes. Place the pumpkin halves on a lightly greased baking sheet with the cut side down. Bake in a preheated 350°F oven until tender, about 30 minutes. Remove from the oven and allow to cool. Scrape out the 3 cups of pumpkin flesh for the recipe. Depending on the size of the pumpkin, you can prepare several pies; they make excellent holiday gifts for your fiery friends. Or, if that sounds like too much work, just use a 29-ounce can of cooked pumpkin, which should yield 3 cups.

DOUG'S HOT-BOTTOM SWEET POTATO PIE

This tasty recipe comes courtesy of Doug "Cupcake" Cuciz of Pleasanton, California. Says Doug, "Doug's Hot-Bottom Sweet Potato Pie is sweet and spicy, like a ride on a country road. The weather is crisp and spicy and the motorcycle is sounding as sweet as can be coming out of the turns. This is a dessert worth waiting for at the end of a ride. I am an instructor for the California Motorcycle Safety Program and Motorcycle Safety Foundation and have been riding for over 40 years. I have competed in hill climbs and drag racing and I now enjoy riding with friends and especially with my wonderful wife, who also rides her own bike. We especially enjoy overnight weekend rides where there are plenty of attractions and fine restaurants where we love to experience wonderfully prepared foods. (Oh, yeah, we like it *spicy*.)" What more is there to say but try Doug's pie.

One 9-inch pie shell

3 large sweet potatoes (not yams), scrubbed

½ cup (1 stick) butter, melted

¼ cup unsalted shelled sunflower seeds

¼ cup walnuts, chopped

¼ cup honey, heated until liquid

1 teaspoon cayenne pepper

¾ cup packed light brown sugar

½ cup granulated sugar

2 large eggs, beaten

¼ cup half-and-half

1 teaspoon ground cinnamon

1¼ teaspoons ground nutmeg

¼ cup Torani vanilla syrup

3 walnut halves

1. Refrigerate the piecrust while you make the filling.

2. Bring a large pot of lightly salted water to a boil over high heat. Add the sweet potatoes, reduce the heat to medium, and cook until

tender when pierced with a knife, about 30 minutes. Drain and run under cold water until cool enough to handle. Peel the sweet potatoes and place in a medium-size mixing bowl. Mash with an electric mixer on medium speed until very smooth. Measure out a generous 3 cups of mashed sweet potatoes, keeping any extra for another use, and set aside.

3. Preheat the oven to 400°F. Uncover the pie shell and brush the interior with some of the melted butter. Add the sunflower seeds and chopped walnuts to the warm honey and stir in the cayenne. Sprinkle ¼ cup of the brown sugar evenly over the bottom of the pie shell. Evenly spread the honey mixture over the brown sugar. Bake until the crust is set and just beginning to brown, about 15 minutes (if the pie shell puffs up, do not prick it).

4. Meanwhile, using an electric mixer on low speed, mix together the mashed sweet potatoes, the remaining melted butter and ½ cup brown sugar, the granulated sugar, eggs, half-and-half, cinnamon, nutmeg, and vanilla syrup until smooth. Spread the filling in the partially baked pie shell, smoothing the top.

5. Reduce the oven temperature to 375°F and bake until a knife inserted in the center comes out clean, about 1½ hours. During the last 15 minutes, place the 3 walnut halves on the top of the pie (in the center in a artistic manner). Let cool completely on a wire cake rack. Cover with plastic wrap and refrigerate until ready to serve.

MAKES 6 TO 8 SERVINGS

Doug "Cupcake" Cuciz with a vintage V-twin Harley composed of Harley-Davidson parts made between 1914 and 1917

DONNA RAWHOUSER'S PEANUT BUTTER PIE

Here is a great recipe from Donna Rawhouser, who is the administrative assistant, Finance, at Harley-Davidson's York Operations. Donna works where they built your beloved Harley. Maybe your ride is so sweet because they enjoy Donna's pie at the factory. Donna told me, "How many people can say they enjoy going to work every day—I sure can. I have a 1998 95th Anniversary 1200 Custom Sportster and a 2002 Fat Boy that I enjoy riding. There is a group of employees at the plant who formed a club called The Employee Rider Association and I am the secretary of the group. We plan a whole season of riding to various places. One of the most enjoyable is our annual 'Run to the Sun' in Ocean City, Maryland—we pretty much book the whole motel we go to. Our group also sells raffle bike tickets for the bike given away at the York Open House, proceeds of which go to MDA. It is a treat to be in touch with our customers and help such a great cause. Of course, being able to work at rallies and represent our company is another great plus to my job. Doesn't get much better than that!" I met Donna and some of her club at the Carlisle Summer Bike Fest 2002 in Carlisle, Pennsylvania, where they had a bike raffle and I can attest to the fact they enjoy their work, both at the company and for the MDA.

FOR THE CRUST

1¼ cups chocolate cookie crumbs

¼ cup sugar

¼ cup margarine, melted

FOR THE FILLING

One 8-ounce package cream cheese, softened

1 cup peanut butter

1 cup sugar

1 tablespoon butter, softened

1 teaspoon vanilla extract

1 cup heavy cream, whipped to stiff peaks

1. Combine the crust ingredients in a medium-size mixing bowl. Press into the bottom and sides of a 9-inch pie pan. Bake in a preheated 375°F oven for 10 minutes.

2. Place the cream cheese in a large mixing bowl and beat. Add the peanut butter, sugar, butter, and vanilla and blend well. Fold in the whipped cream.

3. Pour the filling into the cooled pie shell and refrigerate for at least 4 hours. Freezes well (if you have any left!).

MAKES ONE 9-INCH PIE

LESLIE HUDSON'S TO DIE FOR PEANUT BUTTER PIE

When Leslie told me about this recipe and its strong family connection, I knew it had to be in this book—good food and motorcycling are both strong bonds in so many of our families. Here is what Leslie told me: "My sister, Kate, and I have always been peanut butter fanatics and when Mom made this pie growing up, we just loved it. I had always thought that my mom was the creator of this recipe, but when I was putting it down in writing for the book, I checked with my sister to see if she knew for sure. She thought that it was from our aunt, Sue Beichner. Well, after a call to Aunt Sue in Pennsylvania, where I grew up, I found out that it actually came from a friend and co-worker of hers at Keystone High School (my alma mater), Pat Dittman. Unfortunately, Pat is now deceased, as is my mother. But, this peanut butter pie will always remind me of my mom, and I thank Pat for that."

FOR THE TOPPING
1½ cups confectioners' sugar

¾ cup peanut butter

One 9-inch deep-dish pie shell, your own recipe or store-bought (regular and graham cracker are both nice), partially baked

¼ cup cornstarch

⅔ cup granulated sugar

¼ teaspoon salt

2 cups milk

3 large eggs, slightly beaten

FOR THE MERINGUE

3 large egg whites

¼ teaspoon cream of tartar

6 tablespoons granulated sugar

½ teaspoon vanilla extract

1. Mix the confectioners' sugar and peanut butter together in a medium-size mixing bowl until crumbly. Spread one third of this mixture in the pie shell.

2. Preheat the oven to 400°F. Combine the cornstarch, granulated sugar, salt, and milk in a medium-size saucepan, bring to a boil over medium to high heat, and let boil for 2 minutes, stirring *constantly*. Add about one quarter of this hot mixture to the beaten eggs in a small mixing bowl, beat together, return this to the saucepan, and cook for 2 more minutes, stirring *constantly*. Immediately pour into the baked pie shell.

3. Sprinkle the remaining confectioners' sugar/peanut butter mixture on top, then mix it into the pudding as best as you can.

4. In a medium-size mixing bowl with an electric mixer, beat the egg whites and cream of tartar together until foamy, then add the granulated sugar 1 tablespoon at a time, whipping until stiff peaks form. Beat in the vanilla. Spread the meringue evenly over the top of the pie, making sure it covers the filling all the way to the edge of the crust.

5. Bake until the peaks of meringue are light brown, about 8 minutes.

MAKES ONE 9-INCH DEEP-DISH PIE

TAHINI BITES PIE

This sweet, nutty dessert looks like a cross between a pie and breakfast cereal from hell. One bite and you will be hooked; just like riding your Harley, you will want more. So run into the kitchen and whip up this killer dessert and while it bakes, maybe you can polish some of that chrome on your Hog.

Canola oil

1 cup honey

½ cup tahini (sesame paste)

½ teaspoon cayenne pepper

3 cups spoon-size shredded wheat cereal

½ cup Craisins (dried cranberries; look for them where raisins are sold in your supermarket)

½ cup unsalted shelled sunflower seeds

1. Preheat the oven to 350°F. Grease a 9-inch pie pan with canola oil.

2. In a blender or food processor, combine the honey, tahini, and cayenne and process until fully mixed, about 1 minute.

3. In a large mixing bowl, combine the shredded wheat and Craisins and toss well to mix. Pour the honey-tahini mixture over the shredded wheat and toss well to coat. Transfer to the prepared pie pan, spread out evenly, and sprinkle the sunflower seeds over the top. Bake until the top is golden brown, about 30 minutes. Allow to cool before cutting into wedges and serving.

MAKES 6 TO 8 SERVINGS

DEBBIE HORVATH'S COUNTRY APPLE PIE

Debbie Horvath from Hopatcong, New Jersey, sent in this recipe and told me, "We have always loved Harleys and food; my hubby is 6'1" and about 240 pounds! He and his friends love this one. He is on the pit-crew team for Out of Time Racing and away from home a lot. I am now disabled and do not get to ride anymore, but still love Harleys. It's hard for me to be on my feet for longer than two minutes, but I can still make and enjoy this recipe."

> **7 large or 14 small apples, cored, peeled, and sliced**
>
> **½ cup sugar**
>
> **2 tablespoons cornstarch**
>
> **⅛ teaspoon salt**
>
> **¾ teaspoon ground cinnamon**
>
> **¼ cup plus 3 tablespoons molasses**
>
> **¼ teaspoon ground nutmeg**
>
> **1 cup all-purpose flour**
>
> **6 tablespoons (¾ stick) butter**
>
> **One 9-inch pie shell**

1. Preheat the oven to 375°F.

2. In a large mixing bowl, combine the apples, sugar, cornstarch, salt, cinnamon, ¼ cup of the molasses, and the nutmeg, mix well, and set aside.

3. In a medium-size mixing bowl, combine the flour and the remaining 3 tablespoons molasses, then cut in the butter until the mixture is crumbly.

4. Transfer the apple mixture to the pie shell. Sprinkle the crumb topping evenly over the top of the pie and bake until the crust is nicely browned, the apples are tender, and the filling is bubbling, 50 to 60 minutes.

MAKES ONE 9-INCH PIE

BLUEBERRY MANGO SURPRISE PIE

O h, my goodness, this is too good to share—just hide this pie deep in the back of the fridge. If you don't hide it from your buddies, you will be doomed to bake this pie again and again. The tasty combo of mango and blueberries is highlighted by the sweet and tart freshness of the Craisins and the surprise comes from the cayenne fire. Like a highly detailed custom Harley requires a careful visual inspection to appreciate the builder's art, this pie's complex flavors will demand careful inspection with a fork to reveal the baker's art.

> 1 packaged piecrust mix, prepared for a double-crust 9-inch deep-dish pie
>
> 3½ cups fresh blueberries, picked over for stems
>
> 1 cup peeled and seeded ripe mango cut into ½-inch cubes
>
> ½ cup Craisins (dried cranberries; look for them where raisins are sold in your supermarket)
>
> 1 tablespoon fresh lemon juice
>
> 3 tablespoons cornstarch
>
> ¾ cup plus 1 tablespoon sugar
>
> ½ teaspoon ground cinnamon
>
> ¼ teaspoon cayenne pepper
>
> 1 tablespoon heavy cream

1. Preheat the oven to 425°F. Roll out half the piecrust dough and fit into a 9-inch pie pan. Hold the remainder as a ball of dough. Refrigerate both while you prepare the filling.

2. In a large mixing bowl, combine the blueberries, mango, and Craisins, tossing well. Sprinkle the lemon juice over the fruit and toss well. In a small mixing bowl, combine the cornstarch, the ¾ cup sugar, the cinnamon, and cayenne and whisk together. Add the sugar mixture to the fruit, stir well to thoroughly combine, and transfer to the pie crust.

3. On a lightly floured work surface, roll the chilled ball of dough out to ⅛ inch thick. Cut the rolled top crust into 1-inch-wide strips. Lay half of the strips of crust across the top of the pie with a 1-inch gap

between each strip. Turn the pie 90 degrees and lay the remaining strips over the pie with a 1-inch gap between each strip; this will make a lattice top. Pinch the rim edges of the crust and strips together and press the rim with a fork to make a nice edge. Brush the top of the crust with the heavy cream and sprinkle with the remaining 1 tablespoon sugar. Bake until the crust is golden brown and the fruit filling is bubbly, 35 to 40 minutes. Let cool at least 20 minutes before serving.

MAKES ONE 9-INCH PIE

EXTRA PARTS:
USEFUL LITTLE RECIPES

Have you ever had the uneasy experience, when doing bike maintenance or customizing, of finishing the job and finding you have extra parts left over? Not a good thing, to say the least. What do you do? Just hope everything is okay or tear it all apart and start over? At times like these it occurs to you that there might actually be some merit to using the service manual for something besides leveling your homemade workbench.

Writing cookbooks can be a lot like building a custom motorcycle. You start out with an idea and some parts, then you get building. After countless hours locked away in the kitchen with your ideas, tons of food, lots of hungry friends, a smoking computer, and, in this case, contributions from lots of great Harley folks from around America, you emerge with a cookbook. When you look back at the mess you made in the creation process (I always make a mess) and you discover that some great recipes just did not fit anywhere, you come up with a chapter called Extra Parts. So, go ahead and check out what was left on my culinary parts tray; I am sure you will find some creative uses for them.

ANGELA TLACK'S DAMN GOOD BBQ SAUCE

Angela Tlack of Morris Plains, New Jersey, sent in this killer barbecue sauce recipe, which she uses in another great recipe that she shared with me, Angela Tlack's Spicy Baked Beans in Belgian Ale (page 230). She wants you to know that "this recipe takes a little extra effort, but is so worth it, not just for the baked beans, but for any use. It's easily doubled too! Take my word for it, good BBQ sauce = happy biker!" You got it right, Angela. Make Angela Tlack's Damn Good BBQ Sauce, fire up your grill, and make some bikers happy!

1 Spanish onion, cut into several pieces

¼ cup water

1 cup ketchup

¾ cup Belgian-style ale (such as Chimay or Duvel)

1 teaspoon cider vinegar

2 tablespoons Worcestershire sauce

1 teaspoon spicy golden mustard

5 tablespoons molasses

1 teaspoon hot sauce (such as Tabasco)

¼ teaspoon black pepper

2 tablespoons olive oil

1 clove garlic, minced

1 teaspoon chili powder

Dash of cayenne pepper

1. In a food processor, process the onion until it is finely chopped, about 45 seconds. Pour the water over the onion in the processor, then transfer to a strainer placed over a medium-size mixing bowl. Press the solids for as much liquid as possible, then discard solids and reserve the onion juice. Add the ketchup, ale, vinegar, Worcestershire sauce, mustard, molasses, hot sauce, and black pepper and mix well.

2. In a medium-size heavy-bottomed saucepan, heat the oil over medium heat until it moves freely in the pan. Add the garlic, chili powder, and cayenne and cook, stirring, for 30 seconds. Stir in the ketchup mixture and bring to a boil over medium-high heat. Reduce the heat to low and simmer, uncovered, until thickened, 25 to 30 minutes. Let cool for 10 minutes before using.

MAKES 3/4 CUP

WYATT BARBEE'S H-D BBQ SAUCE

Here is another barbecue sauce recipe—yes, we bikers like our barbecue. This one comes from Wyatt Barbee of Dahlonega, Georgia, who tells me he "loves to cook and this is a homemade original that beats any sauce for BBQ." Give Wyatt's sauce a try at your next H.O.G. barbecue. Oh, and Wyatt says you gotta use the bacon grease—no substituting allowed.

¼ cup bacon grease

1 onion, chopped

1 clove garlic, minced

1 cup honey

1 cup tomato ketchup

1 cup red wine vinegar

½ cup Worcestershire sauce

1 tablespoon dry mustard

1½ teaspoon salt

1 teaspoon dried oregano

1 teaspoon black pepper

1 teaspoon white pepper

1 teaspoon red pepper flakes

½ teaspoon dried thyme

1. In a large saucepan, heat the bacon grease over medium heat. Add the onion and garlic and cook, stirring, until softened. Add the remaining ingredients and bring to a boil, stirring constantly. Reduce the heat to low and cook 5 minutes longer.

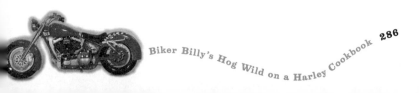

2. Use to baste chicken or pork while grilling.

3. Put the sauce that is left in a small pitcher or gravy bowl to be used at the table during the meal.

MAKES ABOUT 4 1/2 CUPS

IRON HORSERADISH SAUCE

Like the twin-cylindered motorcycle it is named for, this recipe packs two power pulses of fire. Dip your favorite munchies or veggie in this dip for a real taste treat. This sauce is great with Biker Toothpicks (page 22).

1 tablespoon prepared horseradish

1 tablespoon chopped garlic

1/2 cup plain yogurt

1/2 cup buttermilk

1/2 teaspoon white pepper

1/2 teaspoon salt

1/4 teaspoon cayenne pepper

Place all the ingredients in a blender or food processor and process until smooth, about 1 minute. Refrigerate for 1 hour to let the flavors develop before serving. Serve chilled.

MAKES ABOUT 1 CUP

KILLER QUESO SAUCE

This is a cheese sauce to die for—it makes anything Tex-Mex better. Just try it—like riding, if I have to explain it, you won't understand.

> 2 tablespoons butter
>
> 1 medium-size onion, diced
>
> 1 tablespoon chopped garlic
>
> 2 canned chipotle peppers packed in adobo sauce, minced
>
> ¾ teaspoon ground cumin
>
> ½ teaspoon white pepper
>
> ¼ cup half-and-half
>
> 2 cups shredded mild cheddar cheese

1. Melt the butter in a small skillet over medium heat. Add the onion and cook, stirring, until golden brown, 5 to 7 minutes. Add the garlic and cook, stirring, until the garlic begins to color, 1 to 2 minutes.

2. Fill the bottom half of a double boiler not quite halfway with boiling water and place over medium heat. You don't want the top part of the double boiler to be in direct contact with the water. Every so often, check the water level to ensure that the pot does not boil dry. Keep another pot of water boiling on the stove so you can add water if necessary. Transfer the sautéed onion and garlic to the top of the double boiler. Add the cumin, white pepper, and half-and-half and stir well to dissolve the spices. Add the cheese and stir until it melts and a smooth sauce forms. Keep warm over the simmering water until ready to serve.

MAKES ABOUT 2½ CUPS

HOT ROD RED PEPPER SAUCE

Like a souped-up bike, this sauce will give you a blast. Be creative and try adding it to some of your favorite Tex-Mex dishes and hotrod them Biker Billy style. I have combined four different hot peppers in this recipe to create a unique flavor and a complex fire. The ancho and pasilla are mild and very flavorful, the chipotle is a medium hot pepper and adds a smoky, almost sweet flavor, while the guajillo is most definitely hot and gives the combo a nice blast of fire. All four are dried peppers, with the chipotle being smoke dried, then packed in a tomato-based sauce call adobo. I have removed the seeds, which does lower the heat level some. The reason for removing the seeds is that the seeds from the ancho, pasilla, and guajillo are large and hard, which adds a less than desirable texture to the sauce. The chipotle is used with the seeds, since they are smaller and soft from soaking in the adobo sauce. All of these hot peppers can be found in Latin markets or the produce sections of large supermarkets.

4 guajillo peppers, seeded and torn into small pieces

2 ancho peppers, seeded and torn into small pieces

1 pasilla pepper, seeded and torn into small pieces

2 canned chipotle peppers packed in adobo sauce, minced

6 sun-dried tomatoes

1 cup boiling water

1 tablespoon olive oil

2 tablespoons chopped garlic

½ teaspoon dried oregano

1 teaspoon dried cilantro

1 tablespoon cider vinegar

1 teaspoon molasses

½ teaspoon salt

½ teaspoon black pepper

Juice of ½ lime

2 teaspoons sugar

1. In a small heatproof mixing bowl, combine all the peppers, the sun-dried tomatoes, and boiling water. Set aside and allow to cool to room temperature.

2. Transfer the chiles, tomatoes, and their soaking liquid to a blender or a food processor and process until smooth and no large pieces of pepper remain, about 1 minute.

3. In a small saucepan, heat the olive oil over low heat, add the garlic, oregano, cilantro, vinegar, molasses, salt, black pepper, lime juice, and sugar, stir well, and simmer for 1 minute. Add the pureed chile mixture and simmer, stirring often, until the sauce thickens and darkens, 10 to 15 minutes.

I keep this sauce warm over low heat while I prepare other dishes, as a little extra cooking only deepens the flavor. Serve warm.

MAKES ABOUT 1 1/2 CUPS

OUCH OIL

This is a flavored olive oil that I keep on my counter and use for frying everything from eggs to burgers to veggies. It adds a nice zip with little effort. I call it ouch oil for one simple reason; it will make any small cut or your eyes sting if you get it in the wrong place.

2 tablespoons dried basil
4 dried Thai peppers, pierced with a sharp knife
One 8-ounce bottle extra virgin olive oil

Add the basil and peppers to the oil bottle and shake well.

MAKES 1 CUP

RON JANICKI'S ONION MARMALADE

This tasty little recipe is from Ron Janicki, a Harley rider and member of Ocean State H.O.G. in Rhode Island. Ron uses it as an accompaniment for his Spanish Pork Appetizer (page 31). If you want a vegetarian version, just replace the chicken stock with vegetable stock and enjoy.

2 cups chicken broth

12 cups thinly sliced Spanish onions

¼ cup balsamic vinegar

1. In large pot over medium-high heat, combine the chicken stock and onions, cover, and cook until translucent and very soft, about 45 minutes.

2. Uncover, reduce the heat to low, and simmer for 45 to 60 minutes, stirring occasionally. Add the vinegar and cook until the onions are caramelized, another 30 to 60 minutes.

MAKES 2 CUPS

DAVIDA MATTHEWS'S JAMMIN' JALAPEÑO PEPPER JELLY

Says Davida (Davey) Matthews of Blackville, South Carolina, "I adapted a jelly recipe to accommodate the prolific production from my six Burpee's Biker Billy's jalapeño pepper plants. The end result is a clear, sparkling green jelly that serves up beautifully on a cream cheese block or in a seasonal mold (Christmas trees!) with cornbread crackers. You can also use it as a sauce or condiment to 'heat' up chicken or sandwiches. Nothing goes to waste in this recipe, since the leftover pepper pulp is used to make pepper bark." Now, all you need is to grow some Burpee Biker Billy jalapeño peppers!

This recipe assumes you are familiar with basic canning techniques and know your way around handling hot peppers. The simplest thing for me to suggest is to wear disposable latex or rubber gloves while handling hot peppers. If your skin is sensitive, this is advice well heeded. Even if you're not sensitive, wear gloves if you are handling large quantities of hot peppers or habanero varieties. I suggest disposable gloves, since poorly washed gloves can harbor dangerous bacteria. Even better, use disposable sterile powder-free gloves. However, if you are like me, wearing gloves in the kitchen is not something you want to do. In that case, if you are diligent about washing your hands with warm, soapy water (at least twice) after handling small amounts of peppers, you should be okay. You should wash like this even if you use gloves. While your hands (or gloves) have the juices from hot peppers on them, touching sensitive parts of your body, like eyes, sinuses, mucous membranes, and "private parts" will give you an experience that is close to torture.

Half bucket of jalapeños (about 50, depending on size, 3 to 4 pounds)

1½ cups cider vinegar, 5% acidity

1½ cups apple juice

1 package instant fruit jelly pectin (don't use liquid or you will end up with barbecue sauce, which isn't bad but isn't this recipe!)

½ teaspoon salt

5 cups sugar

Green food coloring

1. Wash the peppers. Remove the stems only and cut large peppers in half. Working in small batches, transfer the peppers to a food processor and process until smooth, using the vinegar as needed to achieve a slurry consistency.

2. In a large mixing bowl, combine the pureed peppers, the remaining vinegar, and the apple juice together. Place this devil's own brew in a glass container (two 1-quart jars work well) and store in the refrigerator at least overnight but no more than a week.

3. Transfer the mixture to a jelly bag or wrap it in several layers of cheesecloth and squeeze out the juices over a medium-size mixing bowl until you get 4 cups. If you come up short, add apple juice to the

already-squeezed peppers and let it sit for just a little while, perhaps while you are measuring out your sugar, sterilizing your jars and lids, and bringing your canning water to a boil. When you get your 4 cups of juice, take the residual pureed peppers, place in a gallon-size zippered-top plastic bag, and flatten it out to make pepper bark. Place it in the freezer and break off pieces of it for use in soups, spaghetti sauce, or chili.

4. Wash out the jelly bag or cheesecloth and run the pepper juice through it 2 or 3 times. This will keep the final jelly from becoming cloudy.

5. Combine the pepper juice, instant pectin, and salt in a large, heavy-bottomed pot. Bring to a boil over high heat, stirring constantly. Add the sugar, keep stirring, and return the mixture to a full rolling boil. Keep the temperature high and keep stirring for a full minute. This ensures a good gel. Remove from the heat. If you created foam, skim it off. Stir in just a few drops of green food coloring to brighten the color.

6. Fill the jelly jars to within $\frac{1}{4}$ inch of the rim. Wipe the rim clean, position the lid, and screw the band down just to the point of resistance, like changing an oil filter. Place the jars in a boiling water bath for 5 minutes.

7. Refrigerate after opening.

MAKES 6 HALF-PINTS

DAVIDA'S TASTEBUD BURNER JALAPEÑO PEPPER RELISH

This is another fiery treat from Davida (Davey) Matthews of Blackville, South Carolina. "I vary the heat by substituting green bell peppers for some of the jalapeños for the weak of heart (and for Christmas gifts) but my family prefers the high-octane version that follows. This relish is perfect for hotdogs, ride-in cookouts, and for gift-giving to the Harley family that has everything."

2 pounds (30 to 40, depending on size) jalapeño peppers, stems removed, large ones cut in half (you can substitute seeded green bell peppers or remove the seeds from the jalapeños to ratchet down the heat)

1 pound onions, quartered (not sliced, because that creates onion skin "strings")

3 cups white or cider vinegar (5% acidity)

1 cup sugar

1 tablespoon pickling salt

1. Place the peppers and onions in a food processor and, pulsing on and off, chop them to the desired coarseness.

2. Combine the peppers and onions, vinegar, sugar, and salt in a large heavy-bottomed pot and bring to a boil over high heat, stirring constantly. Boil for 5 minutes, stirring constantly to prevent scorching.

3. Fill sterilized jars with the mixture up to ½ inch from the rim. Remove air bubbles by running a sterilized rubber spatula down the inside of the jars. Wipe the rims; position the lids and screw on the rings. Place in a boiling water bath for 10 minutes.

4. Refrigerate after opening.

MAKES 8 HALF-PINTS

RESOURCES

Motorcycle Safety Resources

In my mind, the motto Live to Ride and Ride to Live has many meanings. One of the more important ones I want to share with you is the concept of being a well-trained rider. If you feel like I do—that you can't live without riding—then you owe it to yourself and those who love you to be a well-trained rider. I first rode a motorcycle during a time when rider education amounted to, here is the gas, here is the clutch, that's the shifter, and, oh yeah, that's the brake—have fun. Surprisingly, it wasn't so long ago. But there is so much more to know about riding a motorcycle, especially if you want to do it safely. It is also a heck of a lot more fun if you are well trained and know your personal limits and the limits of your machine and the environment in which you are riding. That is riding to live.

Harley-Davidson has taken the concept of Live to Ride and Ride to Live a step further. Through participating dealerships, the company offers two different rider education courses designed to help you get the most out of your riding experience in a safe manner.

The first is the Rider's Edge New Rider Course. Designed specifically to meet the needs of novice riders, it is available at local Harley-Davidson/Buell dealerships around the country. Harley-Davidson has developed the course with the National Association of State Motorcycle Safety Administrators (SMSA) and individual administrators to ensure it will complement existing state motorcycle safety programs.

The course is available at select Harley-Davidson/Buell dealers in Alabama, Georgia, Louisiana, Nevada, New Mexico, New York, Wisconsin, and a growing list of other states.

The Rider's Edge New Rider Course takes place in the dealership and at nearby range facilities, with class sizes ranging from six to twelve students. Lasting a total of approximately 25 hours, the course includes interactive classroom exercises, plenty of riding practice, time to become familiar with different types of motorcycles, accessories and riding gear, and a behind-the-scenes look at dealership operations. Students who complete the course will be issued MSF completion cards, and in some states may be waived from taking the skills or knowledge portion of the state motorcycle licensing test.

The training motorcycle used in the Rider's Edge New Rider Course is the new Buell Blast—an all-new single-cylinder motorcycle designed for casual fun, excitement, and adventure. The Blast model's course-friendly features include a low center of gravity, flexible turn signals, a hidden muffler, and two seat heights that can be adjusted on the spot.

The second available course is the Rider's Edge Group Riding Course. Riding motorcycles in groups, whether large or small, is a unique experience that many motorcyclists enjoy, yet others avoid. The difference in attitude is often rooted in rider skills and knowledge. Rider's Edge—The Harley-Davidson Academy of Motorcycling recently introduced its Group Riding Course, which was developed in cooperation with the Motorcycle Safety Foundation and specifically designed to address the special challenges groups of riders face. The course's video format features discussions about ride organization, communication while riding, riding formation, avoiding hazards as a group, and other group riding educational information.

The single rider version of the Rider's Edge Group Riding Course includes the training video, self-study workbook, evaluation form, and completion pin. A group package is also available and includes the video, leader's guide, 25 workbooks, 25 evaluation forms, and 25 completion pins. For more information on Rider's Edge courses throughout the country, please call (800) 588-2743 or log on to the Web site at www.ridersedge.com.

If a Rider's Edge Course is not currently available at a Harley-Davidson Dealer near you, consider taking a Motorcycle Safety Foundation–approved rider education course at a local private or state run facility. The Motorcycle Safety Foundation (MSF) is a national not-for-profit organization promoting the safety of motorcyclists with programs in rider training, operator licensing, and public information. Since its inception in 1973, the foundation has supported state and independent programs in training more than one million students to ride more safely. The MSF is sponsored by the US distributors of BMW, Ducati, Harley-Davidson, Honda, Kawasaki, Piaggio/Vespa, Suzuki, Victory, and Yamaha motorcycles. To learn more about the MSF rider education courses near you, call (800) 446-9227. Several states now consider successfully completing an approved MSF RiderCourse equal to passing a motorcycle operator licensing road test. For more information, check with your state motor vehicle department.

Safety is a state of mind that starts with knowledge and builds with practice and self-discipline. Always maintain your skills, motorcycle, and equipment. This includes maintaining yourself—alcohol and drugs (including prescription and over-the-counter medicine) don't mix with riding a motorcycle, and even lack of sleep will reduce your abilities. Be Smart, Ride Straight.

The Motorcycle Safety Foundation
2 Jenner Street Suite 150
Irvine, CA 92618-3806
(949) 727-3227
www.msf-usa.org

Motorcycle Organizations

Harley Owners Group—H.O.G.
H.O.G. is the factory sponsored motorcycle club for Harley-Davidson motorcycle owners. Founded in 1983, it has grown from a membership of 10,000 to more than 675,000 by the summer of 2002, making it the world's largest organization of its kind. More than 1,300 chapters are based at Harley-Davidson dealers worldwide, providing a local gathering place for members to share riding, social and charity activities. Membership is open to owners of Harley-Davidson motorcycles

worldwide, and associate membership is available for the passengers or family of H.O.G. members.

Hog Tales is the official communication source for H.O.G. and is published bimonthly. Other H.O.G. benefits include a membership card, pin, and patch; a touring guide; *Enthusiast*; the Fly & Ride Program; special travel and motorcycle shipping rates; optional roadside assistance; and national and state rallies.

Harley Owners Group

3700 West Juneau Avenue

Milwaukee, WI 53208-2865

(800) CLUB-HOG

Fax: (414) 343-4515

www.hog.com

Buell Riders Adventure Group—BRAG

BRAG is the official factory-sponsored motorcycle riding club for Buell Motorcycle Company, started in 1995 to enhance the Buell riding experience. As of the summer 2002, BRAG has 10,000 clubs in North America, 900 in Japan, and 70 local BRAG Clubs, each sponsored by a Buell dealer. Currently full BRAG membership is only offered in North America and Japan (Buell riders in other countries are allowed to join, although their benefits are limited).

BRAG usually hosts two national adventures (events) each year, as well as hospitality and smaller events at the Daytona, Laconia, and Laguna Seca rallies. FUELL magazine is the official communications source for BRAG members and is published bimonthly. Other BRAG membership benefits include a membership card, pin, and patch; *Adventure Atlas*; *Enthusiast*; the Safe Rider Skills Program; the Fly & Ride Program; special travel and motorcycle shipping rates; and optional roadside assistance.

BRAG

3700 West Juneau Avenue

Milwaukee, WI 53208

Phone: (888) 432-BRAG (2724)

Fax: (414) 343-4515

www.buell.com

Harley-Davidson Motor Company
Harley-Davidson Customer Service
3700 West Juneau Avenue
Milwaukee, WI 53208
To speak with a Harley-Davidson customer service representative, call
(414) 343-4056
www.harley-davidson.com

There are a few other groups that, in my opinion, you should join. These are the groups that advocate for our rights as motorcycle riders. We live in an age where freedom is still at risk and it is especially true when it comes to our right to ride motorcycles. There are many people out there who just don't understand what riding a motorcycle is all about. Those people have no qualms about dictating to you what you can ride, where you can ride, and what you must wear when you ride. This is not about helmet laws, which simply is one step in a process that could lead to removing motorcycles from the roads of America. As I am working on this book, the Environmental Protection Agency is devising plans and regulations that could have adverse effects on motorcycling in America under the guise of clean air, which we all do want. Motorcycles are not the problem, but they can be part of the solution, reducing traffic and lowering the national average of fuel use per mile traveled. However, we are an underrepresented group at the political table in America and will get shortchanged in favor of well-funded powerful polluters. It is also not just an issue of what is happening in America; the process of globalization may have negative influences on the motorcycles in your future. I do not claim to be an expert on the ever-evolving issues that swirl around us, but there are people who make it their business to stay informed and advocate for our rights. Those people really need your help, and while I won't go so far as to say you owe it to them and yourself to help, I will say the following. If you Live to Ride and Ride to Live, get involved; join the AMA (American Motorcyclist Association), the MRF (Motorcycle Riders Foundation), and your local state MRO (Motorcycle Rights Organization), such as ABATE (American Bikers Aimed Toward Education).

The American Motorcyclist Association

The American Motorcyclist Association, founded in 1924, is a non-profit organization with more than 250,000 members. The association's purpose is to pursue, protect, and promote the interests of motorcyclists while serving the needs of its members. The AMA is best known as the leading defender of motorcyclists' rights in the United States—and its work benefits not only AMA members, but all American motorcyclists. The AMA is also the world's largest motorsports-sanctioning body—between AMA Sports and AMA Pro Racing, and through the efforts of more than 1,200 AMA-chartered clubs and promoters, the organization sanctions more than 4,000 competition events each year.

American Motorcyclist, the AMA's monthly magazine, covers every facet of the American motorcycling experience. The AMA's award-winning Web site, AMADirectlink, offers late-breaking news and online tools for communicating directly to legislators, decision makers, and the media.

AMA headquarters is home to the Motorcycle Hall of Fame Museum, where visitors can see a collection of vintage bikes and informative displays showcasing the designs and technologies that have placed motorcycles at the leading edge of the transportation industry.

AMA members enjoy a variety of benefits, including discount programs that easily offset the modest annual dues. For more information, visit www.AMADirectlink.com, or call (800) AMA-JOIN.

American Motorcyclist Association
13515 Yarmouth Drive
Pickerington, Ohio 43147
Phone: (614) 856-1900
Fax: (614) 856-1920
www.AMADirectlink.com

Motorcycle Riders Foundation

The Motorcycle Riders Foundation (MRF) is a Washington, D.C.-based Motorcyclists Rights Organization (MRO) that works nationwide with motorcyclists and motorcyclist rights organizations to

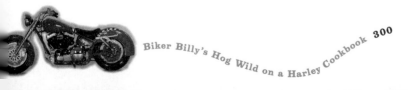

ensure that when motorcycle-related legislation comes up in Washington, D.C., the motorcyclists' voices are heard.

The MRF is a national grassroots organization devoted exclusively to the street motorcyclist and is not financially tied to any motorcycle industry interests or legal firms. The MRF was started in 1988 by motorcyclists and continues to be run by motorcyclists. All financial support for the organization is generated from membership dues, donations from state motorcyclists rights organizations, and motorcyclists rights seminars.

From stopping the denial of federal highway funds to states that adopt adult-choice helmet laws to assuring motorcycle access to America's highways and byways, MRF has been at the forefront of motorcyclists' rights and safety issues since its founding in 1988. These days, MRF is at the vanguard of efforts to fight restrictive emissions regulations, safeguard motorcycling small businesses, and protect our ability to refine our rides. MRF is also pushing an ambitious plan to protect the gains we made in federal legislation in the 1990s while preventing motorcycle accidents in the future by boosting rider training and building motorist awareness of motorcycles. You need to read this important plan—dubbed "Motorcycles Rev the Future"—at www.mrf.org. MRF is also working to rescue health care benefits wrongly denied riders under the implementation of regulations for the 1996 Health Insurance Portability and Accountability Act (HIPAA).

Every rider in America has a stake in these issues, so every rider should join the MRF. Chances are, MRF needs you to call your Congressman today about some burning issue that impacts your rights and your safety on the road. Better join today.

Motorcycle Riders Foundation
P.O. Box 1808
Washington, DC 20013-1808
(202) 546-0983
Fax: (202) 546-0986
www.mrf.org

AMA-Motorcycle Hall of Fame Museum Exhibit

While Harley-Davidson motorcycles are certainly icons of style and sound, it may be that the people who have made them and ridden them are at least as important. In 2003, the Harley-Davidson Motor Company celebrates its 100th anniversary. In honor of the great history of this motorcycle brand, actually the longest-running car or motorcycle brand worldwide, the Motorcycle Hall of Fame Museum, in Pickerington, Ohio, has chosen to mount a special exhibition. Titled "Heroes of Harley-Davidson," the exhibit not only pays tribute to the company's founders, but also to the men and women who have ridden Harley-Davidsons into fame—the racers, like Joe Leonard; the ambassadors, like Dot Robinson; American soldiers on special military machines trained by none other than William S. Harley; customizers like Arlen Ness; and Harley dealers who kept the machines on the road, like Dudley Perkins. Well-researched text, dozens of inspiring photos, more than 40 motorcycles, and some great ephemera tell the story. Understanding where Harley-Davidson motorcycles have been written into the history books over the last century is certainly food for the soul of the serious motorcyclist as well as for those with a taste for American history.

Motorcycle Hall of Fame Museum

13515 Yarmouth Drive
Pickerington, Ohio 43147
Phone: (614) 856-2222
Fax: (614) 856-2221
www.ama-cycle.org

Culinary Resources

Biker Billy Cooks With Fire
P.O. Box 1888
Weaverville, NC 28787
(800) BIKER BILLY
www.bikerbilly.com
E-mail: bikerbilly@bikerbilly.com
Newsletter, Biker Billy products, and fiery stuff.

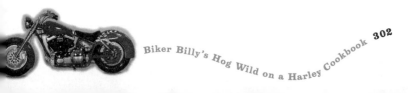

Burpee

300 Park Avenue

Warminster, PA 18974

Phone: (800) 888-1447

www.burpee.com

Chile pepper seeds and garden products and source of the Hot Pepper Biker Billy Hybrid!

Chile Pepper Magazine

1701 River Run Suite #702

Fort Worth, Texas 76107

Phone: (888) 774-2946

Fax: (817) 877-8870

www.chilepepper.com

A magazine of spicy world cuisine.

Kalustyan's

123 Lexington Avenue

New York, NY 10016

Phone: (212) 685-3888

Fax: (212) 683-8458

www.kalustyans.com

Indian and Middle Eastern spices and foods.

Mo Hotta-Mo Betta

P.O. Box 1026

Savannah, GA 31402-1026

Phone: (800) 462-3220

Fax: (800) 618-4454

www.mohotta.com

Fiery foods and products.

Peppers

Rehoboth Outlets #3

1815 Ocean Outlets

Rehoboth Beach, DE 19971

Phone: (800) 998-FIRE (3473) or (302) 227-4608

Fax: (302) 227-4632

www.peppers.com

Fiery foods and products.

INDEX

PHOTOGRAPH CREDITS

All photographs of recipe contributors and their families are re-produced courtesy of the contributors.

The Harvard Common Press also gratefully acknowledges the photo submissions on the following pages:

ii, iii, vii, xi, xv, 1, 11, 19, 33, 51, 65, 95, 169, 223, 283: © Mark Langello

Customized bike at the base of each left-hand page by Lucian Smith, owner of Daytona Pro Street; photograph © Mark Langello

83: Photo of Dot Robinson courtesy of the American Motorcyclist Association (AMA)

105: Photo of Joe Leonard courtesy of the AMA

129: Photo of Sam Arena courtesy of the AMA

193: Photo of Susan Buck © Scott Winn

200: Photo of John Giles by Hatcher & Fell Photography

247: Photo of Windy Lindstrom courtesy of the AMA

255: Photo of Dr. Martin Jack Rosenblum © 2001 by Daniel De Lone

Cover photographs: Biker Billy © W. Atlee Burpee & Co.; chocolate chips © Michael Grand/Stockfood; chili © Colin Cooke/Stockfood